The Urbana Free Library

To renew materials call
217-367-4057

The United States of Storytelling

The United States of Storytelling

Folktales and True Stories from the Western States

Dan Keding

LIBRARIES UNLIMITED

AN IMPRINT OF ABC-CLIO, LLC
Santa Barbara, California • Denver, Colorado • Oxford, England

Library of Congress Cataloging-in-Publication Data

Keding, Dan.
    The United States of storytelling : folktales and true stories from
  the Western states / Dan Keding.
        p. cm.
    Includes bibliographical references and index.
    ISBN 978-1-59158-728-6 (hardcover : alk. paper) 1. Tales—West
  (U.S.) 2. Storytelling—West (U.S.) 3. West (U.S.)—History. 4. West
  (U.S.)—Folklore. I. Title.
    GR109.K43 2010
    398.20978—dc22   2010021572

ISBN: 978-1-59158-728-6

14 13 12 11 10   1 2 3 4 5

This book is also available on the World Wide Web as an eBook.
Visit www.abc-clio.com for details.

Libraries Unlimited
An Imprint of ABC-CLIO, LLC

ABC-CLIO, LLC
130 Cremona Drive, P.O. Box 1911
Santa Barbara, California 93116-1911

This book is printed on acid-free paper ∞
Manufactured in the United States of America

To the children of the United States, who have such a rich and diverse cultural background. I hope these stories help you appreciate your past and those people who went before you, showing you the way. I hope you understand that in our diversity, in our stories, lies our strength.

Also, as always, to my wife Tandy Lacy, who encourages me, inspires me, and fills me with awe. Thanks, Tig.

Contents

Acknowledgments

First I would like to thank my wife, Tandy Lacy, who encourages me, believes in me, and was the first editor of many of these stories. I also want to thank Barbara Ittner of Libraries Unlimited, who came to me and planted the seed for this project. I thank her for her faith in me and for entrusting her idea to my pen. I also thank her for her patience and support as I made a personal journey while collecting Native American stories for this book. I want to thank the staff at The Center for Children's Books at the University of Illinois Graduate School of Library and Information Science, the people who supported me while I haunted their huge collection looking for stories. A debt of gratitude is owed to Art Thieme, not just for the stories he contributed but also for his constant encouragement and friendship throughout the years, and for leading the way for so many of us in our journeys in the folk arts. Thanks to my friends Donald Davis, Kevin Strauss, Tim Tingle, Jenifer Strauss, Alan Irvine, Bob Sanders, Dovie Thomason, Greg Rodgers, and Ceil Anne Clement, who contributed personal, original, traditional, and tribal stories. In addition, I thank the various Native American tribes that gave me permission to use their stories and Professor Debbie Reese from the University of Illinois for her thoughtful insight and advice concerning Native American issues. A special thank-you to Phillip Allen for his story "Choctaw Codetalkers of World War One." I want to thank Paige Osborn, who was my assistant and did endless hours of typing, and Christa Deacy Quinn for suggesting chapter glossaries and always asking, "How's the book?"

Thank-you to all the folks who have encouraged me over the years to pursue my writing and storytelling, friends like Kendall Haven, Kevin Strauss, Betsy Hearne, Amy Douglas, Elizabeth Ellis, Susan Klein, and the all-too-many others.

Most of all, thank-you to the all the children who have listened over the years to my stories. Because of what I saw in your eyes as you listened, and because of your kind words in remembering me as adults, I know that the stories still live in your imaginations and memories and I continue to tell stories. You have given me the gift of purpose, and there are few gifts greater than that.

Introduction

It is diversity that makes America a great nation. Each state in this country is unique, having its own geography, climate, people, and their stories. That uniqueness makes the study of the stories of these states exciting and rewarding. In these pages you will find some characters that you recognize—like Paul Bunyan, Kit Carson, and Jim Bridger—and you will meet some lesser known heroes like Jeanette Rankin, Moses Harris, and Kate Shelley.

Stories are windows that allow us a glimpse of another time. We can see how people differed from us and how they were similar to us, how they acted under severe hardship and how they lived their daily lives. When we look through these windows we see why people laugh and cry, why they try to break through unfair barriers and reach out for the new and exciting. We start to understand why someone fights against injustice and why he or she enjoys spinning a yarn for friends. We can see people's dreams, their fears, their hopes, and their courage. This is the power of the story.

The stories in this collection come from the states west of the Mississippi River. Also included are tales from the U.S. territories and commonwealth states, as well as a selection of tales that cross state borders ("Crossing the Borders"). Some of the tales are traditional stories carried on by native people who resided in the area long before the Europeans arrived, some are transplanted stories brought to America by settlers who came from other countries, and others grew up from the land; some feature historical characters and events, and others the geography, flora, and fauna of a particular state. Virtually every type of story can be found in this collection—true stories, legends, tall tales, pourquoi tales, ghost stories, funny stories, and fictionalized stories based on true events. All, it is hoped, can help readers better understand specific states, their peoples, and their histories.

The chapters of this book by no means provide a definitive collection of the stories of the individual states represented. Instead, they hold a sampling of the stories that are found in the lore and history of the various regions of our country. Naturally it would be impossible to represent every immigrant culture, Native American tribe, historical event, or famous citizen of each state in a collection like this one. Instead, this story collection is meant as a resource—for students, who can find a state and explore some of the stories and legends and people that have made it what it is today, and for educators, who can find state-themed stories to add to curriculum units.

To select these tales I researched hundreds of books and other printed sources, locating several versions of each story before retelling the tale in my own words. I primarily used my own collection and the collections at the University of Illinois Library and the Center for Children's Books at the Graduate School of Library and Information Science at the University of Illinois. In adapting and retelling all of these traditional stories, I have tried to be as faithful to the story as possible—to its voice, content and range of emotions—while still working to make these stories come alive for a twenty-first-century audience.

The stories that come from Native American sources are reprinted here with the permission of each of the various tribes represented, or by permission of recognized Native American storytellers. I contacted tribes from every state. Some tribes gave me permission, a few declined permission, and many others did not respond. Unfortunately, many chapters do not include the stories of the Native Americans who live or once lived in the state. After much consideration and thought, and with the help and advice of my wife Tandy Lacy, Director of Education at the Spurlock Museum at the University of Illinois, and many friends and colleagues, including Barbara Ittner, my editor at Libraries Unlimited, storytellers Dovie Thomason and Lynn Moroney, and Professor Debbie Reese from the University of Illinois, I held back over 100 stories and included only those approved by tribal authorities or Native American storytellers. In all cases this was the decision of the tribes, a decision I honor.

Other tribes and Native American storytellers readily gave their consent, and I greatly appreciate their cooperation and contribution. I believe that the stories of Native Americans belong to them and cannot be treated as a general resource to be pulled from other printed materials and used without any consideration for the people who hold them sacred. Authors and storytellers need to approach American Indian stories as part of living cultures, still vibrant and alive in this country, and not as historical or public domain pieces to be read or told with no regard for their origins and the people who have kept them alive these countless centuries. I hope that my readers will also honor these stories and treat them with the respect they deserve. I encourage other authors and storytellers to do the same.

I also asked several of my storytelling friends to donate a story. Art Thieme, Dovie Thomason, Kevin Strauss, Tim Tingle, Greg Rodgers, Alan Irvine, and Bob Sanders contributed traditional or historical pieces. Donald Davis, Ceil Anne Clement, and Jenifer Strauss gave me true stories from their families or from their own experiences growing up in their home states. These glimpses into the not-too-distant past are meant to entertain and enlighten students, and to let them see that stories are all around them, even in their own lives.

Chapters are organized alphabetically by state name, and each begins with an introduction to the state and its stories. There are four to six stories for each state. At the end of each state's chapter is a short glossary to help the student understand words, people, and ideas that might not be familiar to a twenty-first-century reader, followed by a list of sources, which notes the titles only. The bibliography at the end of this volume lists complete information about all sources. This extensive bibliography can point students and teachers to books that contain more stories. I hope readers will use this resource to discover the many legends that are still told and perhaps some that are almost forgotten and thereby save them from being lost.

People often ask me, "Are stories still important in this modern world of the twenty-first century where computers, cell phones and iPods have become commonplace?" I say that stories and storytelling are more important than ever. Stories help us recognize that we are part of something greater. They help us to be human in the best sense of the word. They engage our imaginations and make us feel alive. Stories teach us about where we come from and what it means to be at this place, at this moment. They even open our imaginations to what the future may bring. Consider the incredible impact of the <u>Harry Potter </u>books, the lasting power of Tolkien's <u>Lord of the Rings</u> trilogy, and the universal popularity of Terry Pratchett's <u>Disc World</u> series. All of these books have one thing in common: they tell great stories. This book, too, is filled with wonderful stories.

I hope that by reading this book students and teachers are encouraged to look into the lore of all states that make up America. Moreover, I sincerely hope readers will connect with the stories of their own states and their own communities, then search to discover more folktales and true stories of their past. I also hope that these tales encourage readers to seek out their elders and discover the living stories that can be more inspiring than any book. Perhaps students will start collecting stories in their own communities or writing their own stories, sharing their memories and thoughts about the places where they live and the people who live there with them. Their stories will become the new legends, myths, hero tales and ghost stories of America's twenty-first-century communities.

Alaska

Alaska was known as Seward's Folly when it was bought from the Russian Empire in 1867. The story of Father Herman, the first Orthodox saint in North America, comes from that Russian colonial period. In 1959 Alaska became the forty-ninth state to join the union. Alaska, which is the largest state by size, is one of the smallest by population. It is home to many Native American peoples, including the Tsimshian and the Tlingit Indians and the Noatak Eskimos.

One of the most dramatic and heroic rescues in American history occurred in Alaska and is told here in the story "The Race Against Death." In 1964 Alaska was the site of one of the most powerful earthquakes ever recorded, the Good Friday Earthquake. No chapter on Alaska would be complete without a tall tale about the cold, and the one we have here is as tall as they get.

Saint Herman of Alaska (a True Story)

In August 1970 clergy, prelates, and laypeople from the Russian Orthodox church gathered in Kodiak, Alaska, to formally proclaim a humble priest from Russia who spent forty years as a missionary in Alaska the first Orthodox saint in North America.

Father Herman was born outside Moscow in 1758 and went to seminary at Holy Trinity-Sergius Skete near St. Petersburg. While there he became deathly ill and prayed to an icon of the Theotokos for help. That night he had a vision that the Virgin was tending to his illness. When he woke the next morning he was healed and he remained devoted to the Virgin for the rest of his life.

As Russia extended its borders eastward the Orthodox Church needed priests to act as missionaries in the new lands. Father Herman was selected and sent to Kodiak Island. He and the other priests taught the Native Aleuts in both their own language and Russian, and the missionaries traveled throughout the Aleutian Islands and to the mainland of Alaska. Within a few years he was alone because the other men in his community died from the extreme conditions. Father Herman seemed to thrive on hardship. His physical strength was a legend among both the Aleuts and the Russians whom he encountered on his travels. He lived on Spruce Island for forty years in a small hut. Nearby he built a school and church, but he always stayed in his humble home.

The story is told that there was once an earthquake and the island community was threatened by a tidal wave. Father Herman brought an icon of the Theotokos to the shore and laid it on the ground. He told his parishioners that the water would not rise past the icon. It didn't. Father Herman loved his people and would often be seen giving out his homemade cookies to the children or visiting long hours with the sick and dying. Stories were told of his talking to the wild animals on the island and even that the huge bears that roamed the Alaskan islands and mainland came to him and ate from his hand like a favorite dog.

Father Herman died on December 13, 1837. He is buried at Saints Sergius and Herman Church on Spruce Island, Alaska.

The Race Against Death (a True Story)

In 1925 the small city of Nome, Alaska, and the surrounding communities were under siege by an enemy so powerful and so cunning that many feared the city would fall. The enemy was diphtheria, a bacterial disease that attacks the throat and upper respiratory system and if untreated is a deadly killer.

Back in 1925 Nome, a city that was only two degrees south of the Arctic Circle, could only be reached by dog sled once the harsh winter set in. The first death from the dreaded disease happened after the last ship of the season left for warmer waters. First one child then another died. The only doctor in the area was Curtis Welch, who practiced medicine with four nurses in the tiny twenty-four-bed hospital. His supply of antitoxin was expired, and new supplies had not arrived on the last boat from Juneau, Alaska. On January 22 Dr. Welch sent a telegram to the governor and also to Washington, D.C., telling them how critical the situation was in Nome and that he needed one million units of diphtheria antitoxin to prevent a horrible epidemic that could kill many of Nome's people and wipe out entire Native Alaskan villages.

Word went out along the west coasts of the United States and Canada to help find the serum. Quickly 300,000 units were discovered, not as much as needed but enough to treat the sick and stave off the disease until more units could arrive. Authorities discussed how to get the antitoxin to Nome. Air service to the far north was still in its infancy, and open cockpit planes could not fly in the 50-degree-below zero or colder weather of an Alaskan winter.

The only way to Nome was by dogsled.

Twenty teams of mushers and their dogs were assembled in relays that would keep fresh men and dogs on the trail. These teams braved temperatures that would drop to 70 degrees below zero and hurricane-force winds that literally made it impossible to see. The mushers relied on their lead dogs to keep them on the trail and find their way through the blizzard. Along the way several dogs froze to death, and several of the men were treated for severe frostbite but in the end the serum arrived and not one vial was broken. The dog teams had covered 674 miles in 127½ hours. The spread of diphtheria was stopped.

All of the men and dogs were heroes, but most agree that Leonhard Seppala and his lead dog Togo were the leaders in this race against death. They left Nome and traveled 170 miles to Shaktoolik, where they picked up the antitoxin and made their way through some of the roughest terrain and coldest weather and carried it 91 miles to Golovin. This brave team covered 261 miles. It was Gunner Kassen who carried the serum the last 53 miles into Nome.

The annual Iditarod Trail Dog Sled Race commemorates this courageous group of men and dogs who braved one of the harshest climates on earth to save the people of Nome.

The Good Friday Earthquake
(Based on True Events)

The whole earth shook. It really did. People felt the earthquake everywhere.

The family ran from their home near the sea. Their house had been shaken so violently that part of one of the walls had come crashing down. They looked at each other and knew immediately what they had to do. They had learned about it in their stories. They ran from the sea. The sea that gave them food, the sea that was their highway on which they traveled was not their friend this day. The family ran as fast as they could and then they heard the roar as the ocean heaved itself up from the floor of its bed and came crashing across the land, wiping out everything in its path. But these people knew the land and they knew the sea, and they had escaped to higher ground along with most of their neighbors. The victory of the earth and sea that day was not complete.

On Friday March 27, 1964, the most powerful earthquake ever recorded in North American history and the third most powerful ever measured by a seismograph hit Alaska. It caused landslides, tsunamis, and fissures in the earth and permanently raised some parts of the land by as much as thirty feet. Since the epicenter was in an area that was sparsely populated, the death toll was lower than it would have been had it hit a major Alaskan city. Tsunamis hit as far away as Hawaii and Japan, while people in California and Oregon were drowned in the massive waves. The death toll was estimated at 131, mostly from the tsunamis, while the property damage totaled over $300 million (almost $3 billion in current U.S. dollars).

Native villages were flattened, highways sank, fires broke out after gas lines ruptured, and bridges were destroyed. Fishing boats in Louisiana were sunk by the huge waves caused by the earthquake. Canadian towns and villages were flattened by the quake.

The people of many coastal towns and villages escaped death only because they ran away from the sea. Whole families clung together as they ran for their lives, pursued by the monster waves that swept up out of the ocean floor and chased them across the land.

The earthquake happened on Good Friday, a Christian holiday, and because of this it is often referred to as the Good Friday Earthquake.

Frozen Flames

We all have heard about the severe cold that roams the wilds of Alaska like a hungry wolf, but the old-timers will tell you that it's much worse than any story. Three men were traveling up in the Dawson City area and found themselves in the wilderness just as the sun was going down. They were coming toward a lake when one of the men happened to see a roaring campfire near the edge of the woods. The three men hiked over to the fire and saw several men sitting around the fire. Now that fire was a big one, with flames that must have been four or five feet in height.

"Excuse me, neighbors," said one of the travelers. "We were wondering if we could warm ourselves by your fire for a while."

There was no answer from the men, who just sat and stared at their campfire.

"Excuse us, but can we share your fire?" asked another of the traveling men.

Still no answer, not even a turn of a head acknowledged their questions.

One of the men walked over to the fire and put out his hand and felt no heat at all. In fact the flame that seemed so warm and inviting was just a frozen tongue from the campfire. It seems that the campfire had frozen solid, and the men who watched it like silent sentinels were frozen just as stiff.

One of the travelers reached out and broke a part of that flame off and stowed it in his pocket. Later that evening when they reached an abandoned cabin and settled down for the night, that flame came back to life and almost burned the cabin down around them.

Yes it was a cold winter in Alaska that year, colder than any story can ever tell.

Alaska Glossary

Alaska: A state that was formerly a Russian colony. It gets its name from the Aleut word "Alyeska," meaning "great land." The United States purchased it in 1867. The capital is Juneau.

Diphtheria: A highly contagious disease that attacks the upper respiratory system and causes swelling that can suffocate its victim.

Dog teams: Trained dogs that pull sleds through ice and snow in Alaska and other areas known for severe winters. Teams are usually made up of between six and sixteen dogs. Often one 50-pound dog can pull up to 800 pounds.

Icon: A beautifully painted picture of a religious figure in the Russian Orthodox Church.

Mushers: Dogsled drivers.

Seismograph: An instrument for measuring the strength of earthquakes.

Theotokos: The name given to the Virgin Mary by the Russian Orthodox Church.

Tsunamis: Tidal waves caused by earthquakes or volcanic eruptions. These waves can be huge and can cause massive destruction.

Story Sources

The Eskimo Storyteller

Folklore from the Working Folk of America

The Greenwood Library of American Folktales, Volume 4

Heroes & Heroines in Tlingit-Haida Legend

Image of a People: Tlingit Myths & Legends

The Magic Calabash: Folktales from America's Islands and Alaska

Northern Tales: Traditional Stories of Eskimo and Indian Peoples

Arizona

Arizona entered the union in 1912 as the forty-eighth state, the last of the contiguous U.S. states. (Alaska and Hawaii are separated from the "lower forty-eight" by Canada and the Pacific Ocean, respectively.) The deserts and mountains of Arizona are home to many Native American peoples, including the Hopi and Navaho. The Hispanic culture is important in this region and is represented by one of the saddest ghost stories in the Americas, "La Llorona" ("The Wailing Woman") and also by a story about a mountain lion who loves a young woman, "The Faithful Lion."

Mining was an important source of income in the state, and the copper-colored star on the Arizona flag signifies that the state was at one time the leading supplier of copper in the United States. We have two stories here from the old mining days, "Belling the Burro" and "The Lost Dutchman Mine." Arizona's stories would not be complete without a tale from the cowboy tradition, and included here is the ballad "The Crooked Trail to Holbrook," which describes the trials of taking cattle from Globe City, Arizona, to Holbrook, Arizona, where the trains took the animals back to eastern slaughterhouses.

Belling the Burro

There was an old prospector who spent almost thirty years in the desert looking for gold or silver or anything that could make him a fortune. It seemed to him that he spent half those years trying to track down his burros. Those donkeys just wandered off all the time and seemed to go deaf whenever he'd call them. He was sure that they hid from him when he went looking for them.

He finally came up with an idea. He put a bell around the neck of his most docile burro, old Sappho. She was like a pet and was the only one who ever came when he called. She also would stay with the others. He figured if he could hear her bell, he'd know where they all were and could easily herd them together when he needed them for work. The idea was working like a charm for a couple weeks, but then he started to notice that he couldn't hear the bell any more. He would go searching for the burros, but he couldn't find them. He would eventually find their tracks and hunt them down, but the bell wasn't helping at all. He thought to himself that maybe he was going deaf.

One day he was coming back to his camp when he passed a small ravine, and there at the bottom he saw his three burros. Sappho was standing still, her head lowered over a flat rock. The other two burros were bringing every other mouthful of grass over to the rock and placing it down in front of her so she wouldn't move her head and ring the bell. There's no doubt about it, burros are smart animals.

La Llorona (The Wailing Woman) (Hispanic)

At one time Arizona was part of Mexican territory and was settled by people of Spanish ancestry. Today, it is home to many Hispanic Americans. This is one of their most well-known stories.

Once a long time ago in Mexico there lived a beautiful woman named Louisa. She came from humble parents and had no money or fame or social position. What Louisa had was incredible beauty, a smile that could brighten a dreary day, and a personality that made her even more attractive.

As Louisa grew up, word of her beauty spread throughout the land. Men came from all around to beg for her hand in marriage, while others came to offer her wealth and a beautiful home as their mistress. She was outraged at the proposals of being a rich man's mistress but soon, when no man of means came forward to ask for her hand in marriage, she saw that the only alternative to living a life of horrible poverty was to accept the offer of being a kept woman. Louisa met one young nobleman, Don Muño de Montes Claros, who fell madly in love with her. He bought a beautiful little house for her and lavished her with gifts. Soon she was as in love with him, as he was always with her and their life was a happy one. Their love was blessed with children, and Louisa always held the hope that one day he would marry her and acknowledge their children as his own and her as his wife.

Don Muno's family kept pressuring him to leave Louisa and find a woman of a respectable family to marry. Louisa knew nothing of the pressure his family was putting on him, until one day he told her that he was leaving their home and marrying a woman of one of the best families in the city. At first she couldn't believe it, but then she cried and argued and told him how much she loved him. He left the house and never returned. Soon she heard that the wedding date had been set.

On the day of the wedding Louisa and her children followed the procession through the city streets and into the church. When the priest asked if anyone had any reason that these two people should not be married, Louisa stood up and proclaimed, "That man is the father of these children." The bride fainted, and rage came over the face of Don Muno.

After that no woman of any respectable family was interested in marrying him.

One evening he came to Louisa's door and demanded she give him the children. "Open up. I want my children now."

"They are my children, too," cried Louisa. "You cannot have them."

He shouted and beat on the door and finally went away, but she knew he would return and take her children. He was a rich Spanish noble and she was a peasant. He would take them from her.

Louisa suddenly felt a madness come over her as she picked up her two youngest children and led the third by the hand and walked to the river behind her house. She threw her children into the river and then calmly walked into the water until it covered her head. She was finally at peace, or was she?

The next morning Don Muno came again to the little house he had once shared with Louisa, but this time he came with the authorities. When there was no answer they broke the door down but found no one inside. They walked through the house and out through the open back door. Don Muno walked over to the river ,where he saw a woman dressed in white with long black hair hovering over the water crying. "Where are my children?" she wailed. She floated down the river crying and asking over and over again, "Where are my children?"

Don Muno died soon after. As his funereal procession made its way through the city streets, a lone woman dressed in white with long black hair followed, crying softly.

They say that Louisa has become La Llorona, the Wailing Woman, who searches the rivers and streams for her drowned children. They say she appears at night in the city and when people see her beauty they follow her and are found dead the next morning staring out with horror in their sightless eyes. Some say she has the face of death; others say her beauty is still there but so contorted by grief that it would bring you to tears. She haunts this world, never touching, just floating above it crying out, "Where are my children? Where are my beautiful children?"

The Lost Dutchman Mine

Jacob Walz was a German, not a Dutchman, but the nickname stuck anyway as nicknames have a habit of doing even if they are wrong. Old Jacob was a hard man with a snow-white beard that framed his fierce face and steely eyes. During one of his trips into the Superstition Mountains, Walz was ambushed by a band of Indians and wounded. He made his escape but lost his horse in the fight, so he walked and crawled until he came upon the camp of three Mexican miners. They tended his wounds, gave him water and food, and took care of the old Dutchman. Walz asked the men why they were out there in the middle of nowhere, and their reply was "gold." The three men had a gold mine, and by the looks of the huge nuggets they showed him it was a mine like no other he had ever heard about in all of Arizona. Distracting the men, Jacob Walz shot them all and buried them there near the opening of the mine. That was the beginning, they say, of the Curse of the Lost Dutchman Mine.

Walz returned to Phoenix and showed off his nuggets and told of his mine. Folks tried following Walz into the Superstition Mountains but the old man knew those mountains better than anyone and had traps and ambushes all laid out along the route to his mine. Many a man left Phoenix determined to find the mine, but none ever returned. They say that one man by the name of Deering had actually found the mine and took out some of its treasure but was killed celebrating his newfound fortune in a Phoenix saloon. He was number seven to die by that curse, at least of all the men that they knew about he was the seventh.

Jacob Walz sent for his nephew in Germany to come and help him. The two of them mined their claim until they had a sizable fortune loaded onto their burros. When they got to town the young man started to spend recklessly and talk about the mine. Walz himself shot his nephew before the young man could blurt out the whereabouts of their hoard.

Walz settled down in Phoenix and finally died from pneumonia. As he lay on his deathbed he tried to tell his friend Dick Holmes about the mine's location. He confessed to killing all the men he had ambushed or who had tried to steal his gold. Before he could complete telling Holmes the directions he died, and the mystery of the Lost Dutchman mine began.

The legend lives on. Perhaps somewhere out there in the Superstition Mountains is a fabulous gold mine cursed by blood and treachery. Perhaps it's all a story.

The Faithful Lion (Hispanic)

At one time Arizona was part of Mexican territory and was settled by people of Spanish ancestry. Today it is home to many Hispanic Americans. This is another one of their stories. The lions found in Arizona are mountain lions.

Once a landowner found a lion cub as he was hunting. He brought the little cub back and gave it to his only daughter as a pet. The lion grew quickly but seemed devoted to the girl.

One of his neighbors warned him that the lion was still a wild animal and could turn on its human friends at any time. The father tried to reason with his daughter about the animal. He wanted to destroy the lion or at the very least turn it loose, but his daughter would have none of it. "Father, the lion is my friend and I will keep him," she said.

Now some local bandits heard that the girl was meeting her boyfriend at a nearby pond and decided to kidnap her and hold her for ransom. They found her, tied her up and gagged her, and raced toward their mountain camp.

Whenever the girl returned from seeing her friend she would always stop and spend time petting and talking to her lion. When she didn't return the lion began to pace and growl and finally it threw itself against its chain and broke its collar. It raced into the brush and disappeared.

Now the bandits had not gone very far when their horses began to shy away from the side of the path and grow more and more nervous. Then suddenly the lion dropped from a branch onto the neck of the leader's horse that was carrying the girl. The leader of the bandits was killed and the others fled into the mountains.

When the girl's father returned he found his daughter and the lion missing. In his mind the beast had gone back to its wild ways and had killed his daughter and escaped. He called his men together and they searched that evening and far into the next day. When they returned from their hunt they found the girl exhausted on the front porch with her faithful lion watching over her.

The Crooked Trail to Holbrook

This song, collected in 1907 by John Lomax, talks about the trials and difficulties of driving a herd of cattle north from Globe to the railroad in Holbrook, Arizona. The trip involved bringing the herd up Mogollon Rim, a 1,800-foot rise that took the cowboys across a dry plateau and on to Holbrook.

Come all you jolly cowboys that follow the bronco steer,
I'll sing to you a verse or two your spirits for to cheer.
It's all about a trip that I did undergo
On that crooked trail to Holbrook in Arizona, oh.

On the seventeenth of February our herd it started out.
It would have made you shudder to hear them bawl and shout.
As wild as any buffalo that ever rode the Platte
Those doggies we were driving and everyone was fat.

We crossed the Mescal Mountains on the way to Gilson Flats,
And when we got to Gilson Flats how the wind did blow.
It blew so hard it blew so fierce we knew not where to go.
But our spirits never failed us as onward we did go
On that crooked trail to Holbrook, in Arizona, oh.

That night we had a stampede; Lord how the cattle run.
We made it to our horses; I tell you we had no fun.
Over the prickly pear and the catclaw brush we quickly made our way.
We thought or our long journey and our girls we'd left that day.

Its long by Sombserva we slowly punched along
While each of us cowboys would sing a hearty song
To cheer up his comrades as onward we did go
On that crooked trail to Holbrook, in Arizona oh.

We crossed the Muggyone Mountains where the tall pines do grow.
Grass grows in abundance and the rippling streams do flow.
Our packs were always turning and of course our gait was slow
On that crooked trail to Holbrook, in Arizona oh.

At last we got to Holbrook and a little storm did blow.
It blew up sand and stones and it didn't blow them slow.
We had to drink the water from that muddy little stream
And swallowed a pound of dirt when we tried to eat our beans.

But the cattle now are shipped and homeward we are bound
With a lot of tired horses as ever could be found.
Across the reservation no danger did we fear,
Filled with thought of wives and sweethearts and the ones we loved so dear.
Now we're back in Globe City, our friendships there to share.
Here's luck to every puncher who follows the bronco steer.

Arizona Glossary

Arizona: A state whose name was probably derived from the Basque words "aritz ona," meaning good oak. Phoenix is the capital of and largest city in Arizona.

Burro: A small donkey.

Doggies: A name for cattle, used by cowboys.

Holbrook: An important city in the days of the cattle industry. The city was a train terminal and had holding pens for cattle before they were shipped east.

Prickly pear and catclaw brush: Desert plants.

Prospector: A person who hunted for precious metals like gold and silver. Usually prsopectors were solitary people and very nomadic, moving from one area to another looking for any sign of gold or silver.

Stampede: Startled cattle running in fear. It was very difficult to stop.

Puncher: A cowboy working with cattle, especially on the trail.

Story Sources

And It Is Still That Way: Legends Told by Arizona Indian Children

Buying the Wind

The Cactus Sandwich & Other Tall Tales of the Southwest

The Corn Woman, Stories and Legends of the Hispanic Southwest

Coronado's Children: Tales of Lost Mines & Buried Treasures of the South West

Cowboy Songs and Other Frontier Ballads

The Eagle and the Cactus: Traditional Stories from Mexico

The Folklore of Spain in the American Southwest

The Greenwood Library of American Folktales, Volume 3

The Hell-Bound Train: A Cowboy Songbook

Mexican Folktales from the Borderland

Mexican-American Folklore

Montezuma's Serpent & Other True Supernatural Tales of the Southwest

Navaho Folk Tales

Navajo Coyote Tales

Tales from the American Frontier

A Treasury of Western Folklore

Arkansas

Arkansas became the twenty-fifth state in 1836. Tall tales are one of the great American contributions to folk literature, and whether we are talking about how cold it can get or how big that fish that got away really was, it's all great storytelling. Arkansas has some great whoppers, and we have two here that deal with how cold it can really get in the state and the slowest train to travel Arkansas's rails.

Arkansas is home to many immigrants, such as the Irish, as well as Native American people, including the Caddo.

Included here is one of America's most famous humorous folk dialogues, "The Arkansas Traveler." Good preachers are hard to come by, especially like the one in the story "The Preacher and the Bully."

The Preacher and the Bully

The mill was a place the community met on Saturdays. People came to get their corn ground and to exchange the local news and gossip. Now once there was a new preacher in this community, and he came to the mill to get acquainted with his congregation and talk and visit with folks. Now that Saturday the local bully was at the mill looking for trouble. He was the kind of man who was always looking to pick a fight with someone or humiliate someone in front of the rest of the town. This bully especially hated preachers and took great pleasure in publicly humiliating every one that came to town.

That day he walked up to the new preacher and started to tease him then taunt him and finally told him that he'd better defend himself because he didn't care who he was, he was going to give him a good beating. Now the preacher was tall and broad shouldered and didn't have the looks of a man who would back down from a loud-mouthed bully.

The preacher looked the bully in the eye and said, "All right son, but before I fight, I always get down and pray to God. So if you'll excuse me just a moment, I'll say my prayers, and then I'll fight you."

The bully smirked as the preacher got down on his knees. The preacher closed his eyes and prayed, "Lord, you know, the last fight I had, I had to kill the man because he was going to kill me. It was his life or mine. And those two other men over in my last parish, that I was forced to fight and eventually take their lives, you understand that it was self-defense Lord and that I had no other choice. And now, Lord, I'm forced to fight again and take the life of another man, and I want you to forgive me, because it's either him or me."

He finished his prayer, sighed, and slowly got up off his knees, then he pulled a long knife out of his boot and he began to sing,

> "Hark, from the tomb a doleful sound;
> Mine ears attend the cry.
> Ye living men come view the ground
> Where you shall shortly lie."

And when he turned around he only saw a little speck of dust down the road. The bully was running for his life. As the preacher allowed himself a slight smile, the folks in town knew that they had a really clever man as their new pastor.

The Night the Lamp Flame Froze

In the winter of 1917, which was the coldest winter in the history of our country, I went up to bed one night, and in those days we had acetylene lights in our house. I went up to bed and lighted the light and got undressed and got ready to go to bed, and when I started to turn out the light, I turned the little screw that was supposed to turn out the light, and nothing happened. Thought that was strange, so I tried to blow it out. I blew and I blew. And the light didn't even flicker—and, lo and behold, when I came to investigate, it was frozen, so I didn't want to sleep in a brilliantly lighted room all night, so I reached up, snapped off the light, went to the window, and threw it out in the yard.

The next morning, one of our old hens thought that was a particularly nice-looking grain of corn, so she swallowed it. Ever since then, until our old hen died, we had hard-boiled eggs for breakfast every morning.

The Slowest Train in Arkansas

Arkansas had the distinction of having the slowest train that ever ran on tracks. One day a man was on this train and it suddenly stopped. He called to the conductor, "Sir, why has the train stopped?"

"There's a cow on the track," replied the conductor.

A little while later it stopped again. "What's happened this time?" asked the passenger.

"Well, it seems we caught up to that cow again," replied the trainman.

The train kept catching up to that cow. The cow insisted on walking down the tracks. After a while it grew a little lazy and slept for a couple hours, but it caught up to the train again and tried to climb into the sleeper car. Good thing they had a cowcatcher on both ends of that train. A lady passenger finally asked, "Conductor, can't this train go any faster?"

"Madam, if you're not happy with the speed of this train, you can get out and walk," the man replied.

"I would," said the woman, "but my family isn't expecting me until the train gets there and I don't want to surprise them by getting in early."

As the conductor collected tickets one woman gave him one and a half tickets. "What's this half ticket for?" he asked.

"My son," she replied.

"Ma'am, adults pay full fare and those under twelve pay half fare. That young man is over twelve."

"He was under twelve when we started this trip," she countered.

An old man walked through the train selling newspapers and candy. "Hey, old-timer," one man called out. "I thought that the job of selling papers and such was usually held by a boy."

The old man turned to the passenger and said, "I was a boy when this train started out."

One of the passengers grew so depressed at how long the trip was taking that he ran ahead of the train and lay across the tracks in order to commit suicide. Trouble was the train was so slow that he starved to death before the train got to him.

At one point the train had a narrow escape from certain destruction. Just as the last car reached the other side of a long wooden bridge, the bridge collapsed into the deep ravine below. One lady asked the conductor, "How did we get across the bridge without falling down with it?"

He looked at her coolly and replied, "Train robbers held us up."

Now there were three classes of passengers on this train: first, second, and third class. One man asked what was the difference between the three classes since they were all riding in the same car. The conductor told the man that his question would be answered soon. In a few minutes the train stopped and the conductor yelled out, "First class passengers stay in your seats. Second class passengers get out and walk. Third class passengers get out and push."

I heard that the train finally made it to its destination. The passengers stayed put and never returned to their original homes. They all agreed that it saved time to just start all over again in a new place rather than chance dying of old age on a return ticket.

The Arkansas Traveler

A traveler on the back roads of Arkansas stops at a small cabin and seeing an old man playing the fiddle decides to ask for directions. What happens next is one of the most famous discussions in American folklore.

"Good afternoon, sir," said the traveling man.

"Hello yourself," said the fiddler.

"Can you tell me where this road goes?"

"It's never been anywhere as far as I know. Its always here when I wake up each morning."

"I was wondering if you had any food?"

"We don't have a thing in the house. Not a piece of meat or a handful of corn."

"Do you have any grain for my horse?"

"I don't have a thing to feed him on."

"I was wondering if I could spend the night? I wouldn't need anything to eat or drink, just a roof over my head."

"Sorry, but the roof leaks. There's only one dry place in the whole house, and that's where my wife and I sleep."

"Why don't you repair your roof if it leaks?"

"Its been raining all day long. I can't repair it in the rain."

"Why don't you fix it when it's dry?"

"It doesn't leak when it's dry."

"Not much between you and a fool, is there?"

The fiddler looked at the traveler and at the space in between them and said, "About three feet."

"Say, how do you do for a living out here?"

"Fine. How about yourself?"

"I mean what do you do for a living? How do you make any money?"

"I sell food and drink."

"I told you before that's what I wanted."

"Food and drink are all gone. Me and Sal ate and drank it all up."

The traveler turned his horse away. The old man kept playing the same few notes over and over again on his fiddle. The traveler couldn't resist one last remark. "Why don't you play the rest of that song?"

"What do you mean?"

"I mean you're not playing the whole song, just part of it. Why don't you finish it?"

"Can you play the fiddle?"

"Yes, a little."

"Well, you don't look like a fiddler, but if you can finish that tune or pull another one out of your head, you can get off that horse and try."

The traveler got off his horse and picked up the fiddle and started to play. He finished the tune the old man had been playing and then played a few more.

The old man was impressed and called out to his family. "Sal, go down to the holler where I killed that buck this morning and bring back the best pieces. Tom, go under the floor boards and get a jug of liquor I've been keeping for a special occasion. Mose, take this man's horse around to the barn and give that animal as much oats and fodder as he can eat."

"How come you didn't offer me those things before?"

"I didn't know you could play the fiddle before now. Keep playing, stranger, and you can sleep in the dry spot tonight."

One Tough Hog

Texas has its long-horned cattle and Maine has its moose, while Florida has alligators. Like these states and so many others, Arkansas also has an animal that it is closely identified with, and that's the razorback. The razorback descended from the European wild pigs that were brought to America with early explorers. They are tough animals that can be ferocious, especially the boars, when cornered.

There was an Arkansas farmer who decided to clear a section of his land. That part of his farm was overgrown with scrub and old trees, and the farmer and his sons worked hard to clear away the area and get it ready for planting. The last thing they had to do was rid the field of a couple of huge old tree stumps. The farmer decided to use dynamite. He placed the stick in a hole right next to a stubborn old stump. He lit the fuse and he and his sons ran back toward the house. Unfortunately the fuse died out and the dynamite didn't go off. Since it was getting late in the day, the man decided to leave it where it was and relight the fuse in the morning.

Early the next morning, before anyone was awake a huge razorback hog started rooting around near the stump and swallowed that stick of dynamite whole. Still hungry, the animal ambled down to the barn and tried to muscle into one of the stalls to steal some breakfast from the farmer's prize mule. Not being an animal that shared his food, the mule reared back and kicked that razorback in the side. It was the last time that old mule would ever kick anything because his hooves connected with the dynamite in the old hog's stomach. The explosion woke folks three miles away.

When a neighbor hurried over to see if there was anything he could do to help the farmer, he found the man leaning on his fence staring at what used to be his barn.

"It looks bad, really bad," said the neighbor, staring at the ruins of the barn.

"Yes, it does," replied the farmer. "The explosion killed my mule, destroyed the barn and the henhouse, and blew out every window on the south side of the house. I also have one sick hog on my hands."

The Gift of Music (Caddo People)

Once, when the earth mother was very young, everyone's heart was heavy. Everyone was sad, and no one knew why. It was because there was no music, but the people didn't know there wasn't any. The only thing they knew was that they felt terrible, and they didn't know why.

At the same time, in the same section of the woods each day everyone would gather to talk about their bad feelings. One day as they were gathering, Hawk was late for the meeting. Hawk went flying over the mountaintops and treetops; she was flying fast, for she wanted her chance to complain. She flew faster and faster, but she knew she would get there too late.

"I know what I'll do," she said to herself. "I'll fly as high as I can possibly fly, and from that vantage point I can see where the meeting is, and I can be there in just a little while."

So Hawk began to fly—higher and higher, on the currents of the wind and in great circles she flew. All of a sudden Hawk began to feel good. She didn't know why—the only thing she knew was that the higher she flew, the better she felt.

Hawk and the Hole in the Sky

Then she saw it—a hole in the sky. From the hole came a sound that made Hawk feel good. Up toward the hole in the sky flew Hawk, but the hole in the sky was high, too high, and Hawk couldn't reach it. She tried again, and again, and again, but the hole was high, too high. Growing very tired, she turned and came back down to where the others were gathered. And there they were, having their usual conversation, talking about their bad feelings when Hawk said, "I felt good today."

"What, Hawk?" They said. "You felt good? How is it you felt good?"

She told them about the hole in the sky. "And the sound coming from the hole," said Hawk, "made me feel good."

"Hawk," they said, "could you find this hole again? Could you bring this sound to us?"

"I'm sure I could," said Hawk. "I'm sure I could."

Everyone was anxious and waiting as Hawk began to fly. Higher and higher, on the currents of the wind and in great circles she flew. And there, just as Hawk remembered, was the hole in the sky, and the sound coming from the hole made Hawk feel good. Up toward the hole in the sky flew Hawk, but the hole was high, too high, and Hawk couldn't reach it. She tried again, and again, and again, but the hole was high, too high. Growing very tired, she turned and came back down to where the others were waiting.

"Hawk," they said, "did you bring the sound?"

"I couldn't," said Hawk. "The hole in the sky is too high, and I couldn't reach it."

Everyone was sad. They all turned and began to scatter when someone said, "Eagle can do it! Surely Eagle can do it."

"Yes," said Eagle, "I can do it. Hawk, where is this hole in the sky?"

Eagle's Attempt

Getting the directions from Hawk, Eagle was ready. Everyone was anxious and waiting as Eagle began to fly. Higher and higher, on the currents of the wind and in great circles he flew. And there, just as Hawk had said, was the hole in the sky; and just as Hawk had said, the sound coming from the hole made Eagle feel good. Up toward the hole in the sky flew Eagle, but just as Hawk had said, the hole was high, too high, and Eagle couldn't reach it. He tried again, and again, and again, but the hole was high, too high. Growing very tired, he turned and came back down to where the others were waiting.

"Eagle," they said, "did you bring the sound?"

"I couldn't," said Eagle. "The hole in the sky is too high, and I couldn't reach it."

Everyone was sad. They all turned and began to scatter when Eagle said, "Let me rest for three days. Surely with three days' rest, I can do it."

On the third day, everyone was anxious and waiting as Eagle began to fly. Higher and higher, on the currents of the wind and in great circles he flew. Up to the hole in the sky flew Eagle, and the sound coming from the hole made Eagle feel good. Up toward the hole in the sky flew Eagle, but the hole was high, too high, and Eagle couldn't reach it. He tried again, and again, and again, but the hole was high, too high. Growing very tired, he turned and came back down to where the others were waiting.

"Eagle," they said, "did you bring the sound?"

"I couldn't," said Eagle. "The hole in the sky is too high, and I couldn't reach it."

Everyone was sad. They all turned and began to scatter when Eagle said, "Let me rest for seven days. Surely with seven days' rest I can do it."

One the seventh day, everyone was anxious and waiting. Eagle was under the tree doing warm-up exercises—stretching his wings, making certain all his muscles were ready, ruffling his feathers to make sure they were all in place. Standing behind Eagle was Thrush, and she said to herself, "Look how soft Eagle's feathers look. I wonder if they feel as soft as they look." Quickly and quietly she walked up and reached out to feel the soft feathers of Eagle. Just as she did so, someone said, "Eagle, it's time to go."

Eagle snapped his feathers shut, trapping Thrush inside, unfelt by Eagle. "I'm ready," said Eagle.

Eagle began to fly. Higher and higher, on the currents of the wind and in great circles he flew. Up to the hole in the sky flew Eagle, and the sound coming from the hole made Eagle feel good. Up toward the hole in the sky flew Eagle; but the hole was high, too high, and Eagle couldn't reach it. He tried again, and again, and again, but still the hole was out of reach. "Surely I can do this thing," said Eagle to himself. He gathered all of the strength of his seven days' rest and tried one more time, but the hole was too high. Growing very tired, he turned and came back down to where the others were waiting.

Just as Eagle turned, a strong wind began to blow, and Eagle's feathers began to ruffle. As Eagle's feathers ruffled, Thrush fell out of Eagle's feathers and flew through the hole in the sky, unseen by Eagle.

Eagle came down to where the others were gathered and waiting, "Eagle," they said, "did you bring the sound?"

"I couldn't," said Eagle. "The hole in the sky is too high, and I couldn't reach it."

Everyone was sad. They all began to scatter, feeling even worse than when they had gathered.

Thrush Hears the Sound

When Thrush got through the hole in the sky, she heard the sound that had made Hawk and Eagle feel good, and it was coming from all around her. The sound she heard was music. She opened her ears and her eyes, and they filled up with music. She opened her mouth, and it too filled with music until she was so full she could hold no more.

Turning away with the sound, Thrush flew back down to where the others had been waiting. But when she got there, everyone was gone. Thrush felt good inside—so good that she jumped up onto a branch of a tree and opened her mouth. The music came forth and filled up the earth. People heard the music, and they all began to feel good inside. Robin heard a song and said, "That's my favorite song." To this day this is the song Robin sings. Meadowlark heard a song and said, "That's my favorite." To this day this is the song that Meadowlark sings. Everyone heard a song that was his or her favorite, and to this day that's the song that person sings.

This afternoon, tomorrow, or the next day, as you are out and about, you will hear a song coming from a bird. Look, and you'll see that it is Thrush. Say thank-you to Thrush for bringing to us the gift of music. You see, because everyone had scattered and gone home, nobody knows that it was Thrush who brought music to us. Ah, but you know, because I've just told you the story.

Used with permission of Dayton Edmonds, Caddo storyteller.

Arkansas Glossary

Arkansas: A state whose name comes from the French pronunciation of the Native American tribe Quapaw. The capital is Little Rock.

Caddo people: A Native American tribe who lived in the Arkansas/Texas area.

Lamp: A glass vessel filled with oil, often whale oil, and lit to produce light, used before the introduction of gas lamps and then electricity.

Razorbacks: European wild pigs. The mascot of the University of Arkansas is the razorback.

Story Sources

American Myths & Legends, Volumes 1 & 2

Arkansas Voices

The Charm Is Broken: Readings in Arkansas & Missouri Folklore

Cowboy Songs and other Frontier Ballads

Dayton Edmunds, Caddo Storyteller

The Devil's Pretty Daughter & Other Ozark Folktales

The Greenwood Library of American Folktales, Volume 2

Myths & Legends of Our Own Land, Volumes 1 & 2

Outlaw Tales: Legends, Myths & Folklore from America's Middle Border

Ozark Folksongs

Stars Is God's Lanterns: An Offering of Ozark Tellin' Tales

Sticks in the Knapsack & Other Ozark Folk Tales

The Talking Turtle & Other Ozark Folk Tales

A Treasury of Southern Folklore

We Always Lie to Strangers: Tall Tales from the Ozarks

California

California became the thirty-first state in 1850 after it had won its independence from Mexico and had established itself as a republic. Because of its history as both a Spanish and Mexican territory, California has a large Hispanic population and the humorous story "Love Mad Lopez and His Pigs" comes to us from that part of California's culture. "The Evil Eye of Governor Salvatierria" is a tale from the Spanish colonial days of California. The old superstitions from that time would almost be funny if the people hadn't taken them so seriously.

Japanese people came to California to seek what all immigrants sought, a better life. During World War II thousands of Japanese Americans, most born and raised here, were placed in internment camps and detained during the entire war, losing their homes, businesses, and possessions. "The Crane Wife" is a traditional Japanese story. When gold was discovered in California it started a race for people to get there and find their fortune. The sea shanty "Banks of the Sacramento" tells about the days of the gold rush.

Love Mad Lopez and His Pigs (Hispanic)

At one time, California was part of Mexican territory, and much of the state was settled by people of Spanish ancestry. This is one of their stories.

Don José Lopez, Love Mad Lopez to friends and admirers, was a man who accomplished great things in his long and illustrious life. He was the first person to teach a coyote to sing, he planted the first crying frijole, he made San Francisco Bay, he planted the Redwood forest, he painted the Painted Desert, he cut the Grand Canyon, he formed Mount Shasta, and he really was responsible for making California look the way it looks today. He traveled around on a flying palm tree chasing the elusive and unknown sangua lima. He was the leader of the Order of Caballeros of the Love Mad Lopez. He was also the man who started the first pig farm in California.

A ship from Spain landed in California carrying a prize boar and some sows. Love Mad Lopez decided that it would be a good idea to raise these pigs for food for his Caballeros. He bought the animals and brought them to his ranch. The pigs had the run of the ranch and ate anything that wasn't moving and a few things that were. The buzzards had to move on since the pigs left them nothing to eat. The pigs grew wild and multiplied until they became quite a nuisance. One day one of his pigs wandered off the ranch and found the mission garden. What it didn't eat it destroyed. The padres at the mission were really angry with Lopez for allowing his pig to eat their vegetables, so they had one of the mission workers shoot the pig.

Now Lopez and his Caballeros never killed anything. They only lived for love. They got the food they needed from the pigs by milking them. They drank pig milk and made pig cheese. They even discovered the art of making pig ice cream.

When Lopez found out that the padres had killed one of his pigs he was heartbroken. He and his Caballeros decided to teach the padres a lesson, so one night they crept into the mission church and stole the bell from the bell tower. You can imagine the chaos the next morning when the bell ringer could not ring the bell and the padres could not hear it and the people coming to church only had to imagine the sound. The mission had to order a new bell from Spain.

Lopez took the bell back to his ranch. He trained the pigs to come to the sound of the bell at milking and feeding time. The pigs were so smart that in no time they would stampede into the milking barn every time they heard the bell ring. The bell was just what they needed on the ranch. Now if anyone needed some pig milk, they just rang the bell and soon they had hundreds of pigs at their disposal waiting to be milked.

After a year or so Lopez and his men knew that they had too many pigs. They just couldn't feed or milk them all. Even though it broke their hearts, they decided they would have to sell some of their beloved friends. When spring came they drove a huge herd of pigs into town. They had to use their singing coyote as a pig dog because none of the sheep dogs would herd pigs. As they were passing the mission the new bell sounded in the bell tower and all those pigs stampeded into the church.

Now the padres were horrified at their new congregation. They ordered their servants to kill the pigs for coming to church.

Before a finger could be lifted against the pigs a new sound was heard in the harbor. A Yankee ship captain had heard the noise and fearing that the townspeople were rioting and would take over his ship, he started to sail away. When he did he rang the bell on his deck to order his sailors to hoist the sails. The pigs heard that bell and started to run toward the harbor. They all dove into the Pacific Ocean and followed that ship all the way to China.

Love Mad Lopez was so disappointed in how his morning had turned out that he rode back to his ranch. He climbed onto his flying palm tree and was soon past the horizon in search of new adventure.

Yearning to Be Free: The Japanese Internment Camps (a True Story)

In 1942 during the early days of World War II the U.S. government made the decision to forcibly relocate the Japanese American population on the West Coast and place the people in interment camps: guarded military camps. Some 120,000 Japanese, 70 percent of them American citizens and the majority Nisei, Japanese Americans born in this country, were sent to these camps from California, Oregon, and Washington. In many cases their homes were looted and their possessions were stolen. Landowners among the Japanese were forced to sell their land before being relocated and were often cheated by corrupt land speculators. The camps were stark and crowded and afforded little or no privacy or decent living conditions. There was a great deal of support among California farmers for this relocation. They didn't want to compete with the Japanese farmers. Most of the people were actually set free from these internment centers in January 1945 while the war in the Pacific raged on, giving rise to the theory that the relocation was not so much a security action as a public relations ploy.

Ironically, while the Japanese Americans were held captive in the relocation centers, the 442nd Infantry Regiment, known as the Purple Heart Battalion, was fighting in Europe. This unit was comprised almost entirely of Japanese Americans who had volunteered to fight in the war. The 442nd became the most highly decorated military unit in the history of the U.S. Armed Forces, with twenty-one Medal of Honor winners.

The Crane Wife (Japanese)

California is home to many people of Japanese descent. This is one of the stories they brought from the old country.

Once a long time ago there was a man named Karoku. He lived deep in the mountains with his elderly mother. Karoku was a charcoal maker and worked hard to provide for his mother and himself. One winter day he was going to the nearby village to buy some new bedding when he saw a crane struggling in a trap. The bird was suffering and desperate to get out of the trap.

As Karoku tried to set the bird free, the man who had set the trap came running up to him. "What are you doing? That is my trap and my bird. Mind your own business."

"I am sorry, but I felt sorry for the animal as it suffered in your trap. Please sell me the crane. I have money that I was going to use for new bedding, but I am willing to buy the bird from you. Please take this money and give me the crane." The man agreed and together they got the trap open and freed the frantic bird. The bird flew off into the sky.

Karoku watched the bird fly away and was satisfied that though the nights might be cold, he did do the right thing. When he got home he told his mother about the bird in the trap and using their money to set it free. "I am sorry that I spent the money we saved for bedding on the bird, but it was a terrible sight to see it in that trap."

"Since it is done it must have been the right thing to do," she answered.

The next evening as night began to fall across the mountains a beautiful young lady came to Karoku's house. They had never seen her before, and her beauty was startling. "Please, may I spend the night here?" she asked.

"My lady, my poor cottage is too humble for someone like you. We are too poor to treat you the way you deserve," he replied.

"I don't mind. Please let me stay," she begged. He finally relented and let her stay there at his home.

After the evening meal she took him aside and said, "There is something I would like to discuss with you."

"What is it?" he asked.

"Please, I beg you, take me as your wife."

Karoku was shocked. "I have never met a woman of your beauty and breeding. I am a very poor man. Sometimes my mother and I don't even know when we will have our next meal. How could I marry a woman such as yourself?"

"Please do not refuse me," she begged him. "Please take me as your wife."

Finally his aged mother joined in and said, "Since you want to marry my son so badly, there must be a reason. Please join our family." Preparations were made and they were married.

Some time after they were married she asked him if he would lock her in a small room and not look in and look at her. She insisted that the room be locked and that he give her his word that he would not look into the room at all until she came out.

Karoku did as she requested, and four days later she came out of the room. She looked tired. Karoku made her something to eat.

"I was so worried about you. Are you alright?" he asked.

She smiled and said, "Yes, I'm fine. But there is something you can do for me. While I was in that room I wove a bolt of cloth. Take it to the market and sell it. Do not ask less than 2,000 ryo for it." She went into the room and came back with a bolt of the most beautiful cloth that he had ever seen.

Hoping to get a better price, Karoku decided to take it to the lord of his province. The lord was so impressed that he offered Karoku 3,000 ryo for it. He then told him that he wanted another bolt of this beautiful cloth.

"I'll have to ask my wife," replied Karoku.

"No need to. I'll just give you the money now and you can bring it to me in a few days."

Karoku agreed. When he told his wife she looked weary but said that she could weave another bolt but that this time she would need a week alone in the room, undisturbed and with no interruptions.

Karoku waited almost until the end of the week, but he started to get worried about his wife. He had not heard from her or seen her, and he started to feel that she might be in trouble. He opened the door to the room to see if she was all right. What he saw was a crane sitting at a loom. She had pulled out most of her feathers and had used them to weave the beautiful cloth. The crane was almost done when he barged into the room.

"Here is the cloth that you wanted, but now that you have seen me like this I can no longer stay here and be with you. I am not a person but the crane that you saved from the trap and set free. I must go home now."

The crane turned toward the west and thousands of cranes came and took her away with them and disappeared over the horizon.

Karoku was now a rich man, but without his crane wife he felt empty inside. He spent months searching for her. One day he lay on a beach exhausted after his search when he saw an old man in a boat coming toward the land. Karoku thought it odd since there were no islands nearby. As he watched the boat came up on the beach.

"Grandfather," called out Karoku, "Where did you come from?"

"I came from the island called "The Robe of the Crane Feathers."

"Can you take me there?"

The old man agreed, and soon they were speeding across the water. In a very short time they came to an island with a beautiful white beach. When they landed Karoku got out, and when he turned toward the boat it was gone and the old man with it.

Karoku walked up the beach and soon came to a pond. In the middle of the pond there was an island, and there stood the naked crane on the island surrounded by hundreds of other cranes that attended to her. She was their queen.

Karoku stayed on the island for a few days. There was a feast in his honor, and when it was time to go the old man and the boat reappeared. Karoku was taken back to his home, where he lived until he was very old with the memories of his beautiful crane wife.

Gold Fever (a True Story)

When gold was discovered in California the promise of quick riches was too much for many people out east. It started one of the most frenzied migrations in American history. Men left their homes, their wives and children, their farms, and their jobs and headed west to the gold fields. They came by horse, by wagon, on foot, and by ship, all dreaming of striking it rich. Following the miners came the gamblers, saloonkeepers, and thieves who preyed upon them, making the miners' camps dangerous places to live.

Gold was discovered at Sutter's Mill on the American River just forty miles from where the American River flows into the Sacramento River. On January 24, 1848, James Marshall, who was building a sawmill for Captain John Sutter, discovered gold in the water. Sutter and Marshall tied to keep it a secret, but word spread like wildfire. Men from all over California, Mexico, and the Southwest flooded into the area. Then the fever spread to the whole United States. The gold rush started in 1849, and the men who traveled to California to look for gold were called Forty-Niners.

The fastest way to get to California at that time was by boat, and soon ships were arriving in San Francisco Bay by the hundreds. Most ships lost not only their passengers but also their crews to the gold fields, and soon there were over a hundred ships rotting at the docks because the captains could not get a crew. (The sea song included here, a capstan shanty, talks about the journey to California and the gold rush fever.)

Banks of the Sacramento

This version of this sea shanty is from the days of the California Gold Rush. The harbor in San Francisco was filled with rotting hulks. Their crews had abandoned the ships to search for gold.

A bully ship and a bully crew,
Dooda, dooda*
A bully mate and a captain too,
Doodah, doodah day.*

Chorus
Then blow ye winds hi ho
For Californio.
There's plenty of gold so I've been told
On the banks of the Sacramento.

Oh around Cape Horn we're bound to go,
Around Cape Horn through the sleet and snow.
Chorus
Oh around Cape Horn in the month of May,
Oh around Cape Horn is a very long way.
Chorus
Ninety days to Frisco Bay,
Ninety days is darn good pay.
Chorus
I wish to God I'd never been born
To go a sailing around Cape Horn.
Chorus
To the Sacramento we're bound away,
To the Sacramento is long, long way.
Chorus
We've formed a band and are well manned
To journey to the promised land.

*These lines repeat in every verse.

Chorus
Oh them was the days of the good old time,
Back in the days of Forty-nine.
Last chorus
Then low ye winds hi ho
For Californio.
There's plenty of stones and dead men's bones
On the banks of the Sacramento.

The Evil Eye of Governor Salvatierra (Based on True Events)

Governor Savatierra was a proud old warrior. He had been a soldier and an officer in Spain's army and was now a governor in California. He wore a patch over his right eye. He had lost the eye in battle to an Indian arrow. The patch gave him the look of a man who had seen the worst in life, and his proud bearing gave him the look of a man who knew how to rule others.

One morning a visitor came to his office, the captain of a sailing ship from America. It was 1797, and Spain ruled California; ships from America could visit but not spend the night in Spanish waters. But the Governor had been expecting this ship and was in a friendly mood, so he ordered a splendid lunch for Captain Scrudder of the ship *General Court*. The food was wonderful and the wine flowed all afternoon. They sang songs and the Governor even showed the Yankee captain how to do a Spanish dance. Soon it was time to go, and Captain Scrudder gave the Governor a small package that he had brought with him. The Governor was grateful and sent the captain back to his ship with wine and food for his entire crew. By sunset the *General Court* was under sail and leaving the harbor.

The next morning Governor Salvaterria went to mass at the church on the square. When he walked in all the people were astonished at what they saw: the Governor now had a right eye. The priests in the church gave special thanks for the miracle that had happened to their beloved Governor. People who usually didn't come to mass during the week came just to see if it was true. But the joy only lasted for awhile.

Soon rumors started that the Governor's new eye could see into a man's soul. People started to confess to crimes when brought before him before they were even asked any questions. Even the priests found themselves telling the old warrior about crimes he had never suspected them of committing. Hearing these things from his people changed him so he appeared sterner and harsher in his judgments. This only fueled the rumors that the evil eye had been given to him as a gift from Satan himself. The people started to cross themselves when he walked by, and the priests started to talk to their peasant congregations about the "evil governor" and how he was Satan's tool and should be destroyed. The Governor knew nothing of these rumors.

One night while he was fast asleep in his bed, four men sneaked into his room. Thinking that it was their duty to rid the world of sin, they had come to kill the unsuspecting old man. One quietly came forward with a knife while the other three waited by the window. As he slowly raised his weapon overhead to kill the sleeping man, the moonlight from the open window struck something on the table next to the bed, and when the man saw the right eye staring up at him from the table he screamed, and he kept on screaming until the Governor awoke and taking up his faithful sword he drove the men from his room. In the fight one of them hit him in his right eye.

The next day people saw that the right eye was once more under a patch, and at the edges of the patch it could be seen to be swollen and dark. The people seemed friendlier, and finally Governor Salvatierra put it all together and figured out what had happened. He continued to wear the patch and once more became the almost fatherlike leader that he had been before. The priests gave thanks in church for the return of their beloved Governor and for the defeat of the Devil.

To his dying day Governor Salvatierra never told them that his "evil eye" was nothing more than a glass eye that the Yankee ship had brought him. You see how simple it is to go from truth to legend.

California Glossary

Caballeros: A Spanish or Mexican gentleman horseman.

California: A state that got its name from the Spanish word meaning "The Land of Calafia." Calafia was a mythical queen who ruled over a tribe of Amazon warriors. Her land was supposedly rich in gold and fantastic beasts. The capital of California is Sacramento.

Capstan shanty: A song that sailors sang to haul up the anchor or to work the pumps that cleared water from the ship. Songs kept the men working at an even speed and made the work go faster.

Cranes: Tall wading birds with long legs and bills. They have large wingspans.

Ryo: Money in medieval Japan.

Story Sources

American Myths & Legends, Volumes 1 & 2

Back in the Beforetime: Tales of the California Indians

The Bodega War & Other Tales from Western Lore

Buying the Wind

The Corn Woman, Stories and Legends of the Hispanic Southwest

Coronado's Children: Tales of Lost Mines & Buried Treasures of the South West

Cowboy Songs and other Frontier Ballads

Folktales from the Japanese Countryside

Folktales of Japan

The Greenwood Library of American Folktales, Volume 3

Heroes, Villains & Ghosts: Folklore of Old California

The Inland Whale: Nine Stories Retold from California Indian Legends

Legends of the Yosemite Miwok

Mexican Folktales from the Borderland

Mexican-American Folklore

Montezuma's Serpent & Other True Supernatural Tales of the Southwest

Myths & Legends of Our Own Land, Volumes 1 & 2

The Parade of Heroes

Tales from the American Frontier

A Treasury of Western Folklore

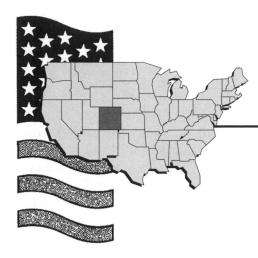

Colorado

Colorado entered the union as the thirty-eighth state in 1876. It is a state dominated by the majesty of the Rocky Mountains, so it is fitting that one of the stories here is about one of the best known of those mountain men, Kit Carson. The mountains also gave rise to an important industry for the state, and we have included a story from those early mining days. Building the railroads through the mountains was difficult and dangerous, and driving those trains over the steep inclines, the snow-covered passes, and the precarious trestles gave us some great folktales, including the haunting story of Marshall Pass.

Native American people, including the Arapaho, Cheyenne, and Ute, roamed these mountains for generations. Tall tales follow wherever American pioneers go, and Colorado is no exception. Where else but in the cold mountain streams would you find fish growing fur? Most communities are blessed by that one person who is so selfless that he or she takes care of those that are in need no matter what the cost, and the story of "Silver Heels" tells about one such person. The Hispanic tradition is presented here with the story "The Eagle and the Lion."

Kit Carson and the Grizzlies
(Based on True Events)

Kit Carson had the great elk in his sights. He squeezed the trigger and watched, as all hunters do, as his shot hit home and the elk dropped to the ground. But the echo of his rifle had not died away when he heard another sound. He knew what animal made this roar, and as he turned he saw two huge grizzly bears charging toward him through the underbrush. It seemed that these monarchs were a bit angry at the mountain man for coming into their kingdom and taking what these huge bears thought was rightfully theirs. Kit barely had time to think, let alone wonder at the situation. He dropped his rifle, wishing that the bullet he had sent through the heart of the elk was now magically back in its chamber so he could use it to defend himself. He took off running, the bears not far behind. Kit knew that his only hope was to make it to the small stand of trees nearby. He ran as hard as he could, the two giant bears in close pursuit. He reached the first tree and jumping as high as he could, he took hold of a low branch and hauled himself up just as a huge paw swept through the air where he had been only a second before.

Knowing that bears can climb trees, Kit took out his big bowie knife and began cutting away at a thick branch. He knew that for all their strength, speed, and power bears were very sensitive on their noses. The bears walked around the base of the tree once or twice and then prepared for their assault. One of the bears took hold of the trunk with his two front legs and started to haul himself up toward the waiting mountain man. As soon as the first bear came close to Kit, he reached down with his wooden weapon and rapped the bear on the nose a few times. The huge monster fell heavily to the earth, rubbing his nose with his paws and howling in rage and pain.

The second bear also tried to reach Kit, but he got hit in the nose too and roared as he slid down the tree. The two huge monarchs of the mountains walked around and around the tree. They were determined that they would not be outsmarted by a mere human. This was now a matter of pride. Kit had beaten them at a foot race, had beaten them up the tree, and now was wounding their pride by beating their noses. They tried over and over again to pull him down from the tree, but all they got for their efforts were more hits on their noses. Kit was clinging to the branches of the tree and desperate to keep them off. They rested for a few moments and then, standing up to their enormous heights, the two tried together one last time, only to feel that hard stick smack their noses over and over again. The two giants walked off, staring over their shoulders at Kit with a sour look in their eyes. Kit waited for a long time before he finally climbed down and found his rifle. He reloaded it right away and walked back cautiously to his campsite.

Of all his adventures, Kit always thought that this was his closest brush with death. His admiration and respect for the mighty grizzly grew that day, you might say, by leaps and bounds.

The Mystery Train of Marshall Pass

Nelson Edwards was an experienced engineer who had recently been assigned to the route that took the passenger train through Marshall Pass. The Marshall Pass was over 12,000 feet above sea level. Nelson had been on the route several months without a problem. One night, that all changed.

The evening was cool and the air was frosty, and it seemed to the seasoned engineer that the night was darker and there was a deeper silence all around him as his engine passed one of the deep canyons that bordered the train track. There had been a report of a defective rail and an unsafe bridge crossing, but assurances were made that repair crews had already been sent to those problem areas. As he passed the first line of snow sheds Nelson thought he heard a whistle that seemed to come from the snowy, ice-bound canyons and at the same time the bell went off in his cab that signaled that the conductor wanted the train to come to a stop.

The conductor walked up beside the engine and looked up at Nelson and asked, "Why did you stop?"

"Why did you signal me to stop?" countered the engineer.

"I didn't give the signal," said the conductor. "You better get going. We have to pass No. 19 at the switches, and I think I hear a train making uptime coming up behind us."

"Behind us?" questioned Nelson. "There are no scheduled trains behind us until the morning."

"Well, I've heard the whistle and I thought I could see her light in the distance when we were on the straightaway back a couple miles."

The conductor went back to his passengers and Nelson and his fireman started up the train and began to gain speed. Now Nelson could clearly hear the whistle of the fast-approaching train. Suddenly he could see the light of the train behind him, and knew he had to put some distance between the two trains. He opened the throttle wide and coaxed every bit of power he could from his engine. The train roared to life but still the train behind them chased them relentlessly through the snow-covered tracks and trestles. If Nelson couldn't come up with a bit more speed, the pursuing train would ram into his rear cars and bring disaster with it. The fireman piled on the wood until he was almost spent with exhaustion, his clothes soaked with sweat and the heat from the boiler filling the engine's cab like a furnace and flames actually leaping from the smokestack. The conductor had alerted the passengers, who dressed themselves in their warmest clothes and lined the windows to get a glimpse of their stalker. Rumors flew among the passengers. They finally came up with the story that an engineer who had gone mad was driving the pursuing train.

When Edwards came to the summit he shut off the steam and let gravity take control of his train. As he looked back he could see the chasing train's engine clearly. The driving wheels on the rear train were larger than his own train's, and he could make out a dark figure standing on top of the engine cab gesturing wildly in the glow of the engine's fire.

As they turned a sharp bend in the track he saw that his pursuer was barely 200 yards behind him and catching up fast. The trains drew closer to each other, and at the next bend Nelson Edwards could see the driver of the other train lean out of the window of the cab and laugh hysterically into the wind. His face was lumpy and looked like bread dough. The wind had gotten fierce and snow was beginning to fall. Huge drifts of snow covered the tracks, but Nelson could not slow down for them but plowed right through, sending giant billowy clouds of snow past the windows of the passenger cars behind him.

Every bridge groaned and creaked as they streaked across them, the wheels of his train seemed to scream in agony at every turn as they gained more and more momentum. The wind howled in his ears as they reached the suspected unsafe bridge, but there was no time to slow down, as they seemed to fly through the air over the deep chasm beneath the bridge. The bridge held and still the two trains sped through the darkness. The switch was in sight, but No. 19 was not there and Nelson and his frightened crew and passengers sped past at full steam. Suddenly he saw a red light about a mile or two ahead. Now the seasoned engineer made a decision. The red light meant an obstacle on the track up ahead. He would be run into from behind as well as plowing his train into whatever lay on the track ahead. Nelson applied the brakes, and he and his fireman leaned on the brake handles with all their strength. Nelson closed his eyes as he heard the whistle of his pursuer getting closer and closer. He and his fireman braced themselves for the crash. He finally glanced behind him and saw the train as it bore down on them. Just before the engine hit the rear car of his train the track before it seemed to spread apart, and the train that had chased him through the passes most of the night seemed to leap into the air, off the tracks and into the canyon below. As it dove into the canyon below it vanished.

The passenger train came to a stop. Nelson jumped from his cab and listened but didn't hear the crash of engines and cars falling down the side of the mountain. He didn't hear the screams of the crew as they fell to their deaths. All he heard was the silence of the mountains. The red warning light in front of them had also disappeared.

The next morning Nelson Edwards reached Green River ahead of schedule. When he climbed down from his cab he walked toward the front of his engine and saw that there were words burned into the black paint. "You have seen the phantom train. We ran off the track and you saw us fall. If you ever bring a train this way again you too will be wrecked." Over a hundred passengers and all the members of the crew had seen the train as it chased them through the mountains. None ever forgot that night. There was no crash. No train had fallen off the track. The phantom train was never seen again around Marshall Pass.

Nelson Edwards quit his job that morning and went back to Denver and took a job as an engineer with the Union Pacific on another stretch of track nowhere near Marshall Pass. He didn't need to be told twice.

The Eagle and the Lion (Hispanic)

At one time, Colorado was part of Mexican territory, and much of the state was settled by people of Spanish ancestry. This is one of their stories, which involves lions. Lions that live in Colorado are mountain lions

Once, a long time ago, eagle was looking for food. It had been very hot for a long time, and food was scarce. Animals had to be careful with their food.

Finally he saw a rabbit running across the desert and he swooped down and killed it. As he sat on the ground eating the rabbit, lion walked by.

"What are you doing," asked lion.

"I'm eating a rabbit I just killed," said eagle.

The lion looked suspicious. "You're not eating some meat that I buried under those rocks, are you?"

"I would never steal food from you. I'm not that foolish to take food from someone like you."

As soon as the lion left the eagle thought to himself, "But thank-you for the information."

After flying up to make sure that the lion had really left, the eagle went searching and found the lion's secret hiding place. The eagle found that lion had hidden a deer under the rocks. He dug it up and ate all of lion's meat. He flew into a nearby tree and rested after his big meal.

When the lion came back and discovered what the eagle had done he was furious. "Why did you steal all my meat?"

"You told me where you hid your meat, so I ate it all. Be careful, I might fly down there and tear at you with my talons."

The lion roared his anger at the eagle. "Because you stole my meat you will have to fight me. We will meet in the field beyond these rocks."

The next day the eagle and lion met in the field and fought. They were both fierce fighters, and by the end of the day neither one could beat the other. They decided to call it a draw. Weary and wounded from their battle, they decided to make peace. They talked and in the end they each claimed to be king over part of the earth. The eagle would rule the skies, and the lion would rule the land, and they would not fight ever again.

That is why to this very day each rules part of the earth, the lion the land and the eagle the sky, separate but equal kingdoms and kings.

Draining the Mine

Young Hal was looking for work when he came to Colorado. His journey had taken him through several states, and he finally found himself in a small mining community. He found work in one of the mines. The owner finally asked him one day if he wanted a real challenge.

"I have a mine that I think has a large vein of silver, but it's flooded. I'll make it worth your while if you can pump out that water. The sooner you do it the more you'll be paid."

The two men talked until a price was agreed upon. The price would double if Hal could do it in less than a week.

The young man manned the pumps, but after two days of pumping the water level had not gone done at all. Hal moved over to a stone that was under the shade of an old oak tree and thought about what seemed an almost impossible task. From where he was sitting he saw what looked like a dead dog in a nearby ravine. That's when he had his idea.

He went and got the dog and tied the body to a large stone, then threw it down into the deep pool of water at the entrance of the mine. Then he tossed in an old coat that he had picked up during his travels. For the final touch he took his hat and threw it into the pool, where it floated on the surface. Then he went to town.

Hal rushed into the sheriff's office out of breath and looking scared. He stammered his story out between deep breaths. "Sheriff, I was camping near an old flooded mine last night and when I woke up this morning I saw something terrible."

The sheriff tried to calm the young man down, "Just relax, son, and tell me what you saw."

"Well, I think there's a body at the bottom of the deep pool at the mine's entrance. I saw a hat floating on the surface and a coat floating underneath the surface and what looks like something at the bottom."

The sheriff sent his deputy over to the mine, who returned quickly with news that the situation was just like Hal had told them. The sheriff and his men went to the mine with pumps borrowed from the firehouse. Hal quietly disappeared during all the commotion.

The sheriff and his men used the fire pumps and hoses and soon the water was pouring out of the mine. They worked all day, and just before sunset they drained the last of the water and found the dog's body tied to a stone.

They were tired and angry and wanted to get their hands on the young man who had reported the drowning, but Hal was nowhere in sight. They packed up the equipment and headed back to town.

Hal, who had been watching the whole thing from a hiding spot above the mine entrance, walked out and went to the mine's owner. He collected his reward for draining that mine and the bonus, too. Hal left and decided he would get a haircut and new shirt and a good supper, but he'd do it in the next town.

The Bearded Fish

A long time ago there was a traveling medicine show that was working its way through Colorado. Now one of the products that this medicine show was selling was a tonic that could cure all disease; improve a man's memory; make children more intelligent; make corn grow higher, hens lay more eggs, and cows give sweeter milk; and grow hair on any bald man. As they were crossing one of the mountain passes a barrel of this elixir fell off the back of the wagon and went crashing down the hill and into the source of one of the biggest rivers in Colorado. The tonic rushed downstream with the spring thaw.

Downstream the first bearded trout appeared and caused an up roar throughout the state.

Folks from all over the country came to Colorado to try to catch one of the elusive, almost legendary bearded fish. As time went by some of the fish began to grow fur all over to protect themselves from the harsh winters.

Now catching these fish was tricky. The fishing pole you used had to be painted just like a barber pole. In order to scale the fish, you first had to shave them, so preparing the bearded trout for dinner took some time. The bearded trout not only were good eating, but if you could get an old one with a lot of fur the pelt from that fish could bring you a pretty price from any fur merchant. The fish were so popular that some of the other fish were feeling a bit neglected and began appearing in the rivers and lakes of Colorado wearing toupees. These were a lot easier to clean.

The bearded trout haven't been seen for many years now, but that's not to say that they are not still lurking in the rivers of Colorado. They might have learned to shave themselves and paint their scales different colors and disguise themselves as rainbow trout. You never know.

Silver Heels (a True Story)

Towering over the city of Fairplay, Colorado, is Mount Silverheels, a beautiful snowcapped mountain that seems to watch over the people who live in its shadow.

Toward the end of the nineteenth century miners came to this area looking for gold. Some struck it rich, while others just toiled away, digging here and digging there always looking for that big strike. The men eventually brought their families, towns grew up around the once lonesome cabins, and soon others came to take away the hard-earned money that the miners chipped away from the mountains and hills and streams. Dance halls and saloons opened where gamblers cheated the miners out of what little they had found.

Among the many people who came to this town looking for a new life was a young woman named Silver Heels Jenny, a dance hall girl. She got the nickname because she wore silver-colored shoes that glittered and shone and seemed to hypnotize anyone who watched whenever she danced. She had a beautiful, almost innocent face and with her pleasant personality she soon became one of the favorites of the men who visited the dance hall. Her generous nature and kindness also made her popular with the other girls who worked with her.

Not long after Jenny arrived in town she met a young miner whom the folks called Buckskin Joe. They fell in love and became engaged. Many a miner pined away when he heard the news that Silver Heels Jenny was to be married.

Soon after they announced their intention to marry a smallpox epidemic fell on Fairplay. Businesses closed; the dance hall and the saloons were empty. Some people packed up and left the area. Most stayed because they had nowhere to go and no money to leave. The horrible disease claimed one life after another, including Buckskin Joe's. Silver Heels nursed him until he died, and then she began to nurse others. She would take care of whole families who were sick and could not even feed themselves. She went from house to house helping in any way she could, washing their clothes, taking care of the children, caring for their animals, nursing them back to health, and taking care of their burial if they fell to the wretched pox. Finally the disease took hold of her. She survived, but her once beautiful face was scarred, and she took to living alone up in the hills overlooking the city in an abandoned cabin.

The miners and their families were so touched by her generous spirit and the way she had taken care of so many of them that they raised some money for her. When they came to give it to her they found the cabin once again abandoned. Silver Heels Jenny had disappeared with all her belongings.

People claimed they saw her, heavily veiled to hide her scarred face, roaming the hills, haunting the grave where her Joe was buried. Still she was never found. The people of Fairplay still wanted to show their appreciation for her kindness and devotion to them, so they named the nearby mountain Mount Silverheels in her honor. And so the mountain sits today looking down on the people who Jenny loved so well.

Colorado Glossary

Colorado—A state whose name comes from the Spanish word for "colored red," referring to the region's red sandstone soil and the silt seen in the river given the same name. The capital is Denver.

Elk: One of the largest species of deer in the world. They can weigh up to 700 pounds and can stand five feet tall at the shoulder.

Grizzly bear: One the largest carnivore in North America, reaching weights of over 600 pounds and standing eight feet tall on their hind legs.

Kit Carson: Christopher Houston "Kit" Carson, born in Richmond, Virginia. The family soon moved to Missouri, where he was raised. He left home at age sixteen to go west, and in the next few years worked as a trapper, lived the life of a mountain man, and was the guide to three of John Fremont's expeditions. He served in the Mexican–American War and the Indian Wars. He later turned to ranching and settled down in Colorado.

Snow sheds: Wooden and concrete reinforced structures used to protect railroads from avalanches in the mountains.

Story Sources

American Myths & Legends, Volumes 1 & 2

Buying the Wind

By Cheyenne Campfires

The Corn Woman, Stories and Legends of the Hispanic Southwest

Coronado's Children: Tales of Lost Mines & Buried Treasures of the South West

Cowboy Songs and other Frontier Ballads

The Eagle and the Cactus: Traditional Stories from Mexico

The Folklore of Spain in the American Southwest

The Greenwood Library of American Folktales, Volume 3

Mexican-American Folklore

Myths & Legends of Our Own Land, Volumes 1 & 2

Outlaw Tales: Legends, Myths & Folklore from America's Middle Border

Tales from the American Frontier

A Treasury of Railroad Folklore

A Treasury of Western Folklore

Hawaii

Hawaii is unique in almost every way from the rest of the forty-nine states. The word Hawaii comes from its native people and means "homeland." The story "Maui Traps the Sun" from the Hawaiian people is included in this chapter. Hawaii is the only state that is not part of the continent of North America and is also the only state completely surrounded by water. The hundreds of islands that make up Hawaii are spread out over 1,500 miles of the Pacific Ocean, with the eight largest being in the southeast part of the chain.

Populated first by Polynesian settlers, Hawaii was a sovereign kingdom under the rule of Queen Liliuokalani when the monarchy was overthrown and ties were made by wealthy American and European landowners to the United States. It became a territory in 1898 and became the fiftieth state in 1959. In 1993 President Bill Clinton and Congress apologized for the illegal overthrow of the Hawaiian monarchy. Hawaii has the largest percentage of Asians of any state; they are represented here by the Japanese story "The Wolf's Debt" and the Filipino story "The Hermit and the Two Worms." One of the first European groups to come to Hawaii in large numbers was the Portuguese, and here we have their story "The Seven Sons." On January 20, 2009, Barack Obama was sworn in as the first Hawaiian-born president of the United States of America.

Maui Traps the Sun (Hawaiian)

Maui was the son of a goddess, a young man of courage and strength. His grandmother had given him a magic club and spear and a magic canoe paddle. Along with his powers as a half god she knew he would need these magical gifts as he made his journey through life.

Now Maui was very fond of his mother, Hina, and visited her almost every day because his stepfather, Aikanaka, was often away. Maui's mother was known throughout the islands for her beauty and for the wonderful tapa, cloth bark that she made. She gathered the bark from mulberry trees and carried seawater to her home in which to soak it. She pounded the wet bark and dried it under the hot sun until it became the tapa for which she was so well known.

One day while Maui was visiting Hina she exclaimed in frustration, "The day is just not long enough. I need more sunlight for my tapa to dry before nightfall comes."

"This is all the sun's fault," cried Maui. "I will go and speak to him and try to convince him that he should slow down and make the days a bit longer so you can finish you tapa."

"My son, that is such foolish talk. The Sun is a god and a great one at that, while we are minor gods and you are only half a god. No one can get close enough to the Sun and live to tell about it."

"Then I shall be the first. I will trap the Sun and make him travel slower as he flies across the sky."

"Please Maui, if you must go take your magic club and paddle with you. You will need all the power you can possibly have if you are to defeat the Sun."

Maui made snares from coconut rope. He took his magic club and placed it in his canoe with the snares. As the Sun faded from the sky and the Evening Star climbed high into the night, he took his magic paddle and with one stroke he was down the river and into the sea. The second stroke took him all the way to the island where the Sun lived.

Maui left his canoe on the shore and walked up the slope of the volcano that rose in the island's center. At the bottom of the volcano slept the Sun covered by a thick blanket of clouds. While the Sun slept Maui took his snares and set them. Then he hid behind some rocks and fell asleep.

Just before dawn the clouds rolled out of the crater and one long ray of the Sun glittered in the first light of sunrise. The ray fell into the snare Maui had set and it sprang shut and held the Sun firm. Maui tied the rope of the snare firmly to a nearby boulder.

"What is this?" roared the Sun.

"You are caught now and are my prisoner," said Maui.

"The world is waiting for me to start my journey across the sky. Let me go now or you will be sorry."

"You aren't going anywhere," said Maui, "until you promise to make your journey a little slower through the sky."

"I go swiftly because then I can rest through the night. If I rest I will be stronger the next day. Why would I promise to go slower for you?" demanded the Sun.

"My mother Hina needs your warmth to dry her tapa."

"Dry her tapa?" roared the Sun. "Do you think I care about something as silly as tapa?"

Maui was done talking. He swung his magic club and struck the ray of the Sun that was caught, breaking off a long piece of it. The Sun brought more of his rays out of the crater, but they too were caught by Maui's snares. The Sun struggled, but the more he did the tighter the nooses on the snares became and the more pain he felt.

"You would not dare to kill me," he said. "If I die then all life dies. Without me there will be no light, no warmth, and animals and plants and men and women will all die."

"Sun, let us make a deal. If you promise to travel more slowly for only part of the year, then I will release you."

"I promise," growled the Sun.

With his magic club Maui broke the cords of the snares, and the Sun leapt up into the sky. Maui paddled back home with the good new for his mother.

After that for part of each year the Sun traveled more slowly through the sky. These days were filled with warmth and sunshine and Hina could make more tapa, and the people of the earth would have longer days, planting food and enjoying the Sun's warmth. The rest of the year the days were shorter and darker, and Sun could sleep a bit longer in his volcano, covered by his blanket of clouds.

Whenever Sun thought about ending his journey too early, he would remember his broken ray and the clever, courageous Maui who had caught him in his trap.

The Hermit and the Two Worms (Filipino)

Many people immigrated to the United States from the Philippines, and many settled in Hawaii. This is one of their stories.

Once a long time ago there lived a hermit. He was a holy man who spent all his time praying and meditating in the cave where he lived. One day he went out to gather some fruit in the forest around his cave. As he walked along he heard a voice call out to him, "Watch where you are stepping."

The old man looked around him and was puzzled that there was no one in sight. He kept collecting fruit until he once more heard the voice. "Be careful, you almost stepped on us. Look where you are going."

The hermit squatted down on the ground and studied the plants in front of him, looking for the source of the voice. He pushed aside leaves and small rocks until he heard, "We're right here behind this rock."

Moving the rock carefully, the hermit found two fat wriggling worms. "Are you all right? Should I move this rock?" asked the hermit.

"We're fine here," said the two worms. "The rock keeps us safe from the trampling feet of humans."

"I'll just step over you and be on my way," said the old man.

"You'll probably step on some other poor creatures as soon as you've left us."

"What do you mean?" asked the hermit.

"People treat all living things as if they are worthless. Humans have no respect for other living creatures. They cut down forests, pollute the land, kill animals and insects, and poison the earth."

The hermit thought about it for a while and said, "Maybe you're right, maybe humans do spoil the earth and destroy nature. How would you two like to do something about it?"

"What can two worms do?" they replied.

"I can turn you both into people, then you can walk among humans and show them how they should act toward nature."

The two worms agreed and in an instant they turned into two people, a man and a woman. They went to live in a small village, where people knew them as Gino and Anna. With the money that the hermit had given them, they bought some land and built a modest house. They also bought some chickens and a couple sows.

Gino and Anna worked hard and made friends easily. At first they told their new friends about their old home in the rainforest. They even traveled to other villages to tell people about the beauty of nature and how all life should be treated with respect.

But after a while their farm demanded more and more of their attention. They started to make more and more money and stopped traveling to other villages. They stopped talking about the beauty of nature and their old lives became a distant memory, fading a little more each day.

Gino and Anna became very wealthy and cut down many of the trees on their land so they could build a bigger, grander home. They had a huge party when they moved in, and the guests were treated to the finest food and the best entertainment. Everywhere folks were walking around the garden, trampling on plants and frightening the small creatures that live just out of the sight of people.

One of the servants came up to Gino and told him that there was an old beggar that was at the front gate and wanted to talk to him and Anna. "Tell him to go away," said Gino.

"He said he won't go away until he talks to you," said the servant.

"Well, he'll just have to wait out there," said Gino. "After a while he'll get tired and go away."

Hours later Anna was saying good-bye to some of the guests when she saw the old beggar standing in the shadows of one of the few trees left near the new house. "Gino," said Anna, "that beggar is still here. What shall we do about him?"

"Unleash the dogs," said Gino. "That will teach him a lesson about bothering his betters."

Suddenly the sky was filled with dark clouds and a bolt of lightening pierced the darkness. Rain poured down in sheets and the guests all hurried inside the house. Then there was aloud crash and the house and everything in it disappeared. The people ran for their homes as fast as they could.

Gino and Anna found themselves soaking wet, standing in the middle of the place their house once stood. The house was gone, their belongings were gone, and weeds filled the garden where their guests had been laughing and talking only minutes before.

"Well, Gino and Anna, I have come for a visit." There was the old hermit, his face dark with rage, standing in front of them.

Gino and Anna fell to their knees. "Please don't take it all away," they cried. "We've worked so hard."

The hermit looked down at them and his voice was full of anger. "You were the ones who were so outraged at the behavior of people. You were the creatures who were going to teach humans how to act, and what have you done? You've become just like them. You cut down trees to build your big house. You chain up your dogs. You live to make money. Your friends trample the little ones in your garden, and all you have to say for yourselves is to beg to keep what you worked hard for? You forgot why you were here and where you came from. Now I'll send you back."

With a flash of light Anna and Gino were transformed back into two fat wriggling worms. Only now their voices were silent.

The Wolf's Debt (Japanese)

Many Japanese people immigrated to the United States, and many settled in Hawaii. This is one of their traditional stories.

Once a long time ago there lived a young farmer, his wife, and their daughter. One day word came to their village that his own father was ill and he was needed at home. His wife told him that she would take care of their farm and that he must go to his parents. The next day he left for his old home with a few belongings and even fewer coins.

Now the walk to his parents' home was a full day and a great deal of the journey was through a dense woods. As the young man walked through the forest he remembered the days of his childhood and how much he loved his mother and father. He was laughing out loud at some memories when suddenly his daydreaming was interrupted by an odd sound: it reminded him of a badger or perhaps an animal wounded or caught in a trap. Now the young man was tender hearted, and the thought of another living creature suffering bothered him. He felt he should find the animal to help it or put it out of its misery.

He left the path and walked through the woods following the cries. He came to a clearing and there in the middle was a huge wolf. The animal wasn't in a trap but just lay on its side, its mouth open wide and growling out that strange sound. At first the young man was frightened, but when the wolf saw him the animal sat up and pawed the air like a big dog, its mouth still open. The young man could see that there was something pushing against the throat of the animal from the inside: a bone or stick must have gotten lodged in the wolf's mouth. He knew that the animal couldn't eat or drink with that caught in its throat and that it would die a slow, terrible death. Slowly he crept toward the wolf. The wolf lay on its side and when the young man knelt beside it the animal put its head in his lap.

"Well friend wolf, it seems that you have a problem. This may hurt, but you have to trust me."

The golden eyes of the wolf seemed to say that he did trust the young man. Slowly the farmer put his hand down the throat of the wolf, past those long sharp teeth till he touched the bone. With a twist he had the bone out.

The wolf jumped to its feet growling, but then it opened and closed its mouth and swallowed and finally came up to the young man and rubbed against his side. The wolf's tail swished once then twice and then it bounded into the forest and was gone.

The man smiled. "A good deed is a good deed whether repaid or not." And he continued his journey feeling happy that he had helped save the wolf's life.

When he finally reached his parents' farm he found that his father was very sick indeed. The crops had rotted in the fields because no one could harvest them, no new crops had been planted, and the debts had piled high.

"First we must get father well again. He needs some good food." But the young man found that there was no food in the house, not even a grain of rice. As the young man looked at the few coins he had brought and tried to figure out what he could buy with them, there was a scratching at the door.

When he opened the door there sat the big wolf. It dropped a pheasant at his feet. "Well brother wolf, have you brought me food?" The long tail swished once then twice and then he was gone. The pheasant was cooked and soup was made and the father began to regain his strength.

The next day the creditors came.

"They owe me this much," said one. "They owe me this much," said another. "We'll take their farm away," said a third.

The coins the young farmer had would not pay off one debt. Then he heard the scratching sound and when he opened the door there stood the gray wolf.

"Well brother wolf, I know you could feed me, but can you pay off our debts, too?" The young man laughed at the thought.

The wolf bent his head and dropped a small leather pouch at the farmer's feet. The long tail swished once, then twice and he was gone.

The little pouch was filled with gold coins. He paid his parents' debts. He bought food to last them and left them with enough money to take care of them till the next harvest. He even kept three gold coins to take home to his wife.

A few days later, with his father on the mend, the young farmer left for home. As he walked through the woods he thought how his kind deed had so helped both the wolf and his parents. Suddenly he heard a sound. As he turned he saw six rough-looking men, swords on their hips, standing behind him.

"Give us your money or we'll take your life." They drew their long swords.

"I only have a few coins."

"Then perhaps we'll sell you as a slave. You look strong and young. You'll fetch a good price."

Suddenly they all heard growling from the woods around them. Then wolves appeared, first one, then another, until a dozen gray wolves surrounded them, lips pulled back and teeth gleaming, sharper than the swords of the thieves. The men dropped their weapons and ran for their lives, the wolves hard on their heels, all except one. That wolf rubbed up against the young farmer and looked into his eyes as if to say, "My debt is repaid."

The young farmer had saved the wolf's life, and the wolf had done the same.

The Seven Sons (Portuguese)

Many people immigrated from Portugal to the United States and Hawaii. This is one of their traditional stories.

There was an old man with seven sons. The man had come to the end of his life. As he lay in his bed he knew there was one more lesson he had to teach his sons before he died.

He asked each of his sons to bring him a branch from a tree and then come to his room.

They did as their father had asked and returned to him, each one holding a branch.

"Give me your branch," he told the oldest. The oldest son gave his father his branch. The old man called his youngest son to his side and gave him the branch. The boy was only seven years old.

"Try to break it," the old man said. The boy took the branch and easily broke it.

"Now break this one," he said, handing the boy the second son's branch. The boy did.

"Now this one," he said, handing the child the third son's branch. The boy again broke it easily.

"Now this one," he said, giving him the fourth son's branch. He broke it again.

"And now this one," he said, and handed him the fifth son's branch. He broke that one as well.

"This one," he said as he handed the child the sixth son's branch. He broke it as easily as the others.

"Now break your own branch," his father said, and the boy broke his own branch.

"Now each of you go and bring me another branch just like the first one you brought to me." The sons, though puzzled by what their father was doing, all went out and again came back with one branch each.

He told the oldest to tie the seven branches all together in a bundle. The oldest son did just that.

"Now," said the father, "break them." The oldest son tried and tried but could not break the bundle of sticks.

"I'm sorry father, but I can't break them," he said.

"Then have your brother help you." So two of them tried but again failed.

"Have another brother help you." But they also failed.

They kept adding more brothers until finally all seven brothers tried together and failed to break the seven sticks tied together in a bundle. The father took the bundle of sticks back and untied them and handed one to the youngest boy and said, "Break it." The child broke it easily.

"This is my last lesson to you, my sons. Do you see what you have learned today? Even the youngest and weakest of you can break these sticks one at a time. But all of you together cannot break them when they are united. The same that is true of branches is true of people. Separated in the world people are weak and vulnerable. But if they are united they are strong and invincible. Together you are strong, alone you are weak. This lesson is the most valuable thing I can leave you, my sons."

The seven brothers learned the lesson well. In everything they did they stayed united and together and soon became a respected, powerful, and rich family in their village and in the countryside around it. Others learned from their example.

It is a powerful lesson, one we should all learn.

Beginnings (a True Story)

In 2003 my wife had gone to a political gathering while I was out of town on business. A young man from the Chicago area, who had been in state politics and was also a professor at the University of Chicago Law School, was going to speak. He was running for the United States Senate. My wife described him to me when I got home. "I'm telling you, this man is amazing. He is an incredible speaker." These were strong words coming from the wife of a professional storyteller. "He just took over the room. He stopped and smiled and shook hands and really talked to people and listened to what they had to say. He has something special about him. I think he is someone who will be a force in this country someday."

That young man went on to win a landslide victory and became the junior senator from Illinois. On January 20, 2009, that same man walked to a microphone in Washington, D.C., and stood there, his hand placed on a bible that Abraham Lincoln had placed his hand on once so long ago. The man began to speak. "I, Barack Hussein Obama, do solemnly swear . . . ." He became our forty-fourth president.

Barack Obama was born in Honolulu, Hawaii, probably the most culturally diverse state in the union. He reflects that diversity in his own heritage. His mother, Ann Dunham, was of European American descent, while his father, Barack Obama Sr., was from Kenya, Africa. They met while students at the University of Hawaii and were married. Their son was born on August 4, 1961.

The young Obama spent his youth in Hawaii except for a couple years when he joined his mother while she was working in Indonesia. Following high school he went first to Occidental College and then to Columbia University in New York. After working as a community organizer in Chicago for three years he went to Harvard to attend law school, where he was the first African American to become the editor of the *Harvard Law Review*. He returned to Chicago, where he taught at the University of Chicago Law School, worked on community projects, was elected to the state senate, then the U.S. Senate, and finally president of the United States of America.

Because of his multiethnic/cultural background, he is a true representative of the melting pot that is America. He has Midwestern roots and an immigrant father from Africa, and was raised by his mother and maternal grandparents in the culturally diverse state of Hawaii. He visits Hawaii often and even stopped his campaign to go back home to Hawaii and visit his terminally ill grandmother, the woman who had helped bring him up and instilled the values he has today.

Hawaii has sent the nation its first Hawaiian-born president. Aloha.

Hawaii Glossary

Filipino: People from the Philippine Islands, an island nation in the South Pacific.

Hawaii: A state whose name means "Homeland" in the Hawaiian language. The capital is Honolulu.

Maui: A hero of the Hawaiian people in their legends and stories.

Tapa: The bark of the paper mulberry tree from which cloth is made throughout Polynesia.

Story Sources

Filipino Children's Favorite Stories

Folk Tales from Portugal

Folktales of Japan

The Greenwood Library of American Folktales, Volume 3

The Legends & Myths of Hawaii

Hawaiian Mythology

Hawaiian Myths of Earth, Sea & Sky

Kauai Tales

Myths & Legends of the Pacific

Polihale & Other Kaua'i Legends

Portuguese Fairy Tales

Tales of Molokai

Idaho

Idaho was admitted to the union in 1890 as the forty-third state. Several Native American tribes have lived and still live in Idaho, including the Flathead, Nez Perce, Shoshone, and Coeur d'Alene peoples, who are represented here by a story told by the Shoshone people. From the Pyrenees in Europe came the Basques, who worked as sheepherders in Idaho. Idaho has one of the largest Basque populations in America, and their story "The Man Who Had No Shadow" is found here.

Like many states there are songs sung about Idaho, and included here is the folk song "Away, Idaho." Many people have unusual pets that come to their rescue. You'll find a pet story here that is a bit unique both in the choice of pet and in how that pet helps its owner. In every grocery store in America you see Idaho potatoes for sale, so many people think of Idaho when they think of potatoes. The story "Idaho Potatoes" tells us about the legendary size of Idaho's best-known vegetable. It may be a tall tale, but then again, maybe not.

The Man Who Had No Shadow (Basque)

A long, long time ago there were three brothers. They lived when the hills of our land were still filled with ogres and fairies and Basa-Juans, wild men who had feet like goats.

Now all three brothers were clever and quick, but the cleverest was the youngest, who was named Axular.

One day he returned to the house he shared with his brothers and told them, "I am going away and I won't be returning for a year and a day."

"Where are you going?" asked his brothers. They were always jealous of their younger brother's wits and they were afraid that he would go on some wonderful adventure and leave them behind at home.

"I don't think this trip will interest you at all," replied Axular.

"Yes it would," they cried. "Please tell us where you are going. Maybe we could all go together?" They begged and pleaded and finally Axular gave in.

"I have heard," he said, "that there is a deep cave high in the mountains where a Basa-Juan lives. The clearing in front of his cave has been a meeting place for fairies and witches and all kinds of creatures for a very long time. I believe that this Basa-Juan has learned their secrets. I am going to ask him if he will teach me their magic. I think that this might be the most valuable knowledge in the whole world."

The two older brothers didn't reply at first. They were afraid of the Basa-Juan. They thought that the idea was too wild and daring. But they also did not want their younger brother to have knowledge that they didn't have, so they decided to join him and share in his adventure.

The next morning they put on their blue berets, threw their coats over their shoulders, and took their makilas down from the hooks on the wall of the kitchen and set out on their journey to find the cave of the Basa-Juan. They traveled for a long time through the hills and mountains until they came to the mouth of a huge cave. They called for the wild man to come out and talk to them.

"We have journeyed far, O Basa-Juan," shouted Axular. "We ask that you teach us the secrets of the magic that you have learned from the fairies and witches and other magical folk who dwell in your mountains and hills."

The Basa-Juan stomped out of his cave and shouted at them. He flew into such a rage that the two oldest brothers almost started to run for home. Axular calmed the wild man down with flattering words and soon he was ready for them to stay with him and learn.

"I will teach all I know, but you must stay here with me for a year and a day, and there is a price," said the Basa-Juan.

"What is the price?" asked the oldest brother.

The wild man laughed and said, "When the year and a day is over the last one to leave my cave will become my slave. Do you agree?"

"I agree," cried Axular in a strong voice.

"We also agree," said the elder brothers, though in much quieter voices.

The very next day the three brothers started their lessons. They learned the language of the fairies and how to fly through the air. They learned how to make themselves into smoke and flow under doors and through keyholes. They learned spells and charms and how to undo the curses that the evil ones place on people. They learned the hiding places of the fairies and how to open the doors that the magical people locked against the outside world. They learned how to make their wands from dogwood trees. After one year they had learned all the secrets the Basa-Juan had learned in the centuries he had listened to the fairies and witches.

The night before the last day, the day they would leave, not one of them slept. They were all thinking who would be the last one out the entrance to the cave and become the wild man's slave. Axular could hear his two older brothers plotting how they would be sure that he was the last one out. Axular had already made his plans, and he prayed that his plans would work and that the Basa-Juan would be deprived of a slave the next day.

"You have all slept too late. Get up, you lazy boys. The sun is shining through the opening of my cave and the time has come for you to leave. Remember, whoever is last becomes my slave."

The three brothers started for the doorway. The two older brothers reached it first and stepped outside into the sunlight, leaving their youngest brother behind. The Basa-Juan came toward Axular with outstretched arms, crying, "You are my payment and will be my slave. You are the last one out of my cave."

Axular stopped and faced the wild man and spoke calmly, "I'm not the last one out. There is one still behind me." He pointed to his black shadow, which looked on the rocky wall of the cave just like a man.

Now in the ways of magic the Basa-Juan might be clever, but his mind worked slowly in the real world, and so he turned and, seeing the shadow, he grabbed it with his long fingers. By the time he realized his mistake Axular was already out of the cave and making his way back home.

From that day on Axular used his new knowledge to help others and fight the evil that lurked in the night. But no matter how bright the sun shone, no dancing black shape followed his steps. He was always known as the Man Without a Shadow.

Away, Idaho

This nineteenth-century folk song gives us the idealistic vision that many settlers and immigrants had when coming to a new land. All the hard times will be gone once they reach Idaho, where they'll never work again but just pick up the gold nuggets and watch their crops grow by themselves. What a dream!

They say there is a land
Where the crystal waters flow
Over beds of ore of purest gold
Way out in Idaho

Chorus:
Away, Idaho,
We're coming Idaho.
Our four-horse team
Will soon be seen
Way out in Idaho.

We're bound to cross the plains
And through the mountains go.
We're bound to make our fortunes there
Way out in Idaho.

We'll need no sieve or spade,
No shovel, pan, or hoe.
The largest chunks lay on the ground
Way out in Idaho.

We'll see hard times no more
And want we'll never know.
When once we've filled our sacks with gold
Way out in Idaho.

Idaho Potatoes

A long time ago the settlers in the Snake River Valley grew some of the biggest crops anywhere in the country. Now I'm not talking about the number of bushels, I'm talking about the size of the plant and the vegetables on it. One old man would come to town and complain that he could not get his crop to town because he didn't have a wagon that could hold any of his pumpkins. "I tried," he said. "But the pumpkin was so big it crashed right through the floor of my wagon and spooked the horses."

After a while some of the folks decided to turn to potatoes, hoping they would grow to a more reasonable size, but no luck. They just kept on growing and growing. During the Depression they had a CCC Camp nearby, and the manager of the camp visited one farmer and asked him if the camp could buy 100 pounds of potatoes. The old farmer shook his head sadly when he told the story to his friends in town. "I told the man I just couldn't do it. I wouldn't cut a potato in half, not even for the CCC."

They grow potatoes big in Idaho.

The Best of Pets

One day a cowboy was riding along when he heard an unusual sound, a hissing and spitting and a slapping in the dusty earth. As he followed the bend in the trail he saw a rattlesnake caught under a large rock. The cowboy got off his horse and walked over to the trapped animal and was just about to put it out of its misery when he had a change of heart. The snake had been pinned for what seemed a long time, and ending its life without a bit of liberty didn't seem right. The cowboy took a long stick and pushed the rock off the snake's back and freed it. He got back on his horse and began to ride back to his cabin in the high country.

As he road along he heard another sound coming behind him. He looked over his shoulder, and there was that snake following the cowboy. The old rattler trailed the cowboy all the way to his cabin and settled in as his houseguest. The cowboy opened a can of milk and poured some in a saucer for the snake, who lapped it up just like a dog.

Now the cowboy lived all alone, and the snake's company was appreciated. After chores were done they would sit on the front porch and the cowboy would play his fiddle and the snake would sway to the music. The man had a few head of cattle, and the snake would help him round them up. The old rattler would sneak up behind the herd and start to shake his rattle, and the cattle would head in the opposite direction, just where the cowboy wanted them. The cowboy also did a little prospecting for gold, and the snake would climb into a large pan and set his tail flapping, and soon all the stones and dirt were gone and the gold dust was settled in the bottom of the pan. They had become partners.

One night the cowboy woke to yelling and cursing. As he jumped out of bed he grabbed his rifle and shouted, "I don't know who you are, but you better identify yourself. I'm holding my rifle, and it might just go off if I don't hear some words of explanation."

"Please get this thing off me. I'm sorry I broke into your cabin to steal your gold dust. Please get this thing off me!"

The cowboy lit a lantern and saw that a man had broken into his cabin. The man was lying on the floor both his legs and arms wrapped tight against his body by the big old rattlesnake. The man looked up pleadingly and the cowboy told the snake to let him go. He tied the would-be robber up and took him to town the next day and deposited him at the sheriff's office.

That cowboy and snake lived together in those hills for some time. Word spread about the old rattler, and folks would stop by and visit just to meet the snake, but nobody ever tried stealing from those two again.

The Golden Cranes (Shoshone)

Once a long time ago there was a flock of beautiful birds who were much loved by the Creator. He loved these majestic birds so much that He gave them feathers of gold.

One day the Creator called the chief of these birds to Him and said, "You are my favorites of all creatures and I have given you your golden feathers to show how much I love you. But because of this you must never leave the territory that I have given you. You and your people must stay where I have placed you. This is my only request of you and your people."

"Why mustn't we leave this place?" asked the chief.

"If you do you will lose your golden plumage. That is my only request of you and your people." The Creator rose into the sky and disappeared.

The chief of the golden birds preened his feathers and then spread his huge wings and rose into the sky. He was going back to tell his people what the Creator had said to him and how it was His wish that they stay in their valley.

As the last of the summer days wore on he saw the first flocks of the geese and ducks as they headed south for the winter. The chief saw the songbirds and all the birds that flew from one place to another when the weather changed start to take flight and leave the place where he and his people were bound to stay. Finally one morning the chief saw that his cranes were the only birds left and that all the others had gone south for the winter. He couldn't resist his urge to follow them any longer, so he called all his people together and told them that they would also be leaving for the winter. Like a giant golden cloud they rose into the air and headed for the southern lands where the lakes and the rivers were free of ice all winter.

When the Creator learned of this He was angry and he told the waters in the southern lands to strip the gold from the cranes' feathers.

The cranes flew for several days and nights until they finally came to the a land where the water glistened and the wind was gentle and warm. The chief circled the first lake he saw and began to descend to its surface. No sooner did he land than a great storm erupted on the waters of the lake and huge waves rose up to come crashing down on the crane people. The raging waters took the golden feathers from the cranes and left them standing in the water dazed and confused at what had just happened to them.

Their chief ordered them to rise once more and fly away, but when they did they rose as a great white cloud, leaving behind the beautiful golden feathers that the Creator had given only to them.

"Perhaps when we return to our valley in the north come springtime our golden feathers will be returned to us," said the chief. All winter he and the cranes waited until they saw the ice begin to melt and the winter sun begin his journey further north to wait until the summer was spent. The chief told his people to follow him home.

They flew all day and all night until they came back to their home. When they came to earth their feathers remained as white as snow. Now the chief knew that by breaking the pact that his people and the Creator had they had lost their beautiful golden plumage forever. When they left their valley they lost their beauty.

Used with permission of the Shoshone-Bannock Tribes.

Idaho Glossary

Basque people: People from the Pyrenees Mountains between France and Spain. They are found in north central Spain and southwest France. Theirs is one of the oldest and most unique languages in Europe. Many Basque came to this country to work as herders in the west.

CCC: The Civilian Conservation Corps, a government organization created during the Great Depression to get men and women back to work. The CCC constructed dams and levees, highways and federal parks, and other government-sponsored projects.

Cranes: Long legged wading birds with long straight beaks.

Coeur d'Alene people: A Native American people who lived in permanent villages and settlements. Their name in their own language was Schitsu'umsh, meaning "the people found here."

Flathead people: A Native American people who call themselves "Salish," meaning "the people." They never have practiced the custom of flattening the head. They originally were found in Montana and Idaho.

Idaho: A state with several different stories about how its name came to be. One is that it was a hoax; another that it was named after a steamboat; another that it is a European pronunciation of the Coeur d'Alene tribe word meaning "gem of the mountains." Its capital is Boise.

Nez Perce people: A Native American people who called themselves "Nimi ipuu," which meant "the people." They lived in mat-covered longhouses during the winter that could reach 100 feet in length, housing an extended family. When the horse was introduced to North America they began to use tepees as they followed game.

Shoshone people: A Native American people found in Idaho, Montana, Nevada, and Utah. They were at first farmers and hunter gatherers, but after the introduction of the horse to North America they began to follow buffalo and elk herds.

Story Sources

American Indian Tales & Legends

American Myths & Legends, Volumes 1 & 2

Blackfoot Lodge Tales: The Story of a Prairie People

Cowboy Songs and other Frontier Ballads

The Greenwood Library of American Folktales, Volume 4

Myths & Legends of Our Own Land, Volumes 1 & 2

Shoshone-Bannock Tribes

Tales from the American Frontier

Tales of a Basque Grandmother

A Treasury of Western Folklore

Way Out in Idaho

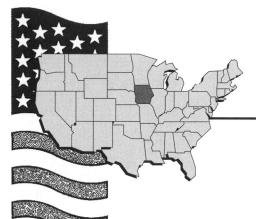

Iowa

Iowa became the twentieth-ninth state in 1846. It is home to several Native American peoples, including the Dakota and the Ioway/Otoe/Missouria people, who are represented here by the story "Ishjinki and the Duck Dance."

All states have ghosts and haunted places, and the story "Now You See It, Now You Don't" is about an on-again, off-again inn on Iowa's Mississippi banks. Two true stories about Iowa citizens are "Kate Shelley Saves the Day," about a young woman's heroism in the face of a raging storm, and "American Gothic," about one of America's most celebrated artists.

Kate Shelley Saves the Day

The Shelley family lived right next to the railroad tracks near Honey Creek about a mile and a half from Des Moines, Iowa. The railroad track was a constant reminder that their father, Michael Shelley, had died as he worked on the railroad, leaving his wife and family of five behind.

The night of July 6, 1881, was filled with the rain, thunder, and lightning of a storm that had blown in that afternoon and was still raging. Kate, at fifteen, was the oldest of the Shelley children. She had already freed the horses and cows from the barn so they could take care of themselves as the nearby creek began to rise dangerously.

As the storm raged on Kate and her mother wondered if the wooden railroad bridge that crossed Honey Creek would hold up to the rising waters. Just after 11:00 p.m. they heard the sound of a locomotive slowly making its way through the storm. The engine had been sent from Moingona, a small nearby town, to inspect the track. It was crawling along backward with two men standing on the rear of the tender looking for any trouble.

As the engine passed the house and started over the bridge, Kate and her mother heard a crashing sound as the bridge collapsed and the locomotive and crew plunged into Honey Creek.

Despite her mother's warnings, Kate grabbed and old miner's lamp and put it inside a lantern, put on her coat, and ran out the door. The water had come so close to the house and was so deep that she had to search to find ground dry enough to walk on as she made her way to the stricken engine. When she reached the creek she saw two of the crew holding on to some trees near the edge of the water. She shouted to them and they shouted back, but neither could understand what the other said over the howling wind.

Kate knew she couldn't rescue the men alone and she also knew that the express passenger train was due at midnight; in this storm it would never see that the bridge was down.

Kate began to run the mile and a half to the Moingona station. When she came to the bridge she was faced with a horrible decision. The bridge only had a narrow catwalk next to the track, and the railroad company had actually taken boards out from this walkway in order to discourage people from crossing on foot. It was a difficult trek to make in daylight in good weather, but in this storm and in the dark Kate was afraid it was almost impossible. Even if she wasn't swept over by the wind or didn't fall through the holes where the boards were missing, there was always the chance she was already too late and the express train might catch her on the bridge. Kate's lamp had gone out and she stood there for a moment in the dark. Then she thought of the men clinging to the trees in Honey Creek and the passengers on the express. She dropped to her knees and began to crawl across the 500-foot bridge. As she crawled splinters tore at her hands and knees and spikes ripped her clothes. She could feel the bridge shake as the water roared underneath her and fallen trees smashed into the supports below her. She saw an enormous tree, earth still clinging to its torn out roots, sweeping toward the bridge. She was sure it would destroy the section of bridge she was on but instead it missed the piers and floated on down the river.

Kate finally made it to the other side and ran the last quarter of a mile to the Moingona station. She burst into the station and started to warn the men who were there. At first they thought she was mad: tattered and muddy and soaking wet from the storm. Finally they understood what she was trying to say. The express was almost at the station when the agent ran out with a red lantern and flagged the train to a halt. The 200 passengers and crew had been saved. Kate guided a rescue train back to Honey Creek where the two surviving crewmembers were rescued.

The passengers took up a collection for Kate, and the state awarded her a medal and a $200 gift. The *Chicago Tribune* started a collection to pay off the Shelley's mortgage and debts. In 1900 the railroad built a new steel bridge and named it after her, the first bridge named after a woman in this country. Kate went on to become a celebrity and gave talks about her adventure. She eventually taught school and in 1903 she became the station agent in Moingona.

For her entire life Kate Shelley was awarded free passage on the trains and door-to-door service when she went for supplies in town and returned to her family home. Sometimes people would wonder why the train stopped in the middle of nowhere and who the older woman was who got off and slowly walked to the small farmhouse. The conductors would take great delight in telling folks that that was Kate Shelley, a true hero in every sense of the word. The passengers would just shake their heads in wonder at that special kind of courage.

American Gothic (a True Story)

Some students were on a field trip to the Art Institute of Chicago when a few of them stopped in front of a painting that depicted rural life in America. They looked at the farmer and his daughter in the picture, the man holding a pitchfork and the younger woman in a cotton dress with an apron. One of the young people said quietly, "It reminds me of my grandfather and aunt. They were farmers in central Iowa. They looked like that all the time."

Another student whose family was city bred said, "You mean they always looked serious?"

"No," said the boy, "they always looked hard working and determined."

The painting was *American Gothic*, by Grant Wood, and it is one of the best-known paintings in America.

Grant Wood was born in Anamosa, Iowa, in 1891. After the death of his father the family moved to Cedar Rapids. Grant Woods was an inquisitive man and was always learning about his art and the world around him. He attended both an art school in Minneapolis and the famed Art Institute of Chicago. He went to Europe four times between 1920 and 1928, studying various styles of painting, including impressionism and postimpressionism.

In 1932 he helped formed the Stone City Art Colony to help artists get through the Great Depression. He also was a champion of regionalism in the arts and lectured around the country. Wood began teaching at the University of Iowa's Art School in 1934. He was a prominent member of the university's community. Grant Wood died in 1942 while he was still teaching at the University of Iowa.

During his lifetime Grant Wood took on many projects that were not based in the artistic community. He painted advertisements, designed building interiors, designed stained glass windows, and taught junior high school before moving on to teach at the university level. During the World War I he served in the army and painted camouflage for concealing guns.

At first many people thought his work *American Gothic* was a critical or satirical depiction of rural America, but during the Depression their view changed and most people thought that it was actually a strong portrait of America's pioneer spirit. The woman in the painting is Wood's sister; the man is the family dentist. It won a prize of $300 and was an instant success when it was first exhibited at the Art Institute of Chicago in 1930.

That painting has become a cultural icon that has been reproduced and satirized thousands of times throughout the years.

The paintings that Wood created depicted a rural America that was already changing quickly. His paintings give us a glimpse into the last of the pioneers, the farmers and settlers who still remembered their homestead days. Grant Wood captured an American spirit and left it as a legacy to be a chronicle of an era.

Ishjinki and the Duck Dance
(Ioway/Otoe/Missouria People)

And so, Ishjinki would go about playing tricks and creating mayhem among the people, they say. He liked to scheme to sneak something to eat, tricking others by calling them as relations, or he would try to attract young appealing women, it seems. And one day, he was alone when he saw many ducks. He went over to them and when the ducks saw him they said one to another: "Uh-oh! Old Man Ishjinki is coming."

"Ho!" said Ishjinki, "Let me sing for you and you all can dance." The ducks agreed to his invitation and so he had them gather in a circle around him. As soon as they gathered around, Ishjinki lay down in the middle of the circle. And so, he said to them, "Shut your eyes, and don't look while I sing. If anyone peeks, he'll have red eyes."

And so he sang, "Iyan annasdan naha isdan sujehiñe e e yo (Someone who looks at me causes red eyes)."

He sang faster and had the ducks dance faster. And he encouraged them to whoop it up, and so they were all saying, "Quack, quack, quack." Soon they danced faster, and Ishjinki reached out and grabbed them by the neck, and stuffed them into a big sack, they say. Soon he had stuffed many of the birds in the bag. He would shout and encourage them, "Ho, good dancing!"

Finally one of the birds became suspicious as it seemed that there were ever fewer "Quack, quacks." So the one duck peeked and he saw Ishjinki grabbing his kins duck people by the neck and filling up his bag with them. He shouted:

"Watch out ! He is killing us!" the duck cried out.

And then all the ducks that were still left flew up and away. And to this day, the Mihgunkciñc (mud hens) still have red eyes, it seems.

And Ishjinki said, "It's good. I have enough to eat now." So he made a fire and let it burn down to a pile of hot coals, they say. He was going to roast the ducks in the hot glowing coals. He made a hole in the ashes and he laid all the ducks in a circle. Then he covered them up with the hot coals. Only the feet were sticking out, they say.

And while he was lying there as they roasted, there stood trees nearby, and the wind made the tree branches rub together. "Kreeeek!" the trees would sound as the wind caused the branches to rub one another. "Buh! Be quiet!" Isjinki shouted out. "You are noisy!" he said. And the wind continued to blow and the trees continued to make the Kreeking noise.

"Be quiet! I'll come there and make you be quiet! Do you hear me!" he shouted.

So the trees only continued to make the noise, and then Ishjinki climbed up the tree. He tried to hit the branches, but they continued to rub together and make noise. He kicked the branches. He wrestled with the branches. The branches continued to rub together and make noise. "I will push them apart and bend them backward," he thought. "Then, when I bend the branch back, it will break," he told himself. At the very place where they rubbed together, he pushed them apart. But the wind blew again, they say. And the branches clamped together and caught his arm. He was caught and he could not get away.

He hollered for someone to help him, and a Wolf heard him. "Ho, my friend, what is the matter?" he said. Ishjinki yelled: "Don't bother my roasting ducks. Just help me get down." The Wolf sniffed the smell of the cooking ducks and saw the fire. Sure enough, the ducks roasted in the live coals. And so, one by one, the Wolf pulled out the cooked ducks. And soon he ate them all up, they say. Ishjinki could not see him. He kept on hollering. And then Wolf piled up the ashes again and stuck all the duck feet back into the ashes, and then he went on his own way.

After the Wolf left, the wind and the tree let loose of Ishjinki, so he climbed down. He was happy when he saw the duck feet sticking out of the ashes. He thought they were yet there. And soon he was disheartened to find only feet. And that is when I started back home.

Used by permission of Jimm GoodTracks, Baxoje Jiwere Language Project.

Now You See It, Now You Don't

A wealthy banker from out east was journeying along the river road on the western shores of the Mississippi River in the later 1800s. His wife and servants, as well as clerks from the main office, accompanied him on his journey from his bank to help him as he visited branches in Illinois, Wisconsin, and Iowa. His traveling group took up two coaches and a wagon with their personal belongings. They had stayed at several inns and hotels along the way but were at least a few hours from Clinton when they came across a quaint country inn nestled in the shadow of a cottonwood tree.

Now this was the perfect stopping place in their travels. They could get a good night's sleep and arrive in late morning in Clinton refreshed and ready to examine another bank.

The banker had made extensive notes about his travels, where they stayed, whom they met, even details about the meals they had along their way. They went inside the inn and talked to the owner, who was more than gracious. He had enough rooms for all of them and dinner was to be served in about two hours. The party went to their rooms to wash up and change for their evening meal. Now the travelers had stayed in some very horrible accommodations and were ready for anything, but to their surprise the rooms were clean, spacious, and light with comfortable beds. After resting and washing up they joined the other guests in the dining room. Instead of the rough and tumble gamblers, traveling salesmen, and wagon drivers they had shared a meal with at other inns and hotels, they were again surprised to find cultured, educated people, the same dinner guests they would have expected at a fancy hotel back east. The food was excellent, the wine first rate, and the conversation stimulating. The only sore spot for the night was one young man at another table who had too much wine to drink. When the conversation turned to ghosts, as it always seems to do among travelers, the young man laughed. He looked at the easterners with a look almost of pity and said, "Our friends here seem to not believe in ghosts. Mark my words, they are real, as real as all of us." They could hear him as he tripped up the steps saying over and over again, "As rcal as us."

As the easterners headed to their rooms they were not only happy but also anxious to make reservations for their return trip after their visit to Clinton.

The next day they made their return reservations and arrived in Clinton later that morning. After such a good night's rest and wonderful supper the day seemed to just go from one easy, happy event to the next. Over dinner that night the banker told one of his new friends at the Clinton branch about the inn they had stayed at on the River Road along the Mississippi. "It must be new," said the man. "There are always new inns and hotels springing up all the time."

The next afternoon, with all the business concluded, they left Clinton and headed back toward the inn by the cottonwood tree on the River Road. The whole party was in high spirits at the thought of another excellent supper and more fine conversation among the other guests. When they turned the bend in the road the coaches stopped and all conversations stopped. There was the cottonwood tree, there was the place where the inn had been, but there was no inn there now. It was just a cottonwood tree. This had to be the spot. It was the right distance from Clinton, there was the old tree, and there was the bend in the road and one in the river, but no inn. Several men got down from the wagons and looked at the ground underneath the tree and found no signs that any building had ever been there. They all looked at each other in amazement. Here was a real mystery. Then they remembered the words of the young man from two nights before, "As real as us."

Turning around quickly, they went back to Clinton and the refuge of the nice and probably not haunted hotel they had stayed in the night before.

Iowa Glossary

Dakota people: A Native American people who are part of the Sioux culture. They lived in tepees made of buffalo hides that were portable so they could follow the herds that they depended on for their food. The tepees belonged to the women. They lived throughout what is now Wisconsin, Minnesota, North and South Dakota, and Iowa.

Iowa: A state named after the Ioway people. Its capital is Des Moines.

Iowa or Ioway people: A plains tribe that called themselves "Baxoje," meaning grey snow. The name Ioway comes from the Sioux word for these people. They lived in earthen lodges made of wood frames and packed earth. They did not follow the buffalo. The Ioway are originally from what is now the state of Iowa.

Old Man Ishjinki: The trickster of Ioway/Otoes/Missouria culture.

Otoe-Missouria people: A Native American people who were originally from present-day central Nebraska and northern Missouri State.

Regionalism: A popular art movement in the United States during the 1930s. Artists who were part of this movement celebrated simpler rural life in America in their art.

Story Sources

American Myths & Legends, Volumes 1 & 2

Ghosts of the Mississippi: Dubuque to Keokuk

Ghosts of the Mississippi: Keokuk to St. Louis

The Greenwood Library of American Folktales, Volume 1

Hearts of Fire: Great Women of American Lore & Legend

Jimm GoodTracks, Baxoje Jiwere Language Project

Myths & Legends of Our Own Land, Volumes 1 & 2

A Treasury of Iowa Tales: Unusual, Interesting & Little-Known Stories of Iowa

A Treasury of Mississippi River Folklore

A Treasury of Western Folklore

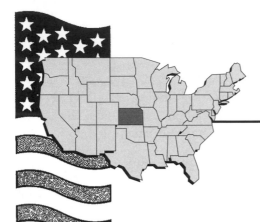

Kansas

Kansas became the thirty-fourth state in 1861. It is in that part of the country often called America's Breadbasket because of its food production. The story "Jack and the Kansas Corn" tells us a little bit about how tall Kansas corn can grow. Before the Europeans came to Kansas, it was home to many Native American tribes, many of whom still live in Kansas, such as the Osage and Pawnee.

During the 1930s droughts came to the plains of America and caused what is called the Great Dust Bowl. The story "Weathering the Storm" gives us a glimpse into that dry and terrible time. Every state has its own special ghost, and Kansas is no exception. "The Ghost on the Hill" tells the tale of a selfless young woman who still watches over her people. "The Traveling Courthouse" is a tale that might be tall or at least very stretched, about the lengths that a small town would go to for its own courthouse.

Jack and the Kansas Corn

One day a farmer sent his son Jack out into the fields to check on the progress of their corn crop. The corn was so tall that Jack couldn't see over it, so he went back to the barn and came back with a ladder. He leaned the ladder up against one of the cornstalks and climbed to the top. From there he could see the whole field of golden corn for miles on end. He knew that his father would be so excited about the wonderful harvest they would have soon. He started to climb down, but as he did he realized that the corn was growing faster than he could climb down. As he stepped from rung to rung he saw that the ladder itself was now caught in the plant and was being carried up and up as the corn grew higher and higher. No matter how fast Jack moved, the corn was growing faster all the time.

His father was worried when Jack didn't return for his lunch, so he climbed up to the top of the old barn and looked out across the cornfield to see if he could spy Jack. Sure enough, there was Jack waving his hat clinging on to the top of a cornstalk. The farmer rang the bell on the side of his barn and soon neighbors from all around came running. After they heard the story of how Jack was caught up in the cornstalk the men all got axes and started to cut down the corn as fast as they could cut. They worked and worked, but every time they made a cut the corn would grow so fast that the next blow would land somewhere else on the cornstalk. The women kept preparing meals for the men so they could work around the clock. After two weeks the weather turned dry and the corn stopped growing, and Jack was able to climb down using all those axe cuts as hand- and footholds on his way down. Jack and his brothers and sisters took some of the corn cobs that fell down, made them into corncob dolls, and gave them to the children of all the farmers and their wives who had worked so hard to get him down. That harvest Jack and his family had a pretty good yield of corn. Of course the vegetable garden was ruined, because the corn blocked out the sun for most of the summer.

Weathering the Storm
(an Original Tale by Dan Keding)

You could hear it before you saw it. The wind howled and moaned and roared and filled your ears with sounds that scared you now and haunted your dreams for years long after the storm was gone. The dogs heard it first. The two little girls were playing near their farmhouse when suddenly the two farm dogs that had been joining in their game of run and scream stopped and looked to the southwest. Their tails stopped wagging and their ears flattened against their heads. Slowly they lowered their heads and growled. Then the girls heard it, too.

All four of them ran back to the house, the girls yelling "Black Roller, Black Roller" at the top of their lungs. Their parents had taught them to do this whenever they heard or saw signs of a dust storm. Their father and brother heard them from the tool shed and started to get their animals into the barn. The chicken coop was long gone, buried under the sand and dust of previous storms. Those chickens that were left and the old rooster had taken up residence in the barn rafters. During one storm the rooster actually went to sleep thinking that night had come and then crowed in the "new" day when the dust storm was over. The animals were frightened. The girls knew that the cats would hide in the barn for hours even after the storm was gone. The few cows they still had and their old mule would moan and snort piteously while the dust storm raged. The dogs always found their way into the house. At first the girl's mother was upset with the farm dogs' intrusion, but now she worried about them and called their names to get safely into the house. It was comforting for the children to stroke the dogs' heads and have something to comfort. It lessened their fear a little bit.

Dad and their brother got the animals into the barn and secured the doors. They had put extra boards up on the roof and upper level of the barn to cover any openings. It helped, they said, but even with the extra protection they would spend two days shoveling out the dust and sand that came through any crack it could find.

Mother had already started to put rags into the spaces by the windowsills and door jams. As soon as the girls got into the house they knew what to do, and they started to help their mother. The dogs found a place under the table to hide and keep out of the way. Several of the house windows had already been boarded up, and the remaining ones were now being stuffed with rags while dad and older brother closed the shutters from the outside.

Mother started to wet down bandanas and cloths for them to wear over their faces so they could breathe during the storm. Without those wet cloths it was hard to take in a breath even in the house.

By now the wind was howling so loud that they had to shout to each other to be heard. They could see the dust storm now. It was a wall of darkness that was heading straight for their farm. It seemed to fill the sky from top to bottom and side to side. When the storm hit it became as dark as night. The girls huddled underneath the dining room table petting the dogs, their heads lying in the girls' laps. The noise and the dust seemed to go on and on forever. You could see it floating in the air inside the house. You could feel the house shake and rock as the wind slammed against its side.

Their father would always start to tell jokes about the dust storms as they sat in the living room and listened to them attack their farm.

"You know," he said, "one day we'll all go down to Texas and look for our farm. I bet we could find it." Mother would always smile. It was better than crying, she said. "I wonder if we have to pay taxes in Texas now since most of our farm is down there?"

"I heard that there was a storm over in Oklahoma that was so bad the prairie dogs thought they were buried and dug up into the storm. When it was over it rained prairie dogs for two hours." Dad shook his head knowingly and the children laughed.

"At school," said their brother, "I heard that some storms have whole prairie dog towns inside them just traveling from state to state."

Even mother laughed at this tall tale.

Sometimes father or mother would read to the children, stories from the Bible or adventure stories like King Arthur and his knights. The kids would close their eyes and pretend they were somewhere else where the wind blew gently and there was no dust that stung your eyes or filled your lungs.

After a few hours the wind started to die down and the darkness outside started to lighten up just a bit. The tenseness that had filled the little house started to creep away, and now they all knew what was ahead of them the rest of day and even part of tomorrow. Digging out. You could already see thick coats of dust all over the furniture and piles near the windows and doors. The color of the dust was red. They wondered where it came from, because the color of the earth in Kansas was black. Their father said it came from Oklahoma. He said there was a lot of iron in the soil down there and it made it red.

When the storm passed father and brother made their way to the barn to tend to the animals while mother and her girls grabbed brooms and mops and buckets and started once more to take back their home.

It would rain again soon.

The Ghost on the Hill

The young woman walked among the soldiers' beds at the fort's hospital trying to console them as the epidemic spread. Cholera had come to Fort Hays, Kansas, and men were dying one after another. Elizabeth Polly was the wife of the hospital steward and helped her husband take care of the sick and dying soldiers. At the end of a long day she would often walk up a nearby hill and stand there, letting the cool evening breeze refresh her after a day of taking care of the sick and the dying. She would close her eyes and pretend she was back at her parents' house, far away from the epidemic that was taking the lives of the young soldiers.

Every day Elizabeth and her husband tended the sick and the dying. The young men would often ask her to write letters for them to send to their folks or sweethearts to let them know that they were thinking of those they loved before they died. Elizabeth would smile and patiently write out the words that each dying soldier spoke to her and send them back to families who would never see their sons or loved ones again. She listened to those who had no one back home and held their hands as they took their last breath. She listened as the older soldiers talked about how unfair it was that they had survived the horrors of the Civil War only to die on the frontier in a hospital bed, murdered by a disease. Day after day Elizabeth listened to their stories and wrote their letters for them, and she never let them see her cry. She cooled their fevered foreheads with water and covered them when the chills took over and their bodies shook. Later she would climb her hill and weep at the stories she heard and the letters she wrote and the young men who had died in her arms as she tried to comfort them.

One day Elizabeth felt very tired. Even a visit to her beloved hill didn't make her feel any better. The next day she couldn't get out of bed. Then she and her husband both knew that she had caught the dreaded cholera. She fought the disease with the same courage she had showed when she had tended the dying soldiers, but there was no hope. As she lay dying her only request was to be buried on top of the hill where she loved to stand and dream of home.

Elizabeth was buried on the hill but not at the top. Her grave was surrounded by four stone columns that were later stolen. Legend has it that the men who stole them all met with violent deaths. Knowing the compassion that Elizabeth showed the rough soldiers when they faced death, it's hard to believe that she would cause harm to the men who took her tombstones.

When Fort Hayes was closed the military graveyard was relocated, as was the cemetery that held civilian workers who had perished, but Elizabeth's grave was left where it was. Over the years the exact location was lost. But it didn't mean that Elizabeth Polly was gone from her hill.

The first sighting of Elizabeth's ghost was by a farmer, who saw a woman dressed in blue walking toward Sentinel Hill, the hill that she used to stand on and dream of home. He followed the woman, who walked into a shed at the edge of his property near the hill and then disappeared. He went in the only entrance, and when he walked into the shed the woman in blue was gone.

After that people started to see the woman in blue more often. Her dress was described as an old fashioned blue dress, maybe a farm dress or one worn by a woman who worked as a nurse or teacher. Folks also started to see blue lights floating across the hill, sometimes lingering on the top as if looking out over the surrounding countryside. People started to call the ghost the "Blue Light Lady." Some visitors have told of footsteps that come up the hill and stop just when they reach the top, but there is no one there.

Another time a police officer called in on his radio that he had just hit a woman dressed in blue near Sentinel Hill. When he got out of his car to look for her there was no body, no trace of a woman, and no damage to his squad car.

The bones of Elizabeth Polly were found and relocated to the top of the hill, where a monument was built. But people still see her, a blue light or perhaps the faint outline of a woman in blue walking along the top of the hill. Is she still crying over the letters of her dead soldiers? Does she still dream of home? Why does she always come back to her hilltop? We'll never know.

The Traveling Courthouse

Kansas was a place to travel through, not to, until the introduction of "Turkey Red" wheat from Russia. This variety of wheat was strong enough to withstand the severe weather and the dry plains of Kansas. Soon farmers started to come to Kansas, and the prairies of this state came to life with people and their farms. Towns sprang up and stores opened. Each community wanted the one symbol of prosperity and approval that only a few could get, a courthouse. Once a small town got a courthouse, they protected it with all the determination and guns they could provide. If the townspeople didn't have enough "guns" to protect the courthouse, then there were always enough outlaws and guns for hire to be had in places like Dodge City.

Probably the strangest story about courthouses came from a place named Occidental City.

The only sound that could be heard was the buzzing of flies. The county clerk had leaned his chair back and was sleeping the afternoon away. The entire town was unaware that hiding in the brush was a group of desperate men from the nearby town of Big Stranger, determined men who had only one goal in mind, to steal the courthouse.

The clerk went home at the end of the day and that evening he joined all the other folks in Occidental City as they slept the deep sleep of the innocent. The men from Big Stranger saw their chance and came out of their hiding place. They sneaked up to the courthouse and pried it loose from its foundations. They hiked that courthouse up and secured wheels underneath it and then hitched several teams of mules to the courthouse. They proceeded to haul the courthouse through the night to Big Stranger and set up their new courthouse in the center of town.

When the folks of Occidental City woke up the next morning they found the hogs that often rooted around the streets of their town were now rooting around the vacant lot where their courthouse had stood the day before. Needless to say, the folks in Occidental were angry and were determined to have their revenge.

About a week later tornadoes were seen all over the county. The sky over Big Stranger turned as dark as night, and the entire town was huddled in their storm shelters or basements waiting for the storm to pass. The men from Occidental City took advantage of the situation and came along and kidnapped their old courthouse. They started to drag it back to Occidental City through the wind and rain.

Suddenly a twister came along and started to lift the courthouse off the ground. Well those Occidental men weren't going to lose their courthouse to another town or to a tornado, so they hung on for dear life as the twister lifted that courthouse about a mile into the air. They held on while the winds tore at their clothes and plucked their beards off their faces. When they finally pulled that courthouse down to earth they were in the middle of Grand Junction, and the folks there were mighty pleased to have a courthouse. The men from Occidental City got out of that town as fast as they could and left their courthouse behind. The Grand Junction folks painted the doors a beautiful yellow and were pretty sure that it was heaven that sent them their new courthouse, not the direction-impaired men from Occidental City.

The folks were so happy that they decided to have a town picnic out by the new church to celebrate their new courthouse. While the whole town was eating and dancing, some men from Rattle Snake Crossing snuck into town and once more hoisted that courthouse up on wheels and stole it right out from under their noses.

Nobody is quite sure what happened to that courthouse. It might be in Rattle Snake Crossing, or maybe folks from Occidental City or Big Stranger or Grand Junction came along and stole it once more. It could even still be out there on the Kansas plains looking for a home where it could just settle down and be safe.

Kansas Glossary

Black roller: The name given to the huge dust storms that plagued the Great Plains during the massive drought of the 1930s.

Cholera: An infectious disease that affects the intestines and is spread by food or drinking water. The disease dehydrates the patient and causes diarrhea. Now we have vaccines and know how to prevent the disease, but in the days of Elizabeth Polly many people died when they caught cholera.

Dust Bowl: A prolonged period of drought and erosion in the central United States, known as the Great Dust Bowl, that lasted from 1930 to 1936 and in some areas until 1940. Drought coupled with extensive farming without crop rotation or erosion prevention caused this disaster. The Dust Bowl covered over 100 million acres. By 1940 over 2.5 million people had left the plains and moved out. When the dust storms came they destroyed the land. They literally picked the soil up and took it away. On April 14, 1935, known as "Black Sunday," twenty of the worst dust storms hit the Great Plains at the same time. Much of the richest soil in America was carried away and deposited in the ocean.

Jack: A folklore character found in stories across the country, especially wherever English, Irish or Scottish people settled. Jack tales are very popular in the Appalachian area.

Kansas: A state that was named after the Kansas River, which had been named after the Native American people called the Kansa. The capital is Topeka.

Osage people: A Native American people who lived in round earthen lodges and used tepees only for hunting trips. They were well known for the quality of their bows. They lived in Oklahoma, Missouri, Kansas, and Arkansas.

Pawnee people: A Native American people who were farmers and hunters and lived in Nebraska and Kansas. Like the Osage they lived in both round earthen lodges and tepees. Pawnee men often shaved their heads and wore one long braid of hair down their backs.

Story Sources

American Myths & Legends, Volumes 1 & 2

Cowboy Songs and Other Frontier Ballads

The Greenwood Library of American Folktales, Volume 3

Indian Sleep-Man Tales: Legends of the Otoe Tribe

Myths & Legends of Our Own Land, Volumes 1 & 2

Outlaw Tales: Legends, Myths & Folklore from America's Middle Border

Pawnee Hero Stories & Folktales

Tales from the American Frontier

A Treasury of Western Folklore

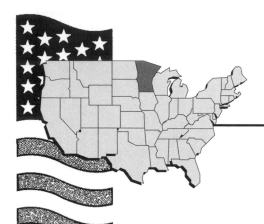

Minnesota

In 1858 Minnesota became the thirty-second state to enter the union. Native Americans settled in the rich forests and plains, and these tribes included the Ojibwa and the Dakota. Immigrants from northern Europe, especially Scandinavia, were attracted to Minnesota and are represented here by a story from Norway about a husband and wife who trade places. During the American Civil War there was a short, little-known war between the Dakota people and the white settlers, whose story is told here. Every state has its monsters, either real or fictional, and Minnesota has its mosquitoes, very big mosquitoes, as you'll find in the story from Grand Rapids by Kevin Strauss called "The Giant Mosquitoes." Sometimes heroes are quiet and arrive on your doorstep at just the right time, as in the story by Kevin Strauss, "Pillsbury vs. the Grasshopper Plague."

The Giant Mosquitoes
(as Told by Kevin Strauss)

The year was 1868 when Paul Bunyan arrived in the winter woods near what is now Grand Rapids, Minnesota. Some people say it was Paul who moved the rivers and made those rapids so big, so they would carry his logs to the mill downstream. But that is a different story. This story is about a different problem, because you see, when loggers arrived near Grand Rapids, Paul Bunyan wasn't the only giant in the woods.

Paul knew something was wrong when loggers began disappearing, first one at a time and then in small groups. Paul sent search parties out to look for the missing men. It was dangerous to stay outdoors in a Minnesota winter. If loggers were just lost, they might not last the night.

But those search parties didn't come back either. That's when Paul knew he had some real trouble. He gathered his men in the dining hall for a late night talk. That's when they heard the buzzing and felt a banging on the windows and doors. In the dark, it was hard to figure out what they were. At first they looked like big birds, but then Paul saw the long, strawlike beaks on their faces. Then he realized what they were, Giant Minnesota Mosquitoes.

Those mosquitoes were a good eight feet long from tip to tail. And when they swarmed out of the swamps, it was like a cloud blotting out the full moon. Luckily the loggers had their tools with them. So when a giant mosquito broke through a window, the men would nail a table or chair over the opening.

The men had plenty of food in the dining hall. But those mosquitoes were hungry, too, and when they couldn't get in through windows and doors, they got angry. The whole swarm of them grabbed onto the roof of the dining hall and began prying it off.

Paul had to think fast. If a log building and a wooden roof couldn't keep them safe, what could? But then he got an idea.

"Get to the bean pot," he yelled to the men.

While the giant mosquitoes were busy lifting the dining hall roof, the loggers burst through the front doors and ran across the camp to the field where the camp cooks boiled up beans for Paul and his 500 loggers. Paul grabbed the giant pot and tipped it over. The loggers climbed inside.

Of course, this didn't fool the giant mosquitoes. They dropped the roof and flew over to the pot. Paul figured that a pot with cast iron sides ten inches thick would stop any mosquito.

But he was wrong.

First he heard a tapping, then a banging, and then he saw the beaks of those giant mosquitoes stabbing right through the sides of the pot.

But then Paul had another good idea. Grabbing a nearby rock, Paul pounded on a mosquito's beak and bent it over just like a nail. He told his men to use their heavy peavey poles to do the same. Suddenly, the mosquitoes couldn't get loose.

Paul figured that was the end of it, but it wasn't. The mosquitoes buzzed even louder, and they pulled and pulled and beat their wings and lifted that giant pot into the air. They raised the pot over the trees and disappeared into the woods.

A few days later Paul heard that a timber cruiser had spotted the giant mosquitoes and the pot flying over Red Lake. But apparently the mosquitoes were getting a little tired, because the man saw the pot sink lower and lower over the lake until it crashed into the ice and disappeared beneath the water, never to be seen again.

And that's why we no longer have giant mosquitoes in Minnesota, and why we never found Paul's giant cooking pot.

"The Giant Mosquitoes," "Aunt Gretchen's First Drink," and "The Hodag's Lament" have been reprinted from The Reading Ranger's™ Guide to 50 Fabulous Folktales That Everyone Should Read and Hear, *by Kevin Strauss. ©2008 by Kevin Strauss. Reproduced with the permission of Trumpeter Press, Eden Prairie, MN.*

The Husband Who Stayed at Home
(Norwegian)

Minnesota is home to many people of Norwegian and other Scandinavian descent. This traditional tale harkens back to Norway.

Once a long time ago there was a husband who was always in a bad mood because he felt that he did all the work around the farm while his wife stayed home and did nothing. He was a man who could never see what was right in front of his nose.

One evening he came home complaining and telling his wife how hard his day was in the fields and how easy her life was at home.

His wife looked at him and said, "Do you think you could do the work in this house better than I?"

He laughed gruffly, looking around the room. "Of course I do. Any man could do this work easily."

The wife smiled sweetly and said, "Well then, tomorrow we trade places. I will go to the fields and work and you will stay home and do my daily chores."

Early the next day the wife put a scythe over her shoulder and went to the hayfield to mow. The husband stayed behind, planning to do her chores and have a little nap as well.

He decided to churn the butter first. After he had churned for a while he was thirsty, so he went into the cellar to tap a glass of ale. He had just taken the plug out when he heard the pig grunting in the kitchen. With the tap still in his hand he ran up the cellar steps and saw that the pig had overturned the churn and was eagerly lapping up the cream.

The farmer became so angry that he chased the pig and fell face down in the cream that now had spread all over the floor. He reached out and caught the pig and hauled himself to his feet. He was so mad that he gave the pig a swift kick in the head. He kicked the pig so hard that the poor thing fell over quite dead. It was then that he looked down and saw the plug in his hand and ran down to the cellar only to see the last drop of ale fall from the barrel onto the floor.

There was still no butter for their dinner, so he left the house and went to the barn in search of more cream. He skimmed off just enough to fill the churn and once more began to work. As he churned, he remembered the cow had not been milked or taken to the pasture and had been kept in the barn all morning with no food or water. When he had milked the cow he had no time to take her to pasture, because he still had to churn the butter for their dinner, clean the cream up off the floor, and butcher the dead pig. So he decided to get the cow up on the cottage roof. It slanted just a little, was covered with sod, and sat close to a steep hill. He was sure he could put a couple of planks from the hill to the roof and coax the cow over to the fine crop of waiting grass.

Just about this time, as he held the lead of the bellowing cow, he heard the baby begin to cry. Knowing it was too hungry, he didn't want to leave the churn still filled with cream in the kitchen where the baby was crawling around in search of food, so he hoisted the churn onto his back and tugged on the cow. When he managed to get the cow on the roof he remembered that the poor thing had not had any water, so he decided to get some from the well. As he bent over to pull up the bucket, all the cream from the churn went spilling over his head and into the well. He was so angry that he took the churn and threw it across the yard, where it hit the side of the barn and splintered into a hundred pieces.

Now the farmer thought that since there would be no butter, and the baby was crying and no doubt covered in spilt cream, and he had not even started dinner, he had better at least make some porridge. He hurried back into the kitchen, stepping over the dead pig and trying not to slip in puddles of cream. He grabbed up the soaking, screaming baby, filled a pot with water, and put it over the fire to boil. It was at that point that he heard the cow above and remembered that he had failed to tie her to a tether. What if she fell off and broke her leg? What would he do then?

He dropped the baby and ran to the barn, where he grabbed a length of rope. He climbed up on the roof again, tied the rope around the cow's neck, and then hung the rope down the chimney so he could tie it to something solid in the kitchen.

When he returned to the kitchen he saw the water boiling and threw some oatmeal into the pot. The baby, still crying, was crawling near the fire. The husband hurriedly wrapped the rope around his ankle so he could pick up the baby and put him back into his cradle. With the baby screaming in the cradle, the man went back to the fireplace to stir the porridge, which bubbled over and down into the fire. At this moment, the cow fell off the roof and the man was pulled halfway up the chimney, dangling by his ankle, above the overturned porridge and the smoking fire. It was then that his wife came home.

Now, the wife had had a fine day mowing and had cut down seven lengths and seven breadths of the field. She had expected her husband to call her to dinner, but when no call had come she decided to return home.

When the wife arrived in the barnyard she saw the broken butter churn and the cow dangling near the ground, hanging from the roof of the house. She ran up and took her scythe and cut the rope so the cow could be freed. This caused her husband to come falling down the chimney face first into the spilt porridge and dying fire. The wife rushed into the house past the dead pig, over the floor smeared with cream, up to her crying baby, and her poor husband groaning in the fireplace.

In silence the husband and the wife cleaned up the baby and the house, hung the pig up to be butchered, and put the cow out to pasture. As the wife comforted the baby, they sat down to a meager dinner of stale bread without butter, porridge, or ale.

Soon the wife turned to her husband and smiled. "No matter, dear. Tomorrow is another day, and I'm sure you'll get the hang of running the house."

The husband held his aching head and slowly chewed his bread. "I think that I am better suited to the simple task of farming and that the work of a woman can only be done by a woman," he said.

That night, when together in bed, the husband and wife laughed about his misadventures and the farmer never again complained about his work or how easy it must be for his wife to keep the house.

The Dakota War of 1862
(Sioux Outbreak of 1862) (a True Story)

The U.S. government had repeatedly broken every agreement with the Dakota people throughout the 1850s. Finally the Dakota felt they could no longer stand by and watch as their lands were stolen and their people humiliated. In the summer of 1862 a band of Dakota warriors attacked and killed five settlers. The Dakota decided to expand on this and began attacking settlements throughout the Mississippi River valley in an attempt to drive the white settlers from their land. The government sent in the army, and though the Dakota fought bravely and won an early battle the uprising was soon ended. The estimates for civilian deaths are between 400 and 800. The Dakota who surrendered were jailed or placed in camps.

By December 1862 the war was over and 303 Dakota warriors were convicted of murder and sentenced to death. Many of these trials lasted less than five minutes. The Dakota had no lawyers and most did not speak the language, nor were the proceedings translated for them. Henry Whipple, the Episcopal bishop of Minnesota, was a supporter of Native American rights and urged President Abraham Lincoln to review the trials and the sentences. President Lincoln commuted the death sentences of 264 prisoners. One other prisoner was later granted a reprieve. The 38 remaining Dakota were executed by hanging on December 26, 1862, in what is still the largest mass execution in U.S. history.

The hardships for the Dakota did not end there. The remaining prisoners were sent to Rock Island, Illinois, where they stayed in confinement for over four years. When they were finally released, one-third of the men had died from disease. Over 1,600 Dakota women and children and elders were held in an internment camp, where more than 300 died of disease. In April 1863 the U.S. Congress declared all treaties with the Dakota to be null and took away their reservation lands, forcing them to relocate first to the Crow Reservation in Dakota Territory and later to the Santee Reservation in Nebraska. A bounty of $25 per scalp was placed on any Dakota found in Minnesota.

Eventually the Dakota did return to Minnesota, and the Lower Sioux Indian Reservation and the Upper Sioux Indian Reservations were established. There are several monuments that commemorate the settlers killed during the short war. A monument in Reconciliation Park in Mankato, Minnesota, honors the 38 Dakota who were hanged.

Pillsbury vs. the Grasshopper Plague (a Minnesota History Tale, Sort of, Based on True Events, by Kevin Strauss)

John S. Pillsbury was already a business success in timber and flour milling when he ran for governor of Minnesota in 1875. You have likely heard his name because of the flour company that still bears his family name.

But when Pillsbury took office on January 7, 1876, he knew that he'd have work to do. His flour mills lined the Mississippi River. But flour mills needed wheat to mill, and the rich farmlands of western and southern Minnesota were in the grips of a grasshopper plague of biblical proportions.

Starting in the summer of 1873, farmers in southwestern Minnesota looked west to see a dark cloud that "just didn't look right." The cloud had a sickly yellow-green hue, and it moved faster than the few ragged clouds that marked the calm blue sky. As the farmers watched, they saw things dropping from the cloud. Was it hail? No. It was grasshoppers, the biggest, ugliest brown grasshoppers (actually Rocky Mountain locusts) anyone had ever seen. As they settled on the land, the grasshoppers seemed to know right where the gardens and the wheat fields where. Their chewing sounded like the rooting of a hundred hogs or the buzzing of a sawmill, and it didn't stop. Day after day the grasshoppers ate crops, tree leaves, clothes left out on the line, even green paint. They never *stopped* eating.

Although the first clouds of hoppers decimated farms in just thirteen Minnesota counties, the locusts laid eggs, and in the spring of 1874 this home-grown generation spread out from Mankato in the south to Moorhead in the northwest, clearing a path through farm fields, gardens, and prairies. By some accounts, the hoppers piled up two feet thick. Trains ground to a halt as dead grasshoppers made the rails too slick; horses had trouble moving through the fields. Farmers tried everything they could think of, from burning nearby prairies, to smoking the insects with burning manure piles, to dragging the field with tar-covered sheets of metal called "hopperdozers" to trap the critters. Although the burning and the traps might have killed millions of grasshoppers, they barely made a dent in the billions of hoppers in the state.

The state got a breather in 1875 when a cool spring seemed to knock back the grasshopper population. But the insects swarmed back with a vengeance in 1876. At first Pillsbury, being a businessman, agreed with his Republican contemporaries that government support was only for large business concerns, like corporations, not the family farm.

Pillsbury did support new game laws to protect grasshopper predators, like pheasants, and laws to set a bounty of $1.00 a bushel for grasshoppers caught and killed before May 25 and a $.50 per gallon bounty on the gray, wormlike grasshopper egg pods. The state also created a reward for the best hopperdozer design, but Pillsbury was against any direct aid to farmers, fearing that government charity would demoralize farmers and make them dependent on government aid.

Being a businessman also meant that Pillsbury didn't wait for the government to do everything. He figured that any biblical plague also required divine intervention. So he made a proclamation that everyone in the state of Minnesota should set aside April 26, 1877, as a day of prayer and fasting. He even closed his own mills so his workers could devote themselves to the act. By many accounts, more Minnesotans of all creeds, or no creed at all, prayed on that day than any day before or since.

According to many accounts, the next day a freak April storm blew in with sleet and snow and that seemed to but an end to the plague. Being a smart politician, Pillsbury took advantage of the change in the weather and the subsequent end to the plague.

Years later, he was still taking credit for the weather, telling folks that it froze every grasshopper in the state stiff!

After that day of prayer in 1877, wheat production in the state returned to almost pre-grasshopper levels, and Pillsbury's mills were busy again. Critics say that the April storm didn't really affect the grasshoppers all that much; they point to summer storms that blew the hoppers out east, some say as far as ships on the Atlantic Ocean. Others say that the western prairie drought that drove the grasshoppers to Minnesota ended and the hoppers returned to their western home. No one knows for sure. But the prayer probably didn't hurt much.

What few people know about Governor Pillsbury is that although he didn't believe in government charity, he was of that rare breed of wealthy men who believed strongly in private charity. During the summer of 1876, he knew that many immigrant farmers had lost everything in the grasshopper scourge. So he dressed in common workers' clothing, loaded up a wagon, and headed southwest from his home in St. Anthony (now part of Minneapolis). When he reached a farm that had been devastated by the grasshoppers, he knocked on the door; when the man or woman of the house answered, he would hand them a rolled-up bundle of dollar bills. It was always enough money so the family could buy food for the next year and buy seeds for next year's planting season.

When someone would ask him who he was, Pillsbury would just smile and say, "a friend," and then he'd turn and walk back to his wagon again.

And that's how John S. Pillsbury put an end to the grasshopper plague. He believed that with government, God, and generosity, you could handle just about anything, even a plague of grasshoppers.

Minnesota Glossary

Beak: A term used by some loggers for the proboscis (needlelike mouth) of giant mosquitoes

Dakota people: A Native American people who are part of the Sioux culture. They lived in tepees made of buffalo hides that were portable, so they could follow the herds that they depended on for their food. The tepees belonged to the women. The Dakota lived throughout what is now Wisconsin, Minnesota, and North and South Dakota.

Minnesota: A state whose name comes from the Dakota word meaning "sky tinted water." The capital is St. Paul.

Ojibwa people: A Native American people, also called Chippewa. They are one of the largest tribes in North America. They settled in the Michigan, Wisconsin, and Minnesota area.

Paul Bunyan: A giant logger who roamed the pages of folktales with his great blue ox, Babe. Stories about Paul are found coast to coast. Though he started out as a literary character, he soon entered the world of folktales, and his stories spread throughout lumber camps and sawmills.

Peavey: A heavy, spearlike pole that loggers use to push logs down a river during a logging run.

Timber cruiser: A man who scouts and maps forests for logging companies.

Story Sources

American Folktales from the Collections of the Library of Congress, Volume 1

American Folktales from the Collections of the Library of Congress, Volume 2

American Myths & Legends, Volumes 1 & 2

Daylight in the Swamp

The Greenwood Library of American Folktales, Volume 1

Lumberjack Lingo

Mythical Creatures of the North Country

Mythical Creatures of the U.S.A. and Canada

Myths & Legends of Our Own Land, Volumes 1 & 2

Paul Bunyan

Paul Bunyan Swings His Axe

Tall Timber Tales: More Paul Bunyan Stories

A Treasury of Mississippi River Folklore

Missouri

Missouri was admitted to the union in 1821 as the twenty-fourth state. Two of its most famous sons are equally famous but were very different. The outlaw Jesse James, one of the most celebrated of America's outlaws, is remembered here in story and ballad. Mark Twain was a writer, one of the greatest novelists of American literature and a splendid performer who recited excerpts from his books all over the world. The Ozark region of Missouri is represented by a story about a doll that could catch a thief. The Otoe/Missouria people lived in the Missouri area before the European settlers came here, and their story about Kétan and the first warrior expedition is included. St. Louis and Missouri were a part of North America that was explored and settled originally by the French and then sold to America by Napoleon Bonaparte to raise money for his wars. It's from St. Louis that Lewis and Clark started their epic journey of exploration.

Jesse James (Based on True Events)

One day Jesse and Frank James and their men were traveling on horseback somewhere in northern Missouri. It being about noon, they were hungry. They pulled off the main road and found a woman alone on a small farm. They asked her if she could supply them with something to eat.

At first the woman hesitated. The men displayed money and assured her they would be glad to pay for what they ate. She then proceeded to prepare what little food she had on hand. As she was making coffee and cooking eggs, the James crowd sat around the room. They noticed that she was weeping; tears were rolling down her cheeks, sobs were heaving her bosom.

Jesse was always tender hearted and couldn't stand a woman's tears. He asked her why she was crying. She tried to smile it off, and said that seeing men around the house reminded her of the happy time when her husband was living and had other men now and then helping him do the farm work. She was just thinking how sadly things had changed since his death, and that was what made her cry.

Jesse kept on asking questions. The woman said she had several children at school, some miles down the road. There was a mortgage on her farm, she went on to say, for $1,400. It was overdue and this was the last day of grace.

"Aha!" said Jesse, "and so that's really what's making you cry—you're afraid you're going to lose your home. I see."

"Yes, that was it," she admitted. That very afternoon, said the weeping widow, the man who held the mortgage was coming out from town to demand his money. He was a hardhearted old miser and she didn't have a dollar to apply on the debt. The man would be sure to foreclose and turn her and her helpless little ones out.

"Huh!" said Jesse, "that so?" his eyes blinking fast and furiously. "Well, now ma'am, I don't know about that. I think maybe you won't lose your farm after all."

The widow looked rather puzzled. She put the food on the table. After they finished eating, Jesse produced a sack and counted out on the table $1,400.

"Here, lady," said Jesse, "you take this money and pay off your mortgage."

The lady was amazed. "I can't ever pay you back," she said, "and so I won't borrow it."

"But it's no loan," said Jesse, "it's a gift."

The widow said she couldn't believe it was anything but a dream, things never happened that way. Jesse assured her it was no dream. The money was good money and it was for her and her children. Jesse then sat down and wrote out a form of receipt, which he had the woman copy in her own handwriting. He put the original into his pocket, so that his handwriting wouldn't get into other hands. Jesse instructed the woman to pay the mortgage holder the $1,400 and have him sign the receipt in ink. He then handed her extra money for food and clothing for her and her children.

Jesse asked the grateful widow to describe the man who held the mortgage. She did so, telling the kind of rig he drove and about what hour she expected him, and the road by which he would come out from town. Jesse and Frank said good day and mounted their horses. The widow was still weeping, but weeping for joy.

They rode some distance from the house and hid in the bushes beside the rocky road along which the mortgage man was to come in his buggy. Presently they saw him driving toward the widow's house. Pretty soon he was driving back, looking very happy indeed. He was humming a tune as he came down the road. Jesse stepped in front of him, held him up, and took back the $1,400.

Jesse James's life and death were immortalized in a ballad, of which the following version is the best known.

Jesse James
Jesse James was a lad, who killed many a man.
He robbed the Glendale train.
He stole from the rich and he gave to the poor.
He had a hand, a heart, and a brain.

Poor Jesse had a wife to mourn for his life,
Two children, they were brave.
But that dirty little coward that shot Mister Howard
Had laid poor Jesse in his grave.

With his brother Frank they robbed the Gallatin bank,
They carried the money from the town.
And in this very place they had a little race,
For they shot Captain Sheets to the ground.

It was on a Wednesday night, the moon was shining bright,
They robbed the Glendale train.
And the people they did say for many miles away,
It was robbed by Frank and Jesse James.

It was Robert Ford, the dirty little coward,
I wonder how he does feel.
For he ate of Jesse's bread and he slept in Jesse's bed,
Then he laid Jesse James in his grave.

It was on a Saturday night, poor Jesse was at home,
Talking to his family so brave.
Robert Ford watched his eye, and shot him on the sly,
And he laid Jesse James in his grave.

The people held their breath when they heard of Jesse's death,
And wondered how he ever came to die.
Robert Ford's pistol ball brought him tumbling from the wall,
For he shot poor Jesse on the sly.

Jesse went to rest with his hand upon his breast,
The Devil will be down upon his knee.
He was born one day in the county of Clay,
And he came from a solitary race.

This song was made by Billy Gashade,
Just as soon as the news did arrive.
He said there was no man with the law in his hand
That could take Jesse James when alive.

Telling the Story (Based on True Events)

The man walked slowly onto the stage, his white suit matching his white hair and flowing mustache. He stood there for a moment looking at the audience with a mixture of curiosity and humor and then started to speak. "You don't know about me, without you have read a book by the name of *The Adventures of Tom Sawyer*, but that ain't no matter. That book was made by Mr. Mark Twain, and he told the truth, mainly."

The speaker was Mark Twain, born Samuel Langhorne Clemens in Florida, Missouri, on November 30, 1835. Halley's Comet was in the sky. Mark Twain always told the truth, mainly.

Clemens and his family moved to Hannibal, Missouri, on the banks of the Mississippi River. Hannibal would be the inspiration for his fictional town of St. Petersburg, the home of Tom Sawyer and Huckleberry Finn. The Mississippi River would be one of his passions both as a man and as an author.

He became a printer's apprentice at twelve and moved to New York City at eighteen to work in the printing trade. In the evenings and on his days off he would haunt the public library, reading books and learning as much as he could about any subject that caught his fancy. Four years later he returned to Missouri, and on a trip to New Orleans on a steamboat he fell in love with the mighty Mississippi. He followed his dream and became a pilot on a steamboat. A steamboat pilot's job was difficult because the river was always changing, so charts and maps also had to constantly change. A pilot had to know the river and be able to see the signs that warned of a sunken log or rock that could sink a steamboat. Later Clemens was to take on the writing name of Mark Twain, a measurement called out when a steamboat was in dangerously low waters.

At the outbreak of the Civil War Twain and his brother Orion traveled west to Nevada. Samuel tried his hand at mining but gave that up to become a reporter for the Virginia City newspaper, *The Territorial Enterprise*. Twain's adventures traveling west and living among the pioneers and miners were the source of his book *Roughing It*. He moved to San Francisco, where he continued to write and speak about his experiences. He traveled to Hawaii and the Mediterranean. On one of his trips to Europe and the Middle East he wrote a collection of letters about his travels, *Innocents Abroad*.

During his travels he met Charles Langdon. Charles was talking about his family one day and showed Clemens a photo of his sister. Twain later said it was love at first sight. He and Olivia were married in 1870. They moved to Hartford, Connecticut, a year later and built a magnificent house. Today you can visit that house and see how Mark Twain lived and wrote.

Two of Mark Twain's most beloved books are *The Adventures of Tom Sawyer* and *The Adventures of Huckleberry Finn*. Both these books are based on Twain's youth in Hannibal, Missouri, and his time spent on the Mississippi River. Some people have called *The Adventures of Huckleberry Finn* the first great American novel. In it Mark Twain writes about a boy faced with what he thinks is right while society thinks it's wrong. He also wrote *The Prince and the Pauper*, *A Connecticut Yankee in King Arthur's Court*, and many more novels and short stories. Often his stories seemed light and even funny, but underneath it all he had a way of telling the truth.

Mark Twain met some of the most remarkable people of his time. He was a neighbor of Harriet Beecher Stowe, the author of *Uncle Tom's Cabin*. He was a close friend of the inventor Nikola Tesla and was a frequent visitor to his laboratory. He knew Frederick Douglass and William Dean Howell. Through his friend Henry Rogers he met Helen Keller and her teacher, Anne Sullivan, and the great educator Booker T. Washington.

In 1909 Mark Twain said, "I came in with Halley's Comet in 1835. It is coming again next year, and I expect to go out with it. It will be the greatest disappointment of my life if I don't go out with Halley's Comet. The Almighty has said, no doubt, 'Now here are these two unaccountable freaks, they came together, they must go out together'."

Mark Twain was right. He died the next year.

Mark Twain's life was filled with travel and people. He saw the world around him and told us all about its weakness and its beauty. He always told the truth, mainly.

The Doll That Caught a Thief

It happened a long time ago that all the folks who were staying at a certain tavern were robbed. Now in those days the taverns were places where travelers could spend the night, resting up before they continued their journeys. On this particular night, all the doors and windows of the establishment were locked and bolted and in the morning no one was missing from among the guests. The owner, who was an honest man, decided that all the folks who spent the night should stay, and together they would try to sort out the problem.

"The reputation of my house is on the line here," he said. "We have to recover those valuables or folks won't want to stay the night under my roof."

It turned out that everyone had lost money, so much money that the sum they calculated was about 3,000 gold pieces. Several gold watches and a snuffbox were missing, too. "That snuffbox has been in my family for generations," said the owner. "I would not part with it for $100."

Everyone searched the house, but nothing could be found. Finally an old woman among the travelers spoke up, "My doll can find the thief." Everyone turned and gave her a strange look, a look of disbelief.

"It's true," she said and walked into a room at the back of the tavern, where she pulled a little wooden doll from her bag and set it on the table. Then she took some walnut juice and spread it all over the doll. When she came out of the room she turned to the owner and said, "You have those travelers go in there one by one. Each person must go in alone and grab the doll and swear that he or she did not steal anything last night. The doll will stay quiet when touched by an honest person but will scream and holler when the thief grabs hold of it." The guests all thought this was foolishness, but at this point they would agree to try anything. One by one, each person went into the back room with the doll and then came back out again.

When they were all through the old woman asked if everyone had taken hold of the doll. They all insisted they had, so she asked them to line up and hold their hands out with their palms up. She looked at each one's hands and then pointed at the man who had claimed that his snuffbox was stolen. "He is the thief," she said. At first he denied it, but when a rope was produced the man spoke up loudly.

"If you hang me you'll never find your money. I hid it where no one could find it, but if you promise to let me go I'll tell you where it is hidden."

Well, the owner of the tavern wanted to hang him then and there, but the other folks wanted their valuables back. They promised to release him and took an oath on the Bible. He told them to look in a hollow log at the bottom of the woodpile near the old cook stove. When the money was found the thief was freed and given a head start. It wasn't really necessary for him to run, because no one was bothering to chase him anyway.

The travelers decided to have a celebration at the thief's expense by raffling off his watch. The man who won the watch turned and gave it to the old woman. A hat was passed and many a silver or gold coin found its way into that hat. The tavern owner turned to the woman and said, "All this money is yours if you can tell us how you caught that thief."

"Well, didn't you hear my doll scream and holler?" she asked. Everyone said no, they didn't.

She smiled and said, "You folks are all honest, and so you went into the room and grabbed hold of that doll. But a thief is suspicious, and he probably knew there was a trick to it all, so he never touched the doll. All I did was look for the one person whose hands were not stained with walnut juice."

The owner handed her the hat full of money and thanked her for saving his good name. The old woman smiled and put her doll back in her bag.

Kétan and the First Warrior Expedition
(Ioway/Otoe/Missouria)

Kétan the Turtle decided to go on a war journey. He started out of the village and he was seen leaving by NathájeThéwe, the Black Cricket.

"Ho! Hintádo, Táan wastá je." ("Greetings, my friend! Where are you going?")

"I am going on a war journey expedition," Kétan replied.

"Well! Let me go, too."

And so NathájeThéwe, the Black Cricket walked along with his friend. And as they continued along, Rawáñe, the Mosquito, saw the two going along.

"Ho! Hintádo, Táan wastáwi je." ("Greetings, my friends! Where are you all going?")

"We are going on a war journey expedition," Kétan replied.

"Ho! Hinráwi tahó." ("Well! Let's all go!") So said Rawáñe.

And so it was, Kétan, NathájeThéwe, and Rawáñe all went together on the war expedition.

They came upon an enemy village, and they decided to pick out a lodge and overwhelm the residents in a swooping attack. And so this is just what they did. In a force of three, they entered into a lodge of a lone man, who had a pot of boiling water over the fire to cook something to eat.

The cricket chirped and chirped to distract the man, while the mosquito similarly buzzed around his head. Meanwhile, Kétan moved steadily forward to count coup by biting his foot. The man tried unsuccessfully to stomp on the cricket, who finally retreated under the bed. The man flailed his arms about and eventually shooed away the mosquito, who flew out the smoke hole in the roof of the lodge.

But when the turtle grabbed the man's foot, he hollered out and then said:

"Ho! Wakánda, warígroxi ke; warúje pi unk^un ke." ("Well, Creator of all Things, I thank you for giving me something good to eat.")

And when he said that, he grabbed the turtle by the tail and threw him in the pot of boiling water to cook himself some turtle meat soup.

And so that is why up to this time, we still can find crickets getting into our houses, find mosquitoes occupying the wetland areas, and the turtles are always somewhere in, near, or around water.

Aré hagú ke. (And that is when I started back home.)

Used by permission of Jimm GoodTracks, Baxoje Jiwere Language Project.

Missouri Glossary

Halley's Comet: The most famous reoccurring comet in history. It appears every seventy-five to seventy-six years. It was discovered to be a regular visitor to our solar system by Edmond Halley and is named after him.

Ioway/Otoe/Missouria people: Native American people who lived in the Missouri, Nebraska, and Iowa area.

Jesse James: At one time a soldier in the Confederate Army with his brother Frank. After the Civil War they returned to Missouri only to find that the Union officials did not welcome people like themselves and they were unable to make a living. They turned to crime and were probably the best-known outlaws of their era.

Missouri: A state that was named after the Missouri River, which in turn was named after the Missouria people. The capital is Jefferson City.

Mister Howard: The alias Jesse James used when he visited his family.

Steamboat pilot: The member of a steamboat crew who guided the boat through the waters of the big rivers of America. These pilots were keen eyed and had to be very knowledgeable about the waters and the constantly changing currents and obstacles that could sink their boats.

Story Sources

American Myths & Legends, Volumes 1 & 2

Ballads & Songs

The Charm Is Broken: Readings in Arkansas & Missouri Folklore

The Devil's Pretty Daughter & Other Ozark Folktales

Ghosts of the Mississippi: Keokuk to St. Louis

The Greenwood Library of American Folktales, Volume 1

Indian Sleep-Man Tales: Legends of the Otoe Tribe

It's Good To Tell You: French Folktales from Missouri

Jimm GoodTracks, Baxoje Jiwere Language Project

Myths & Legends of Our Own Land, Volumes 1 & 2

Outlaw Tales: Legends, Myths & Folklore from America's Middle Border

Ozark Folksongs

The Parade of Heroes

Stars Is God's Lanterns: An Offering of Ozark Tellin' Tales

Sticks in the Knapsack & Other Ozark Folk Tales

Stockings of Buttermilk

The Talking Turtle & Other Ozark Folk Tales

A Treasury of Southern Folklore

We Always Lie to Strangers: Tall Tales from the Ozarks

Montana

Montana was admitted to the union as the forty-first state in 1889. The state is home to several Native American tribes, who are represented here with a story from the Assiniboine people. Montana was also home to many of the first Europeans to come west, the mountain men. "Jim Bridger and the Remarkable Wolves" is a story that comes from one of the most famous of those early mountain men. Like most states Montana has its share of tall tales, and we have one here called "Too Tough for Me" about a town that was probably too tough for anyone. Jeannette Rankin was the first woman elected to the U.S. Congress, and her story is one of strong convictions and hard decisions. Charles Russell came west and grew to love it so much that he painted its wonders and became one of Montana's and the country's most renowned artists. The singing and recitation of songs and poems is strong in the West to this very day, and included here is song about being a cowboy in Montana.

The Courage to Stand (a True Story)

Jeannette Rankin stood on the floor of the House of Representatives six days after the bombing of Pearl Harbor in 1941. She had stood in this place before when she had been elected to Congress the first time, in 1916, and she had voted against going to war in Europe and entering World War I. Now twenty-five years later she stood up and voiced the lone vote in Congress that day against going to war. But Jeannette Rankin was a woman of conviction, a person who tried to always be led by what was right.

She was born on June 11, 1880, the oldest of eleven children, and spent her early years on a ranch. She had been a schoolteacher; a seamstress; attended Montana State University, graduating with a degree in biology; and studied furniture design before she found her true calling working for social justice. She worked with poor children in Spokane, Washington, and later moved to New York and started her lifelong commitment to women's rights through the National American Woman Suffrage Association. She moved back to Montana to work on organizing women in the suffrage movement. It was her brother who came up with the idea of her running for Congress, and Jeannette embraced the idea not only because she thought she would be a good member of Congress but also because she saw it as vital to bringing attention to the suffrage movement. She ran and was elected as the first woman to the U.S. Congress and the first woman elected to a national legislature in any Western democracy.

Jeannette championed social issues that other members of Congress ignored, such as women's right to vote, birth control, equal pay, and child welfare. Finally the day she had waited for came when in 1917 she opened the congressional debate on the Susan B. Anthony Amendment. It passed both houses and was later ratified as the 19th Amendment, giving women the right to vote.

After World War I ended, Jeannette continued to work for social justice, women's issues, and peace through the Women's International League for Peace and Freedom. During these years she also lobbied tirelessly for an end to child labor and for adding an antiwar amendment to the Constitution.

After her second term of office in Congress ended she continued to work for world peace and was a popular speaker worldwide. In 1968 she led a march on Washington, D.C. to protest American involvement in the Vietnam War. Up until her death in 1973 she was still an active spokeswoman for peace and social justice.

President John F. Kennedy said of her, "She was one of the most fearless people in American history."

Jim Bridger and the Remarkable Wolves

One day Jim Bridger was checking his traps along a river when he noticed the fresh tracks of a pack of wolves. He kept an eye open for the pack, but suddenly they appeared at the bend in the river and took Jim by surprise. Bridger went straight for a tree and climbed to safety, the wolf pack hard on his heels. Now Jim knew he was safe from those wolves, and he started to make fun of the pack as they circled the tree, stretching against the trunk but unable to climb up to where he sat, just out of reach. A few of the wolves jumped up, but they just couldn't reach the branch where Bridger sat laughing at them.

Finally the whole pack just sat down and waited. After about two hours the pack left, leaving only two wolves behind to stand guard over the tree and its occupant. When the pack finally returned they were pushing a beaver in front of them. That's when Jim knew he was in trouble. He never underestimated the intelligence of wolves again. If they could get a beaver to chew down that tree, they could do just about anything.

Painting the West (a True Story)

The young man watched as the sun slowly began to set over the tops of the tall pine trees. He studied the colors as the fading rays of yellow and red played off the deep greens of the trees, the browns and grays of the mountains, the coats of the elk and the white clouds high in the sky. He kept it all in his memory so he could re-create it later and bring this scene to life once again. He would bring those colors back to life on canvas. He would show the elk in its majesty and in its fight against nature. He would portray the mountains and the beasts that lived there in such beauty that generations would stare at his paintings and wish they could be there if only for a moment. Charles Russell loved the West and it showed in his art.

Charles Russell grew up in Missouri. He was always interested in drawing and began sketching at an early age. He moved west to Montana when he was sixteen. He worked on cattle ranches, and it was there that he began to draw and paint the beautiful landscapes that would define his career. In the winter of 1886 the weather was cold and harsh and Russell painted a watercolor of a harsh scene. It was a steer under a gray sky being watched by wolves. The ranch foreman liked it so much that in response to a letter from the ranch owner about how the winter was going he sent Charlie's watercolor as his answer. The man liked it so much that it circulated around Helena, Montana. It was even displayed in a shop window. After this demand steadily increased for Russell's paintings. He later redid that first watercolor as a full-sized painting and named it *Waiting for a Chinook*; it was one of his most famous works.

In 1896 he married, and his wife Nancy became a partner in his business. They settled down in Great Falls, Montana, where they would live the rest of their lives. Russell himself was a reserved man, almost shy, so Nancy began to help set up shows of his artwork all over the country and even in Europe.

The beauty of the West was captivating for people, and Russell's paintings caught that beauty and reality as no one had before. He left behind a body of work of over 2,000 paintings that told the story of the West, of the cowboys, the Native Americans, and the land itself. He captured the rugged determination of the people that matched the place they chose to live. Russell's paintings became popular among collectors and lovers of the West. Many early Hollywood stars were fans of his work. Will Rogers, the great Oklahoma humorist and actor, and William S. Hart, one of the first "cowboy movie" stars, were friends and admirers of Russell.

Russell died in 1926. On the day of his funeral businesses shut down and the schools were closed so the children could line the streets and watch as his funereal procession slowly went by, his coffin in a glass coach pulled by four black horses.

Charles Russell loved the West, and through his eyes people around the world grew to love it as well.

How the Morning and Evening Stars Came to Be (Assiniboine) (as Told by Jeremy Fourstar)

A long time ago, a man and his wife and their twin sons lived in a tepee in the woods. The man would go hunting and the woman tanned hides and made clothes. One day when the boys were about seventeen years old, their father told them they had to go on a long journey. Their mother prepared pemmican, dried meat with rosebuds and grease, for their journey. Each boy also had a dog and a horse, which looked just the same as his brother's.

The two boys left the next morning at daylight. They went southeast, traveling while the sun was high and straight over their heads. They came to a fork in the trail. One of the young men said to the other, "You take one of the trails and I will take the other. Every so often we will look at our knives. If the blade of the knife is rusty we will know that one of us is dead." So they each went off on a different trail.

At sundown the boy who took the left trail came to a tepee. The woman who lived there asked him where he was going. He told her he was going on a journey to explore the country. The woman said he could stay and sleep there that night. So the boy tied his horse to a tree, fed his dog, and went to bed. Early the next morning he had breakfast, packed his buffalo robe on the horse, and continued his journey.

That afternoon the boy saw a cow elf and chased it into the woods. When he entered the woods it immediately became dark and he lost the cow elk. The boy tied his horse to a tree and gathered some dry wood. He made a bonfire and started to eat his lunch. All of a sudden he heard something coming through the brush. Out came an old lady! She said, "Grandson, I am cold. Can I sit by the fire and keep warm?"

The boy told her she could sit by the fire and keep warm. He offered her some of his food, but she said she wasn't hungry, just cold. She said, "Grandson, if you get sleepy, you can go to sleep. I will sit here and keep the fire all night." So the boy covered himself with his buffalo robe and went to sleep.

After a long while the old lady tried to find out if the young man was asleep. She said, "Look out, Grandson! The sparks are jumping toward you!" But he did not move. Then she took some of the fire and threw it toward him. Again she said, "Look out, Grandson! The sparks are jumping toward you!" But still he did not move, so she knew he was asleep. The old lady took a stick and put one end in her mouth to wet it. Then she took out her medicine pouch and stuck the stick into it. She touched the young man with the stick. He turned into a tree. Then she went out and touched the dog and horse. They also turned into trees.

About this time the other twin looked at his knife and saw the rusty blade. He knew his brother was dead. The boy turned his horse around and started back to the fork in the trail. When he got there he started on the trail his brother had taken.

The young man went the very same way his brother had gone, with his dog leading the way. He stayed that night at the woman's camp and left early in the morning. He chased the cow elf into the woods and again it turned dark. He made his camp at the very same place his brother had. Again the old woman came, asking to warm herself. But he didn't trust her, and while pretending to be asleep, he watched her through a hole in his buffalo robe. When she threw the sparks at him he did not move. He saw the old woman put the stick into her medicine pouch. She was about to touch him when he jumped out of the way. He grabbed the stick and touched her with it. She turned into an old, crooked tree.

Then the boy told his dog to look for his brother. The dog went sniffing from tree to tree. Suddenly the dog stopped and wagged his tail. The young man took the stick and touched the tree with it. It turned out to be his brother. The dog began sniffing again and stopped by another tree. This time it was the horse. The dog stopped by still another tree. So again the young man touched the tree with the stick. This time it was the dog. After that he took the stick and touched the other trees. They all turned out to be men, and they all told the same story. They had chased the cow elk into the woods and had met the old lady. The young twins told the other men what had happened and that the old lady was a witch. All the men went back to where they had come from.

On their way home the two boys stopped at the tepee where the woman had told each of them to stay. When she saw them both together she knew they were twins. They stayed there that night and started home the next morning.

By sundown the boys were home. They told their parents what had happened. Their father told them, "From this day on you two are going to be useful to the people." He said to one son, "You will go in the direction where the sun comes up. There you will stay. You will be the morning star. The people will know it is time to get up when they see you."

He told the other boy, "You will go toward the direction that the sun sets. And that is where you will stay. You will be the evening star. The people will watch you at dusk. When you disappear on the horizon the people will know it is time to go to bed."

That is how the morning star and the evening star came to be in the sky. From that day on nobody turned people into trees.

Reprinted here with permission of the Fort Peck Assiniboine and Sioux Tribes from their book How the Morning & Evening Stars Came to Be & Other Assiniboine Stories.

Too Tough for Me

One day the people of Butte, Montana, saw a sight most would tell their friends and families about for many years to come.

A little old man came walking down the middle of the street. He was leading a mountain lion on one leash and a grizzly bear on the other. On his shoulder he was carrying a trunk that was almost as big as he was. He walked right up to the door of the best restaurant in town, dropped that trunk to the ground, and tied those beats to a hitching post. "Sit," he told the big cat, and sure as anything that mountain lion sat. He turned to the grizzly bear and said, "Lie down." Sure enough, that bear just lay down like a big dog. The old fellow walked into the restaurant and sat down at one of the tables. He ordered a huge meal and washed it down with a bottle of whiskey. As he was eating his second piece of apple pie he started to twitch a bit in his chair. He reached into his shirt and pulled out a rattlesnake that must have been at least ten feet long. The snake's mouth was dripping with venom.

"Did you bite me again?" said the old man. He threw the snake through the door and said, "Go stay with the others and behave yourself." The snake crawled over to the other wild beasts and curled up sadly and waited.

The people in the restaurant were amazed at the man's courage and strength and the way he handled those wild animals, not to mention the way he ate and drank.

The manager walked over to his table and introduced himself. "Good day, sir."

"Hello," replied the old-timer.

"Where are you from?"

"Me?" said the old man. "Well I'm from a town called Anaconda."

"Really?" said the manager. "Are all the folks in Anaconda as tough as you?"

"Tough? Son, you don't know the meaning of tough. They run off all the weaklings like me out of town a few days ago. Son, that's a real tough town."

My Home's in Montana

This song, often sung to the tune of "The Cowboy's Lament," paints a picture of a land that the singer loves. Though it does give us an idealistic picture of Montana, it also talks of the blizzards and hints at the hardships a cowboy might face.

My home's in Montana, I wear a bandana.
My spurs are of silver, my pony is gray.
While riding the ranges my luck never changes.
With foot in my stirrup I gallop away.

When valleys are dusty my pony is trusty.
He lopes through the blizzards, the snow in his ears.
The cattle may scatter but what does it matter?
My rope is a halter for pig-headed steers.

When far from the ranches I chop the pine branches
To heap on my campfire as daylight grows pale.
When I have partaken of beans and of bacon
I'll whistle a merry old song of the trail.

Montana Glossary

Assiniboine people: A Native American people who have lived in the area known as Montana since the 1300s. They hunted buffalo and other game. The tribe was ravaged by smallpox on more than one occasion after Europeans came to North America. As did most tribes, the Assiniboine used stories to educate their young about their history and culture.

Jim Bridger: A mountain man, guide, and explorer who roamed the mountains of the west trapping and hunting in the early days of the European expansion. He spoke French, Spanish, and several Indian languages as well as his native English. He was born in 1804 and died on his farm near St. Louis in 1881. Fort Bridger, Wyoming, and Bridger, Montana, are named after the great storyteller.

Montana: A state whose name comes from the Spanish word "montana," meaning mountain. The capital is Helena.

Story Sources

Amazing American Women

American Myths & Legends, Volumes 1 & 2

Blackfoot Lodge Tales: The Story of a Prairie People

By Cheyenne Campfires

Cowboy Songs and Other Frontier Ballads

The Greenwood Library of American Folktales, Volume 3

Hearts of Fire: Great Women of American Lore & Legend

The Hell-Bound Train: A Cowboy Songbook

How the Morning & Evening Stars Came to Be & Other Assiniboine Indian Stories

Myths & Legends of Our Own Land, Volumes 1 & 2

Outlaw Tales: Legends, Myths & Folklore from America's Middle Border

The Parade of Heroes

Traditional Narratives of the Arikara Indians, Volumes One, Two, Three & Four

A Treasury of Western Folklore

The Way of the Warrior: Stories of the Crow People

Nebraska

In 1867 Nebraska became the thirty-seventh state to join the union. Before the European migration many Native American tribes made their home in Nebraska, including the Omaha and Otoe/Ioway people. The Otoe/Ioway story "Coyote Medicine Healer and Bear Brothers" is included here.

Nebraska sits on the Great Plains, and its weather can be mild or fierce. Like many of the plains states it is plagued by tornadoes, and there's a story here that talks all about the amazing things these wild winds can do out on the plains. The story "The Joke Session" shows how the people of Nebraska often use humor to make it through disasters like the Dust Bowl. Pioneers encountered terrible hardship in settling the Great Plains, and their story can be found here as well as one about the fictional character Febold Feboldson, the Swede who settled in Nebraska and is their resident folk hero.

Nebraska Tornado Tales

One of the funniest things that a recent cyclone did in this community was to blow our chicken house away. After the storm we all ran out to see about the chickens and found the only rooster we had in a half-gallon jug with his head sticking out, and not even a crack in the jug. We had to break the jug to get him out and found the handle on the inside.

One afternoon a whirlwind swept into our yard and struck the beehives, playing swing your partners right and left with the bees. Then it spun the windlass of the well around like a crank and it followed the bucket and rope right down into the well. When the whirlwind reached the bottom, it shot the bucket sky high and blew the water out with a roar. The water fell a second later like a mighty cloudburst. Pa found the old windlass full of bee stingers drove porcupine-fashion right into the wood. The well was bone dry and has never filled with water since. The bucket was standing by an overturned beehive and was full of clear strained honey.

On April 30, 1888, a cyclone passed over Howard County. This cyclone was not of the mass of windstorms but was a whirlwind with personality. This tornado just craved water. Every well, stream, and watering trough that happened to be in its path was sucked dry of its moisture and left as parched as if on the Sahara Desert. Some wells were dry for weeks and some never filled again; for several days even the cows gave not a drop of milk.

In 1898 we had a cyclone that did considerable damage. That tornado rolled up eighty-nine rods of barbed wire fence, posts and all, and set it on top of a row of cottonwood trees. We had a cow that was so used to walking by that fence that after the tornado she used to climb those trees, go through the barbed-wire fence and down the other side into the cornfield. I saw her do it time and again.

Near the end of a hot afternoon on August 16, 1910, a tornado passed near Hartwell. An agent for a patented scrub brush was demonstrating a sample of his wares at the door of a farmhouse when the storm struck, whirling him in the air and removing every stock and straw from the premises, with the exception of the house. The last gust of the storm dropped the agent once more at the house door. "As I was saying," he began, "this brush is a regular cyclone. It sweeps clean and does a thorough job . . . ."

On April 10, 1917, a very freaky cyclone devastated a section of the country near Mason City. At one place a farmer on the road with a wagonload of oats was picked up, wagon, team, and all, and carried to Arcadia, twenty miles distant, where he was set down, team and wagon in good condition and not having lost an oat. At another place a woman had a hundred prize-winning black Langshan chickens from which the cyclone plucked every feather and pinfeather from every bird in the flock. None of the birds was killed, but that their experience had been horrifying in the extreme was attested by the fact that when the feathers grew back they were snow white. At another place a farmer had just come in from a muddy field and was sitting with his feet in the oven of the kitchen range, drying his socks and reading the daily newspaper. The cyclone blew the socks off the man's feet and carried the stove out the door and five miles over the hills, but left everything else in the house untouched, not even tearing the newspaper that he held spread open before him.

The Joke Session

The town was quiet, the quietness that comes from fear and uncertainty. The general store was open, not that folks had that much money to buy anything, but it was still open. Just like in the good old days when it used to rain it was the favorite place for the farmers to meet and talk and to try and lift each other's spirits.

The old potbellied stove was cold and silent in the corner, but the cane-back chairs had their usual assortment of farmers and old-timers sitting in them talking about the weather. The weather was always the main topic now.

"I'm thinking of rotating my crops this fall," said one man.

"I'm done with that," one man replied knowingly. "The last dust storm rotated all my crops for me. In fact I think it brought a whole field of soy beans over from Arkansas and took my corn to Texas. Now that's crop rotation."

The men laughed that dry, humorless laugh that folks living a nightmare use.

"During the last storm I saw a whole flock of birds flying backward. I guess they were trying to keep the dust out of their eyes." Men nodded solemnly, as if Roosevelt himself had made this statement.

"Last summer during the hottest, driest days my hens were all laying hard boiled eggs. It kept us through some pretty hard times, I'll tell you."

The men nodded knowingly as if every word they spoke was gospel truth.

"I heard that they had a dust storm so thick in the next county that the groundhogs dug right up into it and that groundhogs fell for almost an hour after the storm ended."

One of the farmers looked up and said hopefully, "I hear that it was raining just fifty miles from here. Looks like it could be our turn next."

Another man just shook his head. "Don't matter to me. I've seen rain before. But," and he turned toward his twelve-year-old son, "my boy here, well . . . ."

The men all smiled and then started to chuckle, and they started to laugh out loud, and soon the cares fell off their shoulders for just a few minutes. You know sometimes a good laugh is all you need.

Coyote Medicine Healer and Bear Brothers (Otoe/Ioway/Missouria People)

There were two Bear Brothers living together. The elder Bear became quite ill and seemed close to death. The younger Bear did everything he could think of to heal his dear brother. He did ceremonies and sweat lodges, put medicine on the waters, put tobacco in the fire, and prayed consistently, and yet his Brother seem to continue to fail in health.

Then he heard a rumor of a great medicine person among the Coyote People, so he went to find this person. When he arrived at the Coyote Village, he inquired the location of the rumored great medicine person. And so he found the Coyote Medicine Person, offered him a gift of tobacco, and shared with him the illness of his elder Brother.

In the morning the two journeyed to the Bear's lodge, only to find that the Brother was even more gravely ill. The Coyote Medicine person looked over the dying Bear Brother and thought to himself, "Poor thing! He's not going to live, so what a nice feast he would make for my family." And then he said to Bear, "It would have been good if you came for me sooner, and as it is, it may be too late. But I will try to do what I can."

So he sang his Coyote powwow songs, shook his gourd vigorously, and hopped about in a frantic dance. The sick Bear hardly breathed by now. So he informed the concerned Brother that it was no use, and that he should prepare for the Brother's death. And when he expired, to wrap him up in the usual buffalo hide and tie it up with rawhide strings. However, instead of putting him on a scaffold or up on a tree limb, the Coyote advised him to make a raft, placing the body on it, and send the raft downstream. He also stated that he had important business at home, otherwise he would stay to help with the funeral preparations.

The Younger Brother built the raft, when he found his dear brother had indeed died. So he wrapped up the body, placed it on the raft, sang some prayer songs, and pushed the raft out into the river, with an offering of tobacco.

Meanwhile, Coyote had rushed home and sat with his family on the river bank downstream, as the Bear's raft came floating along. The Coyotes pulled it ashore and butchered the body. They hung up the hide to tan, cut up some of the meat to dry, and cut up some to roast immediately.

And just then a bird flew by, a crow, who asked for some of the meat for his family, which the capricious Coyotes refused and continued their gluttonous feast. So Crow flew over to the Bear Brother and told what the Coyotes were doing to his dear deceased Brother.

Bear was so angered that he charged through the thick woods along the river headed downstream. The Coyotes could hear him from a distance, as he crashed through the brush and trees. Quickly they wrapped up all the meat in the buffalo hide, tied it up, buried the hide, then placed it all back on the raft on the river bank. Then they covered themselves with soot and pretended to cry and wail, as if in great mourning.

And so Bear came upon this bunch of grayish appearing Coyotes of various sizes, mumbling, wailing, seemingly grief stricken as they surrounded the supposed body of the late elder Bear on the bank of the river. The Coyote Medicine person said to Younger Bear, that his family was deeply saddened with his loss and wished to show final respects to his late Brother, before they sent the raft on downstream. Coyote was convincing and so Bear believed him, then thanked him for their honoring, respect, and prayers. And so he went back home, thinking how he had doubted the good Coyote Medicine Man.

And of course, as Bear went out of sight, the Coyotes renewed their feasting again.

This story reminds us that not all "medicine" people are what they seem to be. Sometimes, well-intentioned people come looking for "medicine men," healers and spiritual mystics among the Native Peoples and other individuals of knowledge. But instead of locating such individuals, they get taken and fooled by the Coyotes, and simply are cheated out of their money and other honest gifts for bits and pieces of traditional knowledge out of context. They are unwary as a result of unknowing and inexperience, that there are dishonest and insincere persons living among the good and genuine medicine and spiritual people.

Traditional Native people do not esteem and hold worthy someone because he or she has prominence, prestige, and power in a community. Nor is one esteemed only because he or she is a Keeper of a Sacred Pipe. Traditional people receive their spiritual strength from one another sitting equally around the Sacred Circle, and from the Sacred Pipe itself, not necessarily from the keeper. The ego of any man, even a Native man, does not transcend this sacredness, which needs always to be foremost in mind.

Used by permission of Jimm GoodTracks, Baxoje Jiwere Language Project.

Febold Feboldson Fights the Drought

Febold Febolson was a giant of a man. He came to Nebraska from Sweden. He had all his belongings under one arm, and under the other he had his friend Eldad Johnson, fast asleep as he usually was most of the time. Febold had intended to go all the way to California, but the summer he finally made it to Nebraska was the hottest that anyone could ever remember. The mountains had melted in the heat and then a sudden hailstorm had cooled them off and formed what folks now call the foothills. It was hot.

The heat didn't bother Febold. He was as strong and hardy as a twenty-mule wagon team. But Eldad wasn't used to the heat, and soon he was seeing mirages of rivers and lakes and dreaming of the cool forests and waters of Sweden.

One afternoon Eldad cried out, "Look water, water."

Febold saw a wide ribbon of muddy water floating lazily across the landscape. "Pretty dismal looking river if you ask me," he said.

"I don't care if it is dismal. Can't we stay here for the winter? Please, Febold. You could even call it the Dismal River if want to." Without another word Eldad tore off his clothes and ran toward the water. Unluckily for him the river was only a few inches deep, and when he dove in he broke his neck, but the broken neck was nothing that Febold couldn't fix. They did decide to stay the winter on the banks of the Dismal River and let Eldad rest.

Now Febold had some pet squirrels that he had found during his journey west. When he built his place along the Dismal River he let them go, but the squirrels weren't used to a country with no trees. Try as they might they just couldn't get used to Nebraska. One day they all disappeared. Febold figured they all went back east, but a few days later the squirrels returned. Each one of those animals had a mouthful of seeds and nuts, and they planted them along the Dismal River. Soon trees grew up along the riverbanks. Those trees spread across the state, and that's how those beautiful trees that follow the rivers in Nebraska came to flourish.

The drought that accompanied the hot weather got worse and worse until Febold finally decided to do something about it. He waited at the top of a small rise and watched the sky. He watched day after day until he finally saw what he needed. There was a thundercloud. Now the cloud wasn't letting go of its rain and was just floating across the sky. Febold took out his two revolvers and began shooting holes in the cloud. As his bullets went through the cloud water began to fall from the sky, and the people cheered. Unfortunately for everyone a sudden drop in the temperature caused the rain to freeze, and the falling hailstones were so big that they caused more damage than the drought.

One day Febold decided that his sheep and crops needed water. The Dismal River was dry as a bone, so he walked across the plain until he came to the Platte River. He tore the Platte River out of its riverbed and carried it over to his spread. He gave some water to his animals and then let the river water his crops for a while. Problem was, Febold took a nap, and when he woke up the Platte had flooded the land and everyone's farms and ranches were all under eight feet of water. Waking up, Febold dragged the Platte River back to where it belonged and dug some ditches that drained the water back into the Platte. These ditches became rivers eventually and helped save the folks from spring floods from then on.

Now the folks living in the area were really worried about the drought that accompanied the hot weather. All they could talk about was the weather and the drought. They talked about nothing except the weather. Now Febold saw that this was getting the people down and that they needed something else to talk about.

One day he decided to talk about the government. He complained about every elected office holder from the president down to the lowest county official, from senators to the governor. No one was left out of Febold's criticism. Folks began to see that Febold was right and that his gripes about the government were all legitimate. They all joined in and began to complain and talk about nothing but the government. After twenty-four straight hours of complaining they forgot about the drought. Suddenly it began to rain, and everyone thought it was a mighty nice rain. Too bad those government officials hadn't done their jobs to bring the rain in the first place, the people all said. Talking about politics had taken their minds off the drought, and when the drought realized no one was paying any attention to it any more, well it moved on and the rains came along behind it.

Febold had introduced politics as a substitute for the weather as a topic of conversation.

It doesn't always work, but I have heard that during a presidential campaign Nebraska can be one of the wettest places in the country.

A Pioneer Crossing the Midwest (a True Story)

This story originally came from an interview with Ed Grantham in 1938 during the Federal Writers' Project. The story talks of Ed's family's trek across the Midwest and the Great Plains to their new home in Nebraska. I have adapted it from the original.

We left our home, Talasha, Ohio, on August 4, 1866, on my tenth birthday. After paying farewell visits to both my father and mother's family we got on the train going west at Urbana, Ohio.

Along the way we made several stops, including Indianapolis, Indiana; Terre Haute, Indiana; and Springfield, Illinois. My father had a cousin at Springfield who was a neighbor and friend of Abraham Lincoln. He took us to the Lincoln home and told us many stories of the early life of Lincoln and his days in Springfield.

We boarded the Wabash train for Quincy, Illinois, and crossed the Mississippi River. We took the Hannibal–St. Joe Railroad for St. Joseph, Missouri. There we boarded a steamboat named *City of Denver* and landed two days later on the east bank of the Missouri River opposite Plattsmouth, Nebraska. The landing place was called "Bethlehem Landing." When we got there wagons were waiting to take us to Glenwood, Iowa, our final destination.

Our group was made up of my parents, my four siblings and myself, my aunt Mrs. Robertson, and a Miss Cunningham, both teachers. Father came west to take care of a school started by the Methodist Church of Glenwood. The school was a financial failure and closed April 1, 1867. We crossed the river at Plattsmouth to Nebraska about the middle of April of that year and settled in the then-thriving village of Rock Bluff. Rock Bluff was about seven miles downriver from Plattsmouth.

The railroad had not reached the Missouri River north of St. Joe, Missouri; that's why we took our trip by boat from St. Joe. The Union Pacific began building out of Omaha in the spring of 1867 and had to haul their first engine and cars by ox teams from Atlantic, Iowa, to Council Bluffs some forty miles away. The railroad contracted with the government for so many miles of road and a train of cars by early summer to hold the right to the government land grant, so ties, rails, and train had to be on time. The engine and cars were dismantled and reassembled at Omaha.

The territorial capital was Omaha and was moved to Lincoln the summer of 1867 when Nebraska became a state. Lincoln was a very small town. I visited it with my father and W. F. Chapin in August 18, 1867. There were just a few rude houses in Lincoln at that time. W. Chapin moved to Lincoln shortly after ward and was land commissioner for the federal land office at Lincoln and afterward was elected first mayor of Lincoln.

We lived in Rock Bluff until the spring of 1869. We moved to Saline County to homestead and start a farm. Our home was three-quarters of a mile north of Swan City, at that time county seat of that county. From our first house there was neither a house nor a tree to be seen in any direction.

There weren't any trees on the highlands or even on the bottomlands. Earlier settlers had long since cut down the trees that had once grown so plentiful along the streams and rivers. Prairie fires swept the country, prevented the growth of trees on the great prairie, extending for hundreds of miles. We had everything burned on our place, excepting our dugout, stable, and house, in the spring of 1870.

A neighbor set fire to a tract of land he wished to break up, and the high wind swept the fire down along his buildings and burned all of them except the house. He lost a horse, some 3,000 bushels of wheat, and all of his corn and burned himself so badly his life was despaired of for a time. Not able to work for months, he carried scars to his grave. Fires often swept over our own homestead and burned out hay and fields. Fires were a constant threat to our crops, animals, and even our home.

It started as a normal Sunday. We left for church in the morning, but when we returned in early afternoon our fields of corn were gone. Grasshoppers had come like a dark cloud and had settled on our fields and destroyed our crops. They had left nothing except some rubble and stalks that only rose a few inches above the ground, cleaned to the bone of any leaves or corn. They ate almost anything that grew except for sorghum cane. They especially liked tobacco and devoured our old neighbor's fields. He said that before they moved on to the next farm they all sat on his fence and spit tobacco juice at him.

The next year brought another disaster: drought and hot winds came and burned up the corn. That left the homesteads in bad shape. No food, no money. Of course most of the pioneers were poor and came west to make new lives for themselves. Most of them stuck it out, some too tough to quit and some so poor they had nowhere to go.

We lived, as I mentioned before, in Saline County, and the law, what little there was of it, was taken care of by U.S. marshals. Wild Bill Hickok was Deputy U.S. Marshal back then and one day he brought three prisoners to Swan City for trial. There was no courthouse or jail, and the visiting judge would not convene court until the following October. The sheriff lived two miles west of town, but had no place to keep the prisoners, so it was up to Bill Hickok to "ride herd" on them, which was an old cowboy expression, until their trial would begin. I talked with the marshal many times while he was in Swan City and found him a very quiet and unassuming man. But you could feel what was underneath his outward appearance, and I should of hated to arouse the tiger in him. Those fellows he was guarding felt the same, for they were very lamblike under his watchful eye. He even borrowed shotguns and took those prisoners prairie chicken hunting. When they got to the fields he gave each a gun and had them walk out in front of him. He followed about fifty feet behind them with his hands on both his revolvers. His prisoners just shot chickens and never thought about trying to get the drop on Hickok. They knew better. I went along once, driving the wagon, and saw how easily he could control those men.

I saw Bill practice many times. I have thrown up bottles and empty cans for him to shoot. He would not draw a gun until the target left my hand, then he drew and fired, seldom missing.

Later, Wild Bill went down to Abilene, Kansas, where he was marshal of the town. The town was on the cattle trail, and law was so lax that the gamblers and wild cowboys made living almost impossible there for law-abiding citizens. Wild Bill tamed the town.

Big Bill Staley was one of the most colorful characters of Saline County. When he opened a saloon at Swan City he invited my father, who was a Methodist preacher, to give a sermon in the saloon before he opened up. My father accepted and stood on the bar like it was a pulpit. Just as they started the service, some local bullies thought they would break it up. Bill walked behind the bar and got his two pistols, walked to the door, and told the fellows to "stop that racket" and come into the meeting. He then told them in no uncertain terms that if they continued the racket there would be a funeral instead of a meeting. The troublemakers left and my father finished his sermon.

Those are my memories of growing up in Nebraska.

Nebraska Glossary

Drought: A period during which it stops raining and the groundwater begins to dry up. Some droughts can last a decade or more.

General store: A mercantile establishment in small towns where people could buy just about everything, from groceries to clothes to a new plow. It was also the informal meeting place in most towns.

Nebraska: A state whose name comes from the Otoe word "Ni Brasge," meaning "flat water," probably referring to the Platte River, which runs through the state. The capital is Lincoln.

Omaha people: A Native American people who were found in Nebraska and Iowa. They lived in earthen lodges in the fall and winter and then followed the buffalo herds during the hunting season, living in tepees. Their dogs pulled travois (sleds) that were piled with the Omaha's belongings until the horse was used as a pack animal. The largest city in Nebraska is named after them.

Otoe/Ioway people: A Native American people who were found in the Nebraska, Missouri, Kansas, and Iowa area.

Story Sources

American Myths & Legends, Volumes 1 & 2

Febold Feboldson: Tall Tales from the Great Plains

Federal Writers' Project

The Greenwood Library of American Folktales, Volume 1

Heroes, Outlaws, & Funny Fellows of American Popular Tales

Jimm GoodTracks, Baxoje Jiwere Language Project

Myths & Legends of Our Own Land, Volumes 1 & 2

The Parade of Heroes

Pawnee Hero Stories & Folktales

Tales from the American Frontier

A Treasury of Nebraska Pioneer Folklore

A Treasury of Western Folklore

Yankee Doodle's Cousins

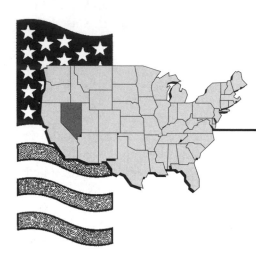

Nevada

Nevada entered the union in 1864 as the thirty-sixth state. It is home to many Native American tribes, including the Paiute and Washo peoples. The Hispanic people have been part of Nevada's landscape for centuries and are represented here by the story "The Magic Bean Pot." Immigrants have come to Nevada to farm and mine and more recently to work in the casinos of Las Vegas and Reno. When the transcontinental railroad came through this area, many Chinese people stayed to open shops and work in the mines. Other Asian people have followed. "The Lost Horse" is a Chinese story about wisdom and the need to look at every day and every change in a new light. When miners came to Nevada from other parts of the world they always brought their stories with them. Sometimes they even brought a little more, as you'll find out in "The Cornish Miners' Friend." Mining, though often dangerous, can have its funnier moments too, as is experienced in the story "The Longest Night." The last story is a "lost treasure" tale about a mine that seemed to open up one day and disappear the next.

The Magic Pot (Hispanic)

At one time, Nevada was part of Mexican territories, and much of the state was settled by people of Spanish ancestry. This is one of their traditional stories.

One day Pedro was out camping all alone. He had lost all his money and was living alone and poor. He wasn't particularly worried since he had been poor before and would be again. He knew that he could get by with his wits and that knowledge was enough to keep him happy.

One day his solitude was interrupted by some mule drivers taking their team across the desert. These were men who lived a rough life, and soon they joined Pedro for supper and a game of cards afterward. The game was fixed, and soon Pedro had lost the little money he had left.

As they were all getting ready to sleep, he overheard them talking about how they had cheated him out of his money. One of them laughed and said, "Perhaps we can get the rest with a card game after breakfast." They all laughed again and went to sleep.

Pedro decided that these men needed to be taught a lesson, and who better to teach them than he? He'd get his money back and some of theirs, too. In the morning he got up before the mule drivers and dug a very small hole in the dirt. He built a small fire inside it. He was very quiet so as not to waken the mule drivers. When the fire had produced some good glowing coals he put his frijole pot over the coals and covered them so it looked as if the pot was cooking on the bare ground with no fire underneath it at all.

The smell of breakfast woke the men, and soon they made their way over to where Pedro was cooking over the pot. They couldn't believe their eyes when they saw the pot boiling away with no fire underneath it. The boss of the mule drivers said, "How does that work? There is no fire underneath that pot, but still it's cooking away. How do you do that?"

"The pot is magic," replied Pedro. "All I need to do is put the beans in the water with some spices and the pot starts cooking by itself. It is the easiest way to cook my meals."

"Where did you get a pot like this? Are there more like it? We've been on the trail for weeks and cooking would be much easier if we had a pot that did all the work for us," said one of the mule drivers.

Pedro leaned closer to the men and spoke in a low voice. "This is the only one of its kind in the whole world. A potter who knew the correct spells made this for me years ago in payment for saving his life. Shortly after he made this pot he died, so this will be the only one."

The leader of the mule drivers looked hard at Pedro and said, "We could steal this from you."

"You could, but then it would be a useless pot. It only works for me." Pedro smiled at the men.

"I'm sure we can bypass the spells that bind it to you if you would sell it to us," he said. "How much would you need?"

Pedro pretended to think long and hard about the proposition. "I'm sure we can come to an agreement." Pedro told them a sum that would pay him back all his losses from the night before and a little extra.

The men thought the price was fair enough, and they gave the money to Pedro. He told them to place the pot carefully on level ground. He told them about the water and beans and the spices. He even said he would leave the spoon he stirred the pot with since the pot had grown used to it.

"We must fool the pot into thinking I am still here or it won't work. When I slip away the first person to put his spoon into the frijoles will be its new master. If I am still here it will always think of me as its master, so I will leave as quickly as possible once we start it cooking." The mule drivers all agreed to the plan.

Pedro packed all his things, including his newfound wealth and piled his bundle under a nearby bush. Then he put in the water and frijoles and spices and started to cook. He quietly handed the spoon to one of the men and moved aside. He waved back at them silently and hurried away from the campsite.

The leader of the mule drivers waited with his men until Pedro was completely out of sight. Then he put his spoon into the pot and said, "Frijole pot, you are mine now. I am your new master." The frijoles just sat there in the water. The coals underneath had gone cold, and nothing would cook in the pot now. When they lifted the pot they saw the coals underneath, and they knew they had been tricked. They were furious, but Pedro was nowhere in sight.

Pedro had won back his money and more and had played a successful trick on another person. It was a good day.

The Lost Horse (Chinese)

In the late nineteenth century, Chinese immigrants came to Nevada to work on the railroad. They brought little with them but their traditional stories, like the one here.

There was a man who lived on the frontier of China. He was a thoughtful man and was always ready to look beyond what was happening at any moment. He was also very good at interpreting what these events meant. One day one of his prize horses ran away and crossed the border into the land of the nomads. His neighbors all tried to console him. All he said was, "What makes you all think this is a disaster?"

The horse returned soon after, followed by a beautiful nomad stallion. His friends were overjoyed at his good luck. All he said was, "What makes you think this isn't a disaster?"

His son loved to ride the new horse and took it every day. One day as he was riding the horse was startled and threw the boy off, and the young man broke his leg. His neighbors all came over and tried to console him. All he said was, "Why do you think this is a disaster?"

A year later the nomads attacked the outpost and came across the border in great numbers. Every able-bodied man took up his bow and sword and went into battle. The battle was horrible, and the frontier lost nine out of every ten men who went into the battle.

Because he was lame from his broken leg, the young man could not fight, and he and his father survived to take care of each other after the war ended.

Blessings can turn into disasters, and disasters can turn into blessings. The world changes, and the changes have no end. No one can understand this mystery.

The Cornish Miners' Friend

The old miner gingerly walked into the abandoned mine and carefully made his way down the tunnel. He had been there the day before and left some bread and cheese just inside the mine hanging from a nail set into one of the supporting timbers. This day he sat down on an overturned bucket and very quietly just sat. He didn't whistle or hum; that was bad luck in a mine. He didn't yawn or move his feet. He just sat very still and he listened. Then he heard the sounds. At first they were faint, almost like someone scratching, then as he listened more intently they grew louder. He could hear the tapping, tapping sound that told him what he wanted to know. He left the mine and walked back into the small mining town. He would find another mine to work.

The next day word came that some new men from out east had gone to that same mine that very morning and had been caught in a cave-in. One of the men had a broken leg and the others were full of cuts and bruises. Most of their gear was lost in the mine.

The old miner sat at his table in the local café and smiled. He leaned across the table to his friend and said, "I bet they didn't feed the bucca. If they did he would have told them what he told me, that the mine was unsafe." The two old-timers smiled at each other and nodded their heads solemnly.

When the men of Cornwall in southwest England came to Nevada they came to work in the mines. Some say that they actually brought the buccas with them, while others say that the buccas are found everywhere, but the folks in Nevada just hadn't learned their ways as yet. Still others say the buccas missed the Cornish miners so much that they followed them over from the old country. What ever happened, happened, and the miners who believed in the buccas were happy to find them here. The buccas are creatures, pixies that live in the mines. If the miners are friendly to them, leaving them food and drink every so often, then the buccas will look out for the miners. They do this by their light tapping. If a miner hears this tapping after he's given the buccas something to eat, then he knows that the mine is unsafe and he should leave it. If, on the other hand, he doesn't hear the tapping noise, he knows that the buccas have told him that the mine is safe and he can continue his work.

Now this might be an old superstition or just an old tall tale that miners like to tell. But if I were you and I were visiting a mine, I'd bring an extra sandwich and some cookies for the buccas just in case.

The Longest Night

The snows can come quickly and heavily in the mountains of Nevada, and in the early spring of 1860 a freak storm came one night to the mountains above Silver City. Half a dozen miners were sleeping in a cavern that was off a tunnel they were mining up in the mountains. While they slept the snow fell, and it fell and it fell, and when it stopped the wind blew and the mountain rumbled when an avalanche covered the entrance to their mine. The men, exhausted from their work, slept through the storm and the snow and the wind and the avalanche. When one of them finally woke up, instead of seeing light streaming down the tunnel as he did every morning, he just saw darkness, so he rolled over and went back to sleep. One man after another woke up to darkness and thinking it was still night just rolled over and continued to sleep the sleep of the innocent and unaware. Eventually, one by one the men woke about the same time and commented on the length of this particular night. They all agreed it was a long night and decided to take advantage of it by getting as much sleep as they could during this unusual but not unwelcome event.

In an hour or so they were all up again, commenting not only on the length of the night but also on the fact that none of them could even force themselves to fall back asleep.

One man finally volunteered to go to the mouth of the tunnel and see if he could witness any signs of the approaching dawn. As he ambled down the tunnel toward the opening, he suddenly walked right into a wall of snow. His cries brought the other miners running, and they understood the reasons behind their unusually long rest. Laughing they took to their picks and shovels and soon had the mouth of the tunnel cleared, only to find that the sun was setting and that they had slept through most of the day. Oddly none of them was a bit tired.

The Lost Hardin Mine (Based on True Events)

The immigrant wagon train moved slowly through northwest Nevada Territory. The people and their oxen and the small herd of cattle that followed the wagons were worn out after their long haul through the mountains and needed to rest. They camped at Double Hot Springs, where there was water and grass for the animals. After a few days' rest they started out again, but three of the men led by a fellow named Hardin left the group to hunt for meat for the rest of the wagon train. They planned to meet the rest of their party again on the other side of a small range of hills and mountains. They trailed some animals but had no luck in bringing any down, and during the hunt they got lost.

They found themselves in the Black Rock Range surrounded by what seemed like burned-out country covered by soft grey ash. Near a shallow gulch they found some curious rocks, some as small as marbles while others were forty or fifty pounds in weight. One of the men had worked on freight pack trains in the mountains of California and identified the rocks as silver. The three men picked up as many as they could possibly carry and continued down the gulch in amazement at the amount of silver that was lying on top of the ground. As the gulch widened out they clambered down to the floor of a valley and found a lone immigrant wagon. The man's ox team was starving, and two had already died. He was busy with a saw, cutting down his four-wheel wagon into a two-wheel cart that his famished animals might be able to pull and get them safely to the next settlement.

Hardin and his companions approached the man and offered him a share in the silver they had found, but hunger and panic had taken hold of the man and he wouldn't even look at them as he worked at his task. He mumbled that they could keep all the silver they found; he only wanted to save his family. The hunters begged and pleaded, but the man just kept working. They walked on a ways, and Hardin threw down the largest piece of silver, telling his friends that they'd never get back trying to haul that much weight. They marked the place where they left the huge piece of silver and divided the smaller nuggets evenly. They resumed their journey and caught up with the wagon train a few days later.

The travelers were amazed when the hunters told their story. Hardin took the silver and began to melt it down. He made a mold out of an axe handle and poured the silver into the molds to make round silver buttons.

When they finally got to California the men told their story and showed people the silver buttons. Experts said it was pure silver, but no one was interested. The gold fever had infected everyone, and gold was much more valuable than silver. The story of the silver was told and retold throughout the area. Most of the immigrants settled down, while Hardin became a blacksmith. A few years after Hardin and his friends had found the silver, another man was crossing that part of Nevada and found the large silver rock that they had left behind. Like the first discoverers of the treasure he left it behind, hoping to return and bring it back with him another day. Another group of settlers found some small pieces of the Hardin Mine, as it had now become known, and brought the silver with them as they headed west into California.

In 1858, almost ten years after Hardin's initial discovery, a party went back to that area to search for the silver. Several dozen men, including Hardin, were in this party, and they searched the area for over three years for the silver deposit but found nothing. The face of the mountains had changed. Perhaps a storm or a landslide had originally exposed the silver and another slide had come along and buried it again. Perhaps water had rushed down the exposed sides of the mountains and washed the silver further down the slopes and covered them again with mud and rocks. The treasure hunters gave up and returned to their old lives. Many years later silver was discovered in that area, but it wasn't the pure silver that Hardin had found. That silver mine is lost and is still waiting for its next discoverer.

Nevada Glossary

Nevada: A state that got its name from shortening the Spanish Sierra Nevada (meaning snowy range) to its present form. The capital is Carson City.

Paiute people: A Native American people who migrated throughout the Nevada, California, and Utah area following herds of animals and seasonal plants that were part of their diet. They are divided into Northern and Southern Paiute.

Pedro: The trickster in many Mexican stories. Sometimes he's a bit foolish; other times he's very wise.

Washo people: A Native American people who settled in the area on the border between western Nevada and eastern California. The name is the English pronunciation of their own name, "washiu," which means "person." They lived in the valleys of western Nevada and would often go to the mountains in the summertime to escape the heat.

Story Sources

American Myths & Legends, Volumes 1 & 2

Chinese Fairy Tales & Fantasies

The Corn Woman, Stories and Legends of the Hispanic Southwest

Coronado's Children: Tales of Lost Mines & Buried Treasures of the South West

Cowboy Songs and other Frontier Ballads

The Eagle and the Cactus: Traditional Stories from Mexico

The Greenwood Library of American Folktales, Volume 3

Mexican-American Folklore

Montezuma's Serpent & Other True Supernatural Tales of the Southwest

Myths & Legends of Our Own Land, Volumes 1 & 2

Tales from the American Frontier

A Treasury of Western Folklore

New Mexico

New Mexico became the forty-seventh state in 1912. At one time it was part of New Spain and later Mexico, and because of that heritage the Spanish culture is strong in New Mexico. The Hispanic story "The Three Counsels" is included here. Several Native American tribes also call New Mexico home, including the Pueblo, Tewa, Navajo, and Apache people.

New Mexico has always been known for its beautiful landscapes and healthy environment. At one time many people went to New Mexico because of respiratory problems. A more humorous look at New Mexico's healthy air is found in the story "The Healing Air of New Mexico." "The Rancher and the Greenhorn" tells a story about selling cattle and the importance of trusting the people you deal with. If you don't you may end up in a tall tale, too! Our last story is a ghost story from the days when New Mexico was a territory. Promises are made to be kept, so be careful when you make one.

The Three Counsels (Hispanic)

At one time, New Mexico was part of Mexican territory, and much of the state was settled by people of Spanish ancestry. This is one of their stories.

Once there was a poor man who had a wife and a sixteen-year-old son. Times were hard, so one day he decided to leave his wife and son and go far away from home to seek his fortune. He finally arrived at a place where he found work with a very good master, who treated him very kindly. He made an agreement to work for seven years for seven bags of money.

When the seven years had elapsed, the man said that he wished to go home to see his family. The master then said to him, "I must now pay you your wages, but I wish you would tell me whether you prefer that I give you three pieces of good advice or the seven bags of money."

The man thought for a while and then he said, "I think it will be better for me to accept the three good counsels."

"Very well," said the master. "The counsels are these: never leave the main road for a shortcut, never ask about things that do not concern you, and don't act on the first impulse."

The man heard the counsels, said good-bye to his good master, and left.

Very soon he came to a fork in the road where two men had stopped. One of them said to the poor man, "The main road is too long. If you come with us by the path, we will reach the next place sooner." But the poor man remembered the counsel of the master and refused to go by the short cut. He continued along the main road.

After walking along for about a league, he heard shouts, and turning his head he saw a man running toward him. When he approached, he saw that the man was wounded, and he soon heard what had happened. As they went along the path, robbers had attacked him and his companion, and killed one of them. He, although wounded, had escaped. The poor man thanked heaven that he had followed the first counsel of his good master, for he had escaped injury or death.

Our traveler then arrived at a very large but quiet house. It was nightfall, so he decided to seek shelter there. He knocked at the door, and a very tall and thin man opened the door and asked him to enter. He entered, and the skeletonlike man asked him to sit down in a large, beautiful room. He went away and left the man there alone for many hours. Everything around him was like a tomb. He did not move or make any noise.

About dinnertime, the thin man entered and asked the traveler to go with him into the dining room for dinner. He took him to a long table where there was food in abundance and all sorts of wines. There were cakes and cookies and fruit in great abundance. The table service was of gold and silver. After they had seated themselves and begun to eat, the wife of the thin man came slowly into the dining room and, without saying a word, sat down. The traveler noticed that she had brought in with her a human skull, and it was in this skull that she had her food served. Then she began to eat out of the skull with her fingers. The traveler wondered why she ate out of the skull and many times was on the point of asking what it meant. But he remembered the second piece of good advice of his former master that he should not ask about things that did not concern him. And so he asked no questions. He had already seen how he had escaped death by following the first advice, so he thought he would also follow the second.

After dinner the owner of the house took the poor man to a room where he told him he could sleep. The room was also very large, and everything around was as quiet as a tomb. There the man slept, but not very soundly, for he was thinking of what he had seen and was wondering what it all meant.

The next morning the thin man appeared at the room of the traveler and asked him to go with him to breakfast. The traveler was glad day had come, and entered the dining room. Again the woman entered and ate out of the skull. The traveler asked no questions. When they finished breakfast and the woman had left, the traveler said he wished to continue his way and thanked the thin man for his hospitality. The thin man then said to him, "I am very much surprised that you asked no questions when you saw my wife eat out of the skull. Why didn't you ask about it?"

The traveler answered, "I have been advised not to ask about things that do not concern me."

The thin man then spoke, "Now that you have not asked any questions, I shall tell you the reason. My wife and I do not belong on earth. During our worldly life we were very rich and miserly. God condemned us to live in this way, my wife eating out of that skull. We were condemned to live here in this inn, giving free lodging to all. If any of our guests asked why my wife ate out of that skull, they died. Come and see them."

Then he took the traveler to a deep underground cavern where there were all sorts of corpses, some long dead, others who had died recently. "Now that you have not asked that question, we are free," he said. He then gave him the keys of the whole house, telling him that there was much wealth concealed there, and that all belonged to him now. He had no sooner said this than the man and his wife disappeared, and all the bodies disappeared with them. The poor man was in possession of the house and of all the riches it contained. Very happy at the idea that he had not only escaped death twice, but also had become rich by following his master's counsels, he left the house and continued on to his home and his family.

He arrived home at nightfall. As he approached the house, he looked through the window and saw his wife seated on a bed caressing the head of a young priest. The man became enraged, thinking that his wife had a lover, and was about to enter the house to kill the young priest. But he remembered his master's third and last counsel, not to act on the first impulse. He went to the door and knocked. His wife and the young priest opened the door. He asked her who the young priest was. She at once recognized her husband and said, "My dear husband, he is your son, the son you left when you went away!" The traveler then embraced his wife and his son, and all three wept with joy. He related his adventures and how he had escaped death twice and become rich and avoided killing his son by following the counsels of his good master. And the next day they went to the treasure house that had been given to him.

Who was the good master who gave him such excellent advice? Was it God himself, or one of his saints? We may never know.

The Rancher and the Greenhorn

In the days when cattle was king and the ranchers were the lords of the plains, an Englishman came to the area to buy some cattle. Now the rancher and the Englishman talked and haggled and then talked some more about the price and the size of the herd to be purchased. Eventually the two men came to an agreement on price and that the herd would be several thousand in number, but the buyer, not trusting the rancher, wanted to count the cattle for himself. Now this angered the rancher. He was fairly insulted that the man wouldn't accept his word on the number of animals in the herd, so he decided to get even. The rancher had his men round up two herds of about 500 cattle each. He told them that they should walk these cattle around and around a small hill that stood out on the prairie.

Now the rancher and the Englishman positioned themselves on the hillside so the new owner could get a good view of his new herd. The rancher said that he had broken the herd into groups of about 500 each so they would be easier to count, and he would have them paraded past for the Englishman's inspection. The cowboys started to walk the herd by so he could count the cattle. As they rounded the side of the hill and were out of view, the next herd came up, and so on all day long, round and round they went with the same cattle. The Englishman was counting the same two herds over and over again. In one herd there was a particularly ugly old steer that stood out from the rest because he had lost one horn, his spotted, yellow hide was distinctive from the others, and he had a noticeable limp. By late morning this old steer had gone past the Englishman several times.

"There seem to be several cattle that are lame, old, and rather sore of foot," said the Englishman.

"There's always one or two in any herd," replied the rancher, knowingly nodding his head. The rancher then took his foreman aside and told him to cut the old yellow steer out of the herd so he wouldn't be seen again.

The foreman cut him from the herd and ran him off to graze, but the old boy was now used to walking around that little hill and seemed to enjoy the company of his fellow cattle. The yellow steer made his way back and joined the herd again, parading past the new owner as proud as can be. When they had disappeared around the side of the hill the cowboys again cut him from the herd and drove him off, but again he seemed to enjoy the new routine and he once more joined the herd on its endless walk. Finally the last herd was counted and the deal was concluded, and the Englishman left, satisfied that his herd was indeed the correct number.

That night the rancher woke up from a terrible nightmare. The foreman heard him cry out and ran into his room only to find the rancher soaked in sweat and shaking like a leaf. He told the cowboy that he dreamed that he was tied to the back of the old yellow steer and that he was walking around that hill listening to the Englishman count the cattle and his cowboys were laughing at the sight of him tied to the old steer's back.

The owner got dressed and insisted that he had to go see that old steer and make sure he was all right. He and the foreman saddled up and rode out to the hill where they had tricked the Englishman just that very day. There they saw the old yellow steer, happy as a lark, limping his way around and around the hill, content with his new job. They left him there walking around the hill. They say that the old lame steer walked around that hill most of the time when he wasn't eating and sleeping and that he died on his well-worn path. He's still there, they say; his ghost can be seen in the moonlight walking around the hill, with almost a smile on his old face, tossing his one horn into the air, happy that he was part of such a grand scheme.

The Healing Air of New Mexico

A man who had moved to Albuquerque from back east got a telegram from a friend that he was near death and would like to see his old friend one more time. Packing a bag in minutes, the man rode his bicycle to the train station and got there just in time to board, taking his faithful bike with him.

When he finally arrived in his old hometown he rode his bike as fast as he could to his old friend's house. Fearing it might be stolen, he brought it right into the house and propped it up against the door jam to his invalid friend's downstairs sick room. As he leaned it against the door a tack punctured the front tire and a hiss of New Mexico air escaped from the tire into his friend's room. When the clean, fresh, New Mexico air passed into his friend's lungs, he sat up almost feeling half better than he did before that rush of healing air. When the Albuquerque man saw that, he punctured the back tire and held it to his friend's mouth. The man healed up from all his ills and lived to a ripe old age, swearing that it was the healing power of that New Mexico air that had saved his life.

The Last Waltz

Mary was the center of attention at Fort Union in the New Mexico Territory. She was the younger sister of a captain, and because of her beauty and her wit she was the most sought-after of ladies at every dance or social. It was a wild, untamed country, and the attention that the young woman received soon went to her head as one young officer after another came courting. One young lieutenant was persistent in claiming her attention and came calling almost every day to take her for a ride or a walk or just to sit on the porch of her brother's house and talk about the future. He courted her, but he never really saw her through eyes that weren't clouded by loneliness and infatuation.

One morning word came that there was an incident at a nearby ranch and that a detachment of soldiers were to be sent out to chase the Apache warriors, who had attacked the settlers. The young lieutenant was in charge of the detail. Before he left he told Mary of his love for her and asked her to be his bride. Mary was so flattered by a proposal from a man going off to battle that she accepted and promised that if he didn't return she would never marry but always remain true to his memory.

As the young man rode off with his men he turned in his saddle and called to her, "Nobody will have you as a bride, Mary. I promise that I'll return and claim you for my own." It was the last time that Mary would see the young officer. In a few days his men returned from a bloody encounter with the Apaches; the officer was lost, missing in action. Mary wept for him like any good woman would for the man she promised to be true to forever, but forever is a long time, and soon she was again attending dances and socials and had attracted the attention of another young officer, recently come to New Mexico from the east. Soon, some said too soon, it was announced that the two young people would be married. The wedding day arrived, and the fort was in a festive mood. Food and drink were well provided for the guests, the dances were lively, and laughter and music were heard throughout the mess room.

Suddenly the laughter and the music stopped and all eyes turned toward the open door. There stood a frightening sight, a dead man in the stained and torn uniform of an officer, his scalp gone and bullet holes making an eerie pattern across his chest. His eyes were wide open, burning with a terrible light, and his mouth was set in an awful smile. He walked across the floor and stood in front of Mary as men shrank from the ghost that had invaded their party. He bowed to Mary, and a voice that seemed to come from the bottom of a grave said, "I hope you saved the last waltz for me, my love." He took hold of Mary and began to dance her into the middle of the open floor. The musicians, who later said they had no recollection of ever playing for the strange couple, played faster and faster as the dead man and his beautiful partner twirled around the room. Faster and faster the two danced until Mary became pale and finally her eyes closed in death. The music stopped and the ghost slowly lowered her to the floor, made an awful cry of pain and sorrow, and then rushed out the door and into the night to disappear as mysteriously as he had appeared.

The next day a patrol found the body of the young lieutenant, his chest riddled with bullets, his scalp gone, and his eyes staring toward the horizon, staring in the direction of Fort Union and the woman he loved. They buried them together. He would have wanted it that way.

New Mexico Glossary

Albuquerque: The largest city in New Mexico.

Apache people: A Native American people found throughout the southwestern desert country. The name is actually Zuni. The original name for the Apache tribe was "Ndee," which means "the people." Though they could not be warriors, girls learned how to ride and shoot, and it was not uncommon for them to help protect their villages. In the old days the Apaches lived in wickiups, small houses about the size of a camp tent made of light wooden frames covered with brush mats or buffalo hide.

Courting: Dating in the old days; it often required a parent's or older brother or sister's permission.

Greenhorn: A person who was new to the West, usually a visitor from "out east" or a new settler or maybe just someone passing through who didn't know the ways and customs of the people who lived there.

New Mexico: A state that was called the Province of New Mexico when it was under Spain. The capital is Santa Fe.

Pueblo people: A Native American people who consist of several tribes. They were a settled people who lived in well-organized settlements in houses, often multistoried, made of adobe and stone. They are found in New Mexico, Arizona, and Colorado.

Tewa people: A tribe of the Pueblo people who live in New Mexico.

Story Sources

American Myths & Legends, Volumes 1 & 2

Buying the Wind

The Corn Woman, Stories and Legends of the Hispanic Southwest

Coronado's Children: Tales of Lost Mines & Buried Treasures of the South West

Cowboy Songs and other Frontier Ballads

The Eagle and the Cactus: Traditional Stories from Mexico

The Folklore of Spain in the American Southwest

The Greenwood Library of American Folktales, Volume 3

Mexican Folktales from the Borderland

Mexican-American Folklore

Montezuma's Serpent & Other True Supernatural Tales of the Southwest

Myths & Legends of Our Own Land, Volumes 1 & 2

Myths & Tales of the Jicarilla Apache Indians

Pueblo Stories & Storytellers

Stockings of Buttermilk

Tales from the American Frontier

Tewa Tales

A Treasury of Western Folklore

North Dakota

In 1889 North Dakota became the thirty-ninth state to enter the union when the Dakota Territory was split to create the states of North and South Dakota. North Dakota is home to many Native American tribes, including the Dakota and the Arikara. Ceil Anne Clement gives us a true tale of her grandfather, who came to North Dakota in 1906 as a homesteader. The little story "Wrong Side Down" shares an important lesson about the land and offers a glimpse into the future when the Great Dust Bowl would hit the Dakotas hard. Some legends really get around, and here we have yet another Paul Bunyan story, about Paul's role in North Dakota history, by Kevin Strauss. The last story is my own retelling of two short folktales found in North Dakota and in the northern European tradition of its early pioneers.

Wrong Side Down

Years ago there was a farmer who was doing his plowing. He was turning the prairie grass under and preparing the soil for his crop of wheat. As he plowed an old Native American man watched him from the side of his field. The old man sat calmly, watching as the plow dug into the earth. When the farmer took a break the old man walked over and picked up a piece of earth that still held some prairie grass and turned to the farmer and said, "Wrong side down." The old man replaced the clod with the grass pointed up toward the sky.

For years people thought this was a joke about the way Indians didn't know much about farming, but after the great dust storms in the 1930s during the Dust Bowl era, people realized that the old man was right. They had plowed all the prairie grass under, and when the drought and the heat and the winds came there was nothing to hold the soil down, and it blew away. They had indeed turned it all the wrong side down.

No Place Like Home
(by Ceil Anne Clement) (a True Story)

Springtime on the prairie is a wondrous sight. The ice and snow of winter melt and leave in their wake a carpet of green. Purple crocuses dot the sunny side of prairie buttes, followed by patches of yellow sweet peas and sky blue penstemons. Puffy white clouds float in an azure sky. Soft gentle winds make it easy to forget that the same paths walked on a mild summer day had been paths of great danger filled with snow, cold, and the raw winds of winter six months earlier.

A hundred years have brought many changes to the prairie. Now trees stand tall, sentinels lining towns and farmsteads. Street lamps and farmyard lights are yellow beacons welcoming travelers home. A hundred years ago on this fragile, short-grass prairie only moonlight and the faint reflection of stars lit the way . . . and nothing stopped the wind.

Young Tom came out from Iowa to southwestern North Dakota in 1906. He staked out his homestead and returned a year later, in 1907, the year the Milwaukee Railroad reached the town site of Hettinger, North Dakota. His homestead was two miles west of town, a small sod hut built exactly like those of his neighbors, with one small windowpane on the east wall. Inside were a small cookstove, a narrow cot covered with a buffalo robe, a washstand and basin, and a small wooden kitchen table. The sod bricks kept him cool in the summer and warm in the winter. When the weather grew cool enough, he hung a slab of bacon overhead. Every morning Tom lit a fire in the small stove and brewed himself a cup of strong black coffee, which he drank from a blue enameled tin coffee cup with a white edelweiss painted on the side, a present from his mother when he left Iowa.

Tom worked at a local lumberyard, and every morning just at dawn he hiked two miles into town. He hoisted heavy nail kegs onto the wagons of farmers and did bookwork in the office with the pot-bellied stove, where men gathered to drink coffee and tell stories.

One morning in early October Tom woke up in the predawn darkness. He made a fire in the cookstove, broke a thin skin of ice in his washbasin, and shivered as he washed his face. He fried bacon and brewed his usual pot of morning coffee. He dressed warmly in woolen long johns, woolen pants, and a heavy flannel shirt. Before he left for work he banked the fire in the cookstove, put on a heavy jacket, wrapped a long muffler his mother had knit him around his ear-flapped hat, and pulled on sheepskin mittens.

Frost-crusted prairie grass crunched under Tom's feet. He walked briskly and slapped his arms about his chest to warm himself. He reached town just as the morning sun slid over the horizon.

By mid-morning the cold of early dawn was long forgotten. Tom shed cap, scarf, and jacket. Sweat trickled down his neck as he worked outside the lumberyard doing the demanding physical work his job required.

At noon when he went next door to Barry's Café, he noticed a long line of blue-grey clouds to the northwest, and when he left the café after lunch a strong wind blew before it the first snowflakes of the year.

By mid-afternoon the wind rattled the wooden planks of the lumberyard shed and snow as fine as sugar sifted through the slats, forming little drifts on the ground. By late afternoon the wind roared and heavy snow gathered in the corners of the yard.

When Tom left the lumberyard at 5:00 p.m. the light of day was devoured by gray shrouds of snow. He rounded the corner of the lumberyard and a blast of wind caught him off balance. He staggered through swirls of snow and saw in the darkness a horse and buggy driven by his neighbor Mr. Gustafson. He reined in the horse and said, "Tom, listen to that wind. There's some storm brewing. You'd better spend the night at my place. I've got a funeral to go to in Minnesota. I'm just going to make the train. But you'll never make those two miles tonight. Stay at my place."

"Thanks, Gustafson, but I'm sure I can make it. I want to go home."

Tom continued on his way and rounded Mirror Lake, then headed west. As he plodded along the drifts grew heavier: ankle deep, then calf deep. A sudden gust of wind caused him to lose his balance, and he staggered and fell. When he pulled himself to his feet he had the sensation for the first time in his life of not being able to see a hand in front of his face. Because of the fall he had no sense of which direction he was heading. The wind seemed to swirl from all directions. Where was the big butte with the large rectangular sandstones on the top? If he was south of that butte, there was 100,000 acres of open rangeland. He could wander for miles and not find shelter.

"Push into the wind," said a voice in his head. He bowed his neck and bent into the wind. The wind keened around him, a high-pitched eerie wail overhead and a low moaning sound at his feet. His hands, once warm in the sheepskin gloves, began to feel as if they were being pricked by needles. His feet felt like lumps of lead.

The stories he'd heard the men tell as they had sat around the pot-bellied stove in the lumberyard office began to filter back into his mind. Just yesterday someone had told of the Seim sisters in South Dakota. While walking to a neighboring farm for a visit, they had been caught in an unexpected blizzard. During the night neighbors had thought the wind sounded strange, almost like human voices. In the morning the two women had been found huddled together by one of the outbuildings, frozen to death.

And then came the story of the two men 100 miles up north who worked in a coal mine. Every night the mother of the house lit a lantern and placed it in the window to light their way home. One day a storm came. The lantern ran out of kerosene, and the men were found the next day frozen in the field beyond their house. They had missed the house by inches.

"Stop thinking those thoughts!" said the voice in his head. "Push into the wind."

Thoughts of his childhood home in Bancroft, Iowa, came to him. He could smell catfish frying on the big black kitchen stove. He heard the sound of his mother's voice as she called her seven children to supper. He heard the ring of his father's hammer on the anvil in the blacksmith's shop and the knell of the church bells on the day they buried his favorite sister, twelve-year-old Jessie, dead of pneumonia. He imagined a telegram sent to his parents saying, "So sorry to inform you that your son Tom was found frozen after a sudden blizzard in North Dakota."

"Stop thinking those thoughts!" urged the voice in his head. "Push into the wind."

The wind howled and shrieked and seemed to come from all directions. Every footstep became an effort. The woolen muffler he had wrapped around his head and over his face

---

was ice crusted from his labored breathing. He tasted the wet icy wool. His jaw muscles ached from clenching.

And then . . . a soft, seductive voice swirled into his brain. "Stop. You're so tired. Just stop and rest. Quit fighting and give up. Rest. Sleep."

A wave of lethargic warmth swept over him. He felt his knees begin to buckle and thought what a soft, downy bed the snow would make.

"Push into the wind!" roared the voice in his head. He flailed out at the snow and swung his hands wildly. He struck out at the wind and the snow as if it were a physical force to be beaten into submission. And his hand connected—smack—with the rough edges of sod bricks.

"I've reached Gustafsons'!" he thought and edged his way around to the door. He stomped the drift against the door with half frozen feet and pushed his way into the hut. He slammed the door shut behind him and felt the instant relief from the howling wind that could no longer reach him. He felt the faint warmth of a long banked fire in a cookstove as he stumbled across the floor and fell onto a narrow cot. A buffalo robe pulled over his half frozen body warmed him and a deep fatigue overtook him. The muffled howling of the wind faded from his mind, but not the feeling of being safe from it. He slept the sleep of an exhausted man.

The silence woke him. He peeled back a corner of the buffalo robe and peered into weak sunshine glimmering through a single glass pane. Overhead hung a slab of bacon. On a small wooden table rested a blue enameled tin coffee cup with a white edelweiss painted on it.

Home!

© Ceil Anne Clement. Used with permission.

How Paul Bunyan Logged North Dakota
(by Kevin Strauss)

Everyone knows that Paul Bunyan dug out the Grand Canyon and the St. Lawrence Seaway, and that he made the Mississippi River when Babe the Blue Ox tripped and spilled a giant-sized water tank down a hill, but even those tasks pale in comparison to Paul Bunyan's most amazing job. The strange thing is that he did such a good job that you won't even notice the job he did, that is if you don't know what North Dakota used to look like.

You see, a long time back, North Dakota had pine trees that reached the sky. And it just so happened that news of Paul Bunyan reached Sweden just when the King of Sweden, King Gustav III, had a problem. So he sent Paul a letter.

Dear Mr. Bunyan,

I have a problem. There are too many Swedes and not enough farmland in Sweden. I hear that there is lots of land in America, but most of it is covered in trees. Could you log off a few thousand square miles for me and my subjects?

His Highness,

King Gustav III

Paul wrote back that North Dakota would be perfect for a group of Swedes. It's plenty cold in the winter and nice and breezy in the summer, just like Sweden. So Paul began putting together a work crew big enough to log a whole state. Paul needed so many men that he built a bunkhouse eighteen stories high. It was the tallest building west of the Mississippi until 1950. Loggers on the top floor had to wake up an hour earlier than the loggers on the ground floor just to get to breakfast on time.

Since he was on a deadline, King Gustav wanted his people planting wheat by next spring, Paul had loggers working around the clock. When the sun went down, Paul reached up and lit a bonfire on the moon so the loggers could keep working all night long.

In addition to his regular crew, Paul also hired the famous Seven Axmen of Sweden. These men were all cousins and all named Frank. While you might think that would be confusing in the woods, it actually made things easier, because they all did the same job. All Paul had to say every morning was, "OK, Frank, start chopping," and the Seven Axmen started hacking down trees faster than anyone but Paul Bunyan himself. When their axes got dull, they'd just start chopping at boulders until their blades were sharp again. That's why they say there are so many small rocks in North Dakota today.

The problem was that once the crew got halfway through the state, it got harder and harder to ship logs east to the Minnesota River. Luckily, Paul Bunyan speaks Beaver. So he started up conversations with the local beaver population about some winter work. Sources differ as to what Paul actually offered the country's largest rodents for their help, but rumor has it, it was either all the fresh lettuce and turnips they could eat, or a promise that when the Swedes settled North Dakota, they'd plant it with tasty aspen and maple trees rather than these sticky, sour pines. But in any event, a few days later, 400 beavers appeared at Paul's "Bismarck Logging Camp" (named for one of Johnny Inkslinger's favorite uncles). They got to digging and dug so well, pretty soon, Paul had a river running from the Rocky Mountains right down to the Mississippi. At first the loggers called it the "Beaver River," but unfortunately some city folk in Missouri got their hackles up, and to calm things down, Paul let them name the river the "Missouri River." But to this day, some folks say that North Dakota beavers are still collecting on that agreement with Paul Bunyan.

As winter ended, Paul and his crew had cut down the last tree in North Dakota. And just about that time, the Prime Minister of Sweden came up the Missouri River in a paddlewheel riverboat to look over Paul's work. But as he approached Paul's camp, that finely dressed man had a sour look on this face.

"This simply won't do, *Mr.* Bunyan," the Prime Minister said in a high nasal voice.

"What do you mean?" said Paul.

"Well, my people can't plant wheat in fields full of tree stumps," said the Prime Minister. "You'll simply have to remove all of these stumps."

"Now wait just a minute, the King hired us to cut the trees. He never said anything about the stumps," said Paul.

"Nevertheless," said the Prime Minister, "get rid of the stumps by next week, or we won't pay you a dime!"

It was attitude like that that really stuck in Paul's craw. He wanted to tell the Swedish Prime Minister just what he could do with his money. But Paul had learned a long time before that talking when you're angry is a lot like spitting into the wind. You always regret doing it afterward. So Paul gathered up his work crew and began thinking about how they could get rid of a state full of tree stumps in just one week.

It turned out that Johnny Inkslinger, the camp clerk, came up with the best idea.

"You all know how Babe hates to get his hooves wet, right?"

"Yeah," said Paul.

"Well, how about we put Babe at the foot of the Rocky Mountains. Then we block up the Missouri River by Bismarck and the Red River of the North near Fargo. They'll back up and flood the state. Then you stand in Minnesota and call for Babe. He won't want to get his hooves wet, so he'll hop form stump to stump to get to Minnesota."

So the men got to work, and wouldn't you know it, it happened just like Johnny said it would. When Babe hopped from stump to stump, the huge blue bull pounded those stumps six feet into the ground. When the loggers opened the dams, the floodwaters smoothed out the land, leaving it the North Dakota we know today. Of course, it is possible that Paul taught those rivers a lesson we'd rather they didn't know. To this day the Red River gets tired of flowing in its banks and decides to spread out a bit.

And to this day, folks swear that North Dakota has always been a land of prairie grass, Swedes, and wheat. Paul Bunyan wouldn't have it any other way.

© Kevin Strauss. Used with permission by the author.

The Black Dog

The majority of settlers who came to North Dakota were from Northern Europe, especially Germany and Norway. They brought with them their customs, stories, and faith. Sometimes other aspects of the Old World came tucked away in their imaginations.

The people of the town were mostly Lutherans, with a few Catholics thrown in for a sense of variety. The local keeper of the general store was neither; in fact, he wasn't a religious man at all and was often the talk of wagging tongues and the object of scornful and disdainful looks from the women of the town and surrounding farms. The storekeeper didn't mind and in fact fueled the stories with anecdotes about the work he'd done on Sunday and the waste of time it was to attend church on a day that called for you to go hunting or fishing. When the ladies would tell him that his behavior was horrid he would just laugh and say that there was still time for them to save his soul. Oddly enough, the townsfolk ignored the fact that he was a good man, always there to help his neighbors, just in his dealings at his store, and always willing to forgive a debt to folks who had fallen on bad times. His lack of religion got in the way of their common sense.

The storekeeper became ill one fall and took to his bed. His wife and children tended to him, but he seemed to get worse and worse. One of the children noticed a black dog prowling around the house. At first the dog kept its distance, but as the man grew weaker and weaker the dog became bolder and bolder and was seen actually looking into the house. No one had ever seen the dog before, and soon rumors started to circulate among the sewing circles and church groups about the dog and who it really was that was hanging around the man's house. When the man finally died, folks say the dog raised his head and howled an unearthly scream and disappeared. Now the rumors came out in the open as folks started to tell whoever would listen about the black dog and that it was really Satan, who had come for the man's soul.

The family sold the general store and moved away from the small town and its hateful talk. The man who bought the store turned out to be a good church-going man who cheated his neighbors, never helped a soul, and had little compassion for his fellow man.

I wonder who that black dog was there to punish, anyway?

North Dakota Glossary

Arikara people: A Native American people who called themselves "Sanish" in their own language, which means "the people." They were not migratory and did not follow the buffalo herds, but lived in settled communities in lodges made of wooden frames and packed earth.

Black dog: A symbol of bad luck or the devil in traditional stories.

Dakota people: A Native American people who are part of the Sioux culture. They lived in tepees made of buffalo hides that were portable so they could follow the herds that they depended on for their food. The tepees belonged to the women. The Dakota lived throughout what is now Wisconsin, Minnesota, and North and South Dakota.

Dust Bowl: A prolonged period of drought and erosion in the central United States, known as the Great Dust Bowl, that lasted from 1930 to 1936 and in some areas until 1940. Drought coupled with extensive farming without crop rotation or erosion prevention caused this disaster. The Dust Bowl covered over 100 million acres. By 1940 over 2.5 million people had left the plains and moved out. When the dust storms came they destroyed the land. They literally picked the soil up and took it away. On April 14, 1935, known as "Black Sunday," twenty of the worst dust storms hit the Great Plains at the same time. Much of the richest soil in America was carried away and deposited in the ocean.

North Dakota: A state that was formed from the northern half of Dakota Territory, which was named after the Dakota people. The capital is Bismarck.

Story Sources

American Myths & Legends, Volumes 1 & 2

Cowboy Songs and other Frontier Ballads

The Greenwood Library of American Folktales, Volume 3

Heroes, Outlaws, & Funny Fellows of American Popular Tales

Kevin Strauss

Lakota Myth

Myths & Legends of Our Own Land, Volumes 1 & 2

Outlaw Tales: Legends, Myths & Folklore from America's Middle Border

Tales from the American Frontier

Traditional Narratives of the Arikara Indians, Volumes One, Two, Three & Four

A Treasury of Western Folklore

Oklahoma

Oklahoma was known as the Indian Territory before it became Oklahoma Territory and then the forty-sixth state, in 1907. Several Native American tribes made Oklahoma their home before the European migration, including the Wichita and Caddo people. Oklahoma was also the destination for the Trail of Tears and other forced removals of Cherokee and other native people from their ancestral homes. Almost forty Native American tribes have reservations in Oklahoma and are represented here by the Choctaw story "Lone Hunter and the Swamp Spirit." Also included is a story from World War I about the Choctaw codetalkers, who helped defeat the Germans toward the end of the war. Will Rogers was one of the most famous performers of his era, and he never forgot his Oklahoma roots. Two folklore heroes are present here in the stories "Kemp Morgan and the Oil Wells" and "Paul Bunyan's Oklahoma Farm."

I Never Yet Met a Man I Didn't Like (a True Story)

He was one of the most popular entertainers of his era. His voice was well known to millions. He was admired and loved by people around the world. He was a comedian, a movie star, a columnist, a radio personality, an after dinner speaker, an author, a social and political commentator, and a stage actor. He was one of the most versatile performers to ever capture the American audience and one of the busiest.

Will Rogers was born in Oklahoma on the Dog Iron Ranch near Oologah from parents of Cherokee and European descent. He used to tell people that his ancestors didn't get to America on the *Mayflower* but they met the boat when it docked. His father, Clement Rogers, was a Cherokee senator and a respected member of the community who served as a delegate to the Oklahoma Constitutional Convention. His mother, Mary, was the daughter of a Cherokee chief. He quit school to work on the ranch and then began to wander. He worked for a time in Argentina and broke horses for the British Army in South Africa. He was exceptional with a rope and was named for his feats in the *Guinness Book of World Records*. He got a job with "Texas Jack's Wild West Circus" doing his rope tricks. He left Africa and joined a circus show that toured Australia.

In 1904 he headed to New York to try his hand at vaudeville. He appeared at the Victoria Roof and other theaters doing his act of humor and rope tricks for ten years. He honed his skill as a social and political comedian. He would start each show by saying that he didn't know much except what he read in the papers and then start retelling the day's news through his often biting wit.

Will Rogers got married in 1908 and had four children. He later moved his young family to California and got into movies. He appeared in 71 films and was one of the highest paid actors in Hollywood. He also appeared on stage in plays such as Eugene O'Neil's *Ah Wilderness*. He started a syndicated column that ran from 1922 until 1935, using his wit to make observations on the politics and problems of the times. He traveled around the globe to perform. He was America's Good Will Ambassador to the world. His Sunday night radio show was the most listened to show on the air, while he was also the most widely read newspaper columnist in the country.

Rogers was a great promoter of aviation and loved to fly. He would often go on trips with his friend and fellow Oklahoman, the famous aviator Wiley Post. In 1935 their plane crashed near Barrow, Alaska, killing both men.

He coined lines that are still recognized today. "I never yet met a man I didn't like" and "I don't belong to an organized political party. I'm a Democrat" were just two of hundreds of lines that people in his day would quote. There is a statue of Will Rogers in the Capitol in Washington, D.C. It is the only statue that faces the entrance to the House Chambers. Will wanted it that way so he could keep on eye on Congress.

Kemp Morgan and the Oil Wells

The oil workers watched in silence as the giant of a man crawled along on all fours sniffing at the ground. He was as tall as two men standing one on the other's shoulders and had arms about the size of small tree trunks. This was a big man. But as big as he was, his reputation was even bigger, because this was Kemp Morgan, the most famous man in Oklahoma or Texas, the man who discovered oil. He was the Paul Bunyan of the oil fields and he could smell oil. Kemp kept crawling around on the ground sniffing like some enormous dog looking for a prairie dog. Finally he stopped and slowly stood up. He took his long-handled shovel and began to dig. When he finally had dug to a point where the shovel couldn't reach anymore, he took out his six-shooter and shot a bullet right into the ground. Kemp put his steel drill bit into the bullet hole and started to hammer the drill down. When he finally struck oil he built his derrick around the drill bit. His derricks were tall. They were so tall that sometimes he had to build them with a hinge so the sun and moon could pass by. When the derrick and engine and pumps and tanks were all in place, he pulled that drill out and the gusher came roaring to the top of the derrick. Kemp just capped the well himself and soon the tanks were filling up. This was one big man.

One day Kemp was sniffing for an oil well and he started to dig and drill, but a freeze came up just as the oil gushed to the surface. The oil froze right there as it shot into the sky, thousands of gallons of oil frozen solid and just stood there, a huge pillar of frozen black gold. Now Kemp looked at that giant column of frozen oil and wondered what he would do with it. If he waited for a thaw, then it would just run all over the ground and he'd lose it all. Then he got an idea. Oil was expensive to haul because the railroads charged a lot of money for a tanker, but he didn't need a tanker with that frozen skyscraper of oil. He took his saw and cut that oil into twenty-foot lengths and stacked it up on flatbed railroad cars and sent it off to the refinery before all that oil thawed out. He made a tidy profit off that frozen oil.

Now Kemp always had to be careful not to hit his drill too hard with his big hammer. One day he was pounding away on his drill, daydreaming and not paying any attention to how hard or how deep his drill had gone. Suddenly the sky burst with a gusher, but it was like no gusher Kemp had ever seen, because it was white. He bent down and tasted the white stuff that poured out of his oil well and found that he had hammered all the way to China, and his oil well was gushing rice all over. At first Kemp was pretty annoyed, but then he realized that it was winter and a hard one at that, and he gathered that rice and gave it to all the boomers and settlers and Indians who needed it and kept everyone well fed over a very cold winter.

Kemp kept sniffing out oil wells for all his days and having adventures both in the oil fields and all around Oklahoma. One day he dug the deepest, biggest well in the world. When it gushed the stars had a hard time staying in place, because the oil made the heavens too slippery.

Some folks say Kemp Morgan went out east and settled down. Others say he moved on to the western oil fields. Most folks in Oklahoma say he's still around sniffing out oil wells and having the time of his life.

Lone Hunter and the Swamp Spirit
(Choctaw People)

Lone Hunter respected the old Choctaw ways and cared for his dog, Lukna. But he went against the words of the elders in one respect. "Never hunt alone, and never stay overnight in the swamp," the elders said. They warned of the creatures that lived in the swamp, the dark and hulking ones who rose from the soggy earth in the late night hours.

Lone Hunter did hunt alone in the swamp, and sometimes at night. He knew of the warnings. But by his reckoning, he always traveled with his dog, so he was never alone.

One night, following a long and exhausting day of hunting, Lone Hunter sat by the fire. His catch for the day was four small squirrels. He skinned and roasted two squirrels, one for himself and one for Lukna. He picked the warm meat from the bones and fed Lukna before eating his own meal.

As the fog thickened and the night noises hummed and howled, Lone Hunter settled close to the fire. He was almost asleep when he heard Lukna growl. The dog turned his face to Lone Hunter and spoke.

"The man who comes is no man," Lukna said.

Lone Hunter sat up. The sound of dragging feet slithered through the swamp. Soon a figure cloaked in a black robe stood by the fire. A low-hanging hood covered his face and his sleeves drooped over his hands. Lone Hunter could see no skin.

"You are welcome here," he said, rising to greet the stranger. The figure neither spoke nor moved.

"I have some squirrels. Let me cook you one." While he squatted and prepared the squirrel, Lone Hunter kept an eye on the figure looming over him. Lukna growled his low growl.

When the squirrel was roasted, Lone Hunter stretched his palm to the dark one, thinking, "Now I will see his hand." But the stranger took the squirrel with his sleeves. Lukna growled.

Lone Hunter heard a gnawing and gnashing of teeth, and when the dark one rose, squirrel bones fell to the ground.

"You can sleep there, on your side of the fire," said Lone Hunter. "I will sleep here, by my dog."

The dark one rolled into his cloak, saying nothing. Lone Hunter struggled to stay awake, but soon his eyes closed and his mind drifted. He was awakened by the hot breath of Lukna, close to his ear. *Grrrrrrr.*

Lone Hunter, frozen with fear, saw the dark one rise, move around the fire, and lean over him. The figure pulled back his hood. His skull shone in the faint light of the embers. As he lifted his arms, his sleeves fell away, and skeletal hands with long thin fingers moved to Lone Hunter's throat.

The Choctaw hunter rocked backward and, with an explosive kick, sent the dark one hurtling into the fire. A deep purple cloud, foul-smelling, hovered where the dark one had been.

Lone Hunter and Lukna ran stumbling through the swamp to the Choctaw town. He awakened the leaders and the council met to decide a course of action.

The next night at the same hour, Lone Hunter and Lukna once again lay by the fire. Twenty Choctaw men hid in the surrounding bushes and vines. When the dark one appeared, the Choctaws quickly surrounded the clearing, linking arms to prevent his escape.

The dark one ran to the circle, moving through the Choctaw men like the spirit he was. He dashed through the swamp to a cliff overlooking a quarry. The men followed, with Lone Hunter and Lukna close behind. When he reached the cliff, the dark one never slowed, but flung himself over the edge.

As the Choctaws watched, he twisted into a slow fall. Time stopped as the men watched the dark one fall to his death, a death of years ago. He turned in the air and his cloak disappeared. The skeleton grew skin and a young man screamed before them, smashing onto the boulders below.

Four Choctaws slowly climbed into the quarry. Before them lay dried and powdery bones, all that remained of the dark one. They carried the bones to the clifftop. An *alikchi*, a Choctaw medicine man, stepped forward.

"This young man was not evil," he said. "Years ago he fell to his death, just as we have seen. He never received a proper burial, and his spirit has lingered in the swamp."

At sunrise the next day, Choctaw singers gathered. The wailing began and the sacred bone bundle, the remains of the young man, was buried overlooking the quarry. No one ever saw the wandering spirit again.

Lone Hunter and Lukna continued to hunt in the swamp, but never after dark, and Lone Hunter always remembered the words of the elders: "If you love your dog and treat your dog as part of your family, as if your dog is human, if your life is ever in danger, your dog will speak to warn you." Choctaw elders always speak of dogs with a special reverence.

Used with permission of Tim Tingle, Choctaw storyteller.

Choctaw Codetalkers of World War I (a True Story by Phillip Allen)

Near the end of World War I, the German army was preparing for their final big push of the war, an attack on an American battalion near the French/German border. German infantry surrounded the battalion and began shelling heavy artillery on the American troops. Foxholes were easy targets for German cannons, and casualties were heavy. Several Oklahoma Choctaws were serving in the targeted American battalion.

Germans also broke the Americans' radio codes, which meant they understood every message sent from one company to another on the battle line. When the army tried sending runners instead of using radio communication, one out of every four runners was captured by the Germans.

Company Commander Lawrence, while moving through his troops, happened to overhear Solomon Lewis and Mitchell Bobb conversing in their native Choctaw language. After listening for a few moments, he called Lewis aside.

"Corporal," he asked, "how many of you Choctaw boys do we have in this battalion?"

"We have eight men who speak fluent Choctaw in the battalion, sir," Lewis said.

"Are any of them in Headquarters Company?" asked the captain.

"I think that Carterby and Maytubby are over there," Lewis replied.

"You fellows wait right here," said the captain. He made a hasty telephone call and discovered that, indeed, Choctaws Ben Carterby and Pete Maytubby were attached to Headquarters Company.

"Get the Choctaws and have them stand by," Captain Lawrence told his commanding officer. "I have an idea that might get the Germans off our backs."

The captain told Lewis and Bobb, "Look, I'm going to give you a message to call in to headquarters. I want you to give your friends a message in your Choctaw language. See if somebody there can understand it."

The message was written and Private Bobb translated the words into the Choctaw language. He used a field phone to call the message to another Choctaw soldier, Ben Carterby. Thus the first codetalker message ever sent by the American army in wartime was in the Choctaw language, between Oklahoma Choctaws Mitchell Bobb and Ben Carterby. Carterby then translated the message into English for the Battalion Commander.

Within a few hours, the eight Choctaw speakers had been shifted until there was at least one Choctaw in each company headquarters. The Choctaws began making telephone calls, in only the Choctaw language. They wrote field orders, only in Choctaw, that were carried by runners to other parts of the battlefield. If a runner was captured, the Germans were unable to read the message.

As the battle neared its conclusion, German troops still held the upper hand. They completely encircled the Americans and were planning a morning assault. When the American army learned of the plan, messages were sent out in Choctaw to begin an artillery barrage and, five minutes later, to top the hill and attack the Germans. The Germans were taken completely by surprise.

Twenty-four hours after Choctaw became the U.S. Army's language of choice for telephone and written communications, the tide of the battle turned. In less than seventy-two hours the Germans were retreating. The Allies seized the advantage and were in full attack.

Joseph Oklahombi is quite possibly the most famous of all World War I Choctaw Codetalkers. In addition to his codetalking duties, Oklahomabi was involved in the infantry assault on the Germans. All alone, he discovered a company of 170 Germans encamped in a graveyard in the early morning hours. Oklahombi set up rifles at several positions on the stone fence surrounding the graveyard. Once all guns were in place, he began firing and running, firing and running, until the Germans thought they were surrounded by an entire company of Americans. Bullets came flying from every direction. Many Germans were still asleep, and those awake were enjoying a campfire breakfast, completely unprepared for battle.

The Germans soon waved the white flag of surrender. They threw down their weapons and marched out of the gate of the graveyard, and were stunned to see only one American soldier waiting, Private Oklahombi. He herded the German prisoners to his company headquarters. For this amazing feat, Joseph Oklahombi was awarded France's Croix de Guerre, the Cross of War, that nation's highest military honor.

In October 2008, in a ceremony before the U.S. Congress, eighteen World War I Choctaw codetalkers, or their descendants, were awarded Congressional Medals for their special part in achieving American victory.

Used with permission of Phillip Allen.

Paul Bunyan's Oklahoma Farm

Paul Bunyan tried his hand at farming in Oklahoma. He had heard that there was enough land there so that he and his Blue Ox Babe could stretch a bit. Now Paul had developed a strain of corn that was a lot like him, fast growing. The day after that first plant came through the ground the cornstalk was already six feet tall. Thinking it was a tree, one of his neighbors tied his wagon and team to it when he stopped to talk with Paul. When the sun broke through the clouds that corn really took off. In fact it grew so fast and so big that his neighbor's team of horses and wagon shot up with it. Now Paul's old crew from his lumbering days were still working for Paul, so one of them put on his cleats and climbed that corn just like it was a tall pine. He untied the horses and lowered them down to Paul.

One of the ears of corn fell off the stalk and hit the ground with such force that it dug a well over a hundred feet into the ground.

Now the year before Paul had tried growing his own strain of watermelons. They had grown so big that when one of those melons broke open the juice washed away a nearby dam and almost wiped out an entire town. The only way to harvest those melons was to tunnel through them with dynamite, drive wagons into the melons, and bring the fruit out back through the tunnel.

Paul always carried a walnut walking stick with him when he went out into the fields. One day he stuck it into the ground while he was working and left it there all night. The next day that walking stick was a full-grown walnut tree full of walnuts. When lightning struck that tree later in the year Paul cut it into enough lumber to build himself a nice ten-room house, just the right size for him and Babe.

Even though Paul enjoyed farming, his heart was still in the woods, and he moved west to have more adventures out in Oregon and Washington.

Oklahoma Glossary

Caddo people: A Native American people who were among the original residents of Arkansas, Texas, Louisiana, and Oklahoma. They lived in earthen lodges with thatched roofs, and a wooden wall often surrounded their villages. Inside they had their homes, a sports field, and a place of worship. They were famous for their pottery.

Cherokee people: The largest Native American tribe in America today. At one time they occupied parts of Tennessee, Kentucky, Georgia, the Carolinas, Virginia, and Alabama. They were removed from their lands by President Andrew Jackson and relocated to Oklahoma during what is called The Trail of Tears.

Choctaw people: A Southeastern tribe, one of the Five Civilized Nations. They were removed from their lands by President Andrew Jackson and brought to Oklahoma on what is now referred to as The Trail of Tears, along with the Cherokee, Seminole, Chickasaw, and Creek peoples.

Derrick: The frame and drill used to drill for oil.

Kemp Morgan: A folklore hero who grew up in the oil fields of Oklahoma and Texas.

Oklahoma: A state whose name comes from two Choctaw words, "ukla" and "huma," meaning "red people." Its capital is Oklahoma City.

Paul Bunyan: The folklore hero of the north woods. His stories are found throughout the United States.

Wichita people: A Native American people who at one time lived in beehive-shaped houses that were thatched with grass. Their settlements were permanent, and they sent parties out to hunt buffalo and deer instead of constantly following herds. They lived throughout Texas and Oklahoma. They moved north to Kansas to escape European expansion but were later relocated to Oklahoma.

Story Sources

American Myths & Legends, Volumes 1 & 2

Ballads & Folk Songs of the Southwest

Cowboy Songs and other Frontier Ballads

The Ghost of Mingo Creek & Other Spooky Oklahoma Legends

The Greenwood Library of American Folktales, Volume 3

Heroes, Outlaws & Funny Fellows of American Popular Tales

Montezuma's Serpent & Other True Supernatural Tales of the Southwest

Myths & Legends of Our Own Land, Volumes 1 & 2

Outlaw Tales: Legends, Myths & Folklore from America's Middle Border

Tales from the American Frontier

Tingle, Tim. Choctaw Storyteller

A Treasury of Western Folklore

Yankee Doodle's Cousins

Oregon

Oregon entered the union as the thirty-third state in 1859. The land of Oregon is home to several Native American tribes, including the Klamath and Wasco.

"The Darning Needle" is a wonderful story about the simple, rugged lives many new settlers faced and the kindness that can form new bonds of friendship. "Black Harris" traces the exploits of the legendary African American mountain man Moses Harris. Paul Bunyan makes an appearance in Oregon, too; "The Death of Babe the Blue Ox" spins another yarn about this legendary duo. Gold and pirates and buried treasure haunt the shores of every coastal state, and Oregon is no exception; read about "The Oregon Beeswax Legend."

The Darning Needle (Based on True Events)

The pioneers who traveled west to a new life in California, Oregon, and Washington suffered many hardships, some great, some small. But when the only darning needle in Pass Creek Canyon in Oregon was lost, it seemed like a real crisis. The women passed the needle around from one household to another, each taking turns mending the clothes for her family then passing it on again. It was a prized and well-cared for treasure in the community.

The needle actually belonged to Grandmother Drain, but she knew how important it was to the community and gladly shared it. Mrs. Chitwood had just finished using it and sent it back to Grandmother Drain by her eight-year-old son, Jimmy. She tied a red thread through the eye of the needle and stuck it into a potato so he wouldn't lose it.

Now Jimmy knew how important his mission was, so as he walked the trail through the canyon to Grandmother Drain's cabin he was careful to stay alert. He was tempted to chase the rabbits and squirrels and deer that crossed his path, but he kept on. When he heard the low moan of a mother bear and her cubs he hid behind a serviceberry bush and watched until they passed by. He wasn't really afraid, because he knew that bears kept to themselves and wouldn't bother you if you didn't bother them. He also knew that a mother with her cubs could get a little nasty if she thought her babies were being threatened. The bears took their time stopping and sniffing and eating some berries off an old blueberry bush. Finally they moved on.

Jimmy stood up and stretched and then got back on the path and continued his journey. He walked on, thinking about the beautiful day and the bear mama and her cubs. Then he remembered the needle and realized that he had left it behind when he was watching the bears. When he got back to the spot where he thought he saw the bears he couldn't find the serviceberry bush. He looked and looked and finally ran back to his family's cabin and told his mother. She sent him to find his father, who was working with the other men of the settlement cutting down trees. The men joined the boy in looking for the needle.

"Now Jimmy," said his father, "do you remember any other landmarks besides the serviceberry?"

Jimmy thought for a moment and then said, "There was an odd stump right next to the bush, almost under it."

Everyone looked for the serviceberry with the stump, but it was Jimmy who finally found it. "Jimmy you've got the makings of a real woodsmen," his father said with pride.

"Jimmy, I'm so proud of you. You lost the needle but then you found it," said his mother.

The darning needle was found and everyone in the settlement was relieved. But nothing lasts forever, no matter how well you take care of it. One day while Grandmother Drain was darning a sock the head of the needle broke off. Now all the women in the village just piled the clothes that needed mending to one side and wondered when they'd ever be able to get to them.

One day near the end of November a peddler came through the settlement. His name was Aaron Meier. His older brothers Julius and Emanuel had come to California from Germany to open a general store in Downeyville. Aaron joined them later but decided he would travel the area selling goods as an itinerant peddler. He wanted to see the country, and he was a man who loved meeting new people. His brothers gave him the money to buy the goods he needed to sell and for a mule to haul them around for him. He headed up into Oregon Territory and came into Pass Canyon Creek that day in November for the first time.

The children saw him first, and soon most of the settlement was crowding around the peddler. People crowded around as he spread his wares out on a blanket on the ground.

People looked at combs and knives, clothes and toys for the children, tin ware and pots, buttons and tools. Finally Mrs. Chitwood said, "Do you have any darning needles? The kind that have a large eye in them?" Jimmy's mother told Mr. Meier the story of the only darning needle they had and how they shared it. She told him how Jimmy had lost it and then found it again and how it had just worn out and broke.

"My people don't celebrate Christmas," said Aaron, who was Jewish "but I know that holiday is right around the corner. You all give presents at that time, don't you?" he asked Jimmy, who had stood nearby stroking the neck of Aaron's mule.

"Well, why don't you and I give all the ladies of Pass Canyon Creek an early present?" The peddler reached into one of his sacks and came out with a thin packet. "Here are all the darning needles I have, but there should be enough here for every family," said Aaron with a smile. At first everyone was just stunned, then the smiles broke out on the faces of all the ladies with murmurs of "he's a good man" and "what kindness."

Jimmy helped the peddler pass out the needles to all the women and kept enough to bring a needle to each lady who had not come to the village that day.

It was the first of many visits that Aaron Meier made to that settlement. Later he opened the store of Meier & Frank in Portland. and the same honesty and goodwill that he showed to the folks up in Pass Canyon Creek ensured his success in his new store.

Black Harris

"The snow was fifty feet deep and my friends and I had to eat our moccasins to survive."

So begins one of many tall tales of Moses Harris, the African American mountain man, explorer, and teller of stories also known as Black Harris.

Moses came west from probably South Carolina and became a well-known mountain man in the northern Rockies, especially in Oregon and Montana. He was a trapper and hunter and like many mountain men seldom stayed in one place very long, preferring to roam the vast wilderness of the American and Canadian Rocky Mountains. By all accounts he loved to spin tall tales, and like most mountain men his stories probably had some basis in truth. Few easterners would believe the real stories of the mysterious West, so men like Black Harris made their stories more fantastic with each telling.

He told the story of the Petrified Forest complete with stone birds and animals. "We came out of that fifty-foot snow fall and into a valley that was green and beautiful. I mean it was February and this mountain valley didn't have a flake of snow in it." The mountain men who were listening could see the twinkle in Harris' eyes as the story started to pick up speed. They knew that the folks from back east would soon be caught in the story's trap. "I spied a bird and decided that it was the end of our days of eating old leather. I picked up Ginger, my musket, took aim, and fired. That bird fell right off that branch, but when I got to it and picked it up I found out that the bird was solid stone. Before I could tell the others old Rube decides to start a fire and thaw out our horses. He took an axe and went up to an old cottonwood tree and swung at that tree, and wham! that axe bounced right off that tree. The blade of that axe was shattered, and old Rube was thrown a dozen feet backward. We walked up to some animals, and they had no fear of us at all, and when we got close we could se that every last one of them was made of stone. Well, we started to sharpen our knives on some of the tree trunks. That stone was so fine we had the sharpest edge anyone ever had on a bowie knife. Every blade of grass was stone, too, and it crunched as we walked around. Well, we had to get out of that valley as fast as we could. With a stream where the water was stone and stone grass and stone animals, there was nothing for man or beast to eat or drink." The folks from back east weren't sure if they had been taken for fools or if they had just heard a great storyteller or both.

When the days of trapping started to slow down, Black Harris started leading wagon trains across the mountains into Oregon. He also was known for rescuing wagon trains and settlers who had gotten lost in the mountains or caught by an early snow. He lived in a cabin on the Luckiamute River, one of the few times he had settled down in his life. He went back to St. Louis to organize another wagon train west but died during the cholera epidemic of 1849.

The Oregon Beeswax Legend

The *Acapulco* galleons carried the treasure from Manila to Mexico and on to Spain in the seventeenth century. Storms drove one of the treasure ships off course until it floundered below the mouth of the Columbia River near the sandpits that shelter Nehalem Bay. According to the Indian legends, all the crew had light complexions except one, whose skin was black. There were twenty men who survived the wreck, and when they found there was no hope of getting the ship off the beach, they accepted the Indians' hospitality and built huts on shore. One of the things they brought from the ship was a heavy chest, which they wished to bury, but they were not satisfied with the low, almost featureless Nehalem shore. Five miles to the north they found a high, bare mountain, with the Pacific forever charging in and bursting against its western base—an unforgettable landmark, visible for many miles at sea and on land. The sailors carried their chest to the southwest side, where the mountain rose from a little meadow. Elk were feeding on the grassy slopes that went up toward the sky, and when the castaways saw them they cried, "carne!" which is Spanish for "meat." From then on, according to the Indians, the mountain was called Neacarne, "the place of the meat," which has been corrupted into Neahkahnie.

Near the foot of the mountain the sailors dug a pit into which they lowered the chest, filled the pit, and went back to live with the Indians. But as luck would have it, that time was not to be very long.

One of the habits of the castaways was to ignore the marital arrangements of the local people and take their pick of women in the tribe. When the sailors refused to learn the ways of their more civilized hosts, the people surrounded their huts and killed them all. Peace once again descended on Nehalem. The castaways were buried on the shore where they had been betrayed by their arrogance. The man with the black skin died where the mysterious chest was buried at the foot of the mountain. Fearing places of burial, the Indians avoided the spot and in time forgot its location.

Long afterward, white settlers came to Nehalem and heard the Indian legends of the ship and the buried chest. The ship was still there, with its teak-wood frames sticking out of the sand like an ancient skeleton, and in the meadow at the foot of Neahkahnie Mountain they found a large rock carved with European symbols: crosses, the letter *W*, and *DE* followed by a row of dots above an arrow that pointed toward the mountain. Nearby was a smaller rock with other symbols and an arrow pointing toward the larger rock. It took little imagination to deduce that the long-buried chest held treasure and that the carving on the larger rock was a code for locating it. But who knew the code?

Few people can resist the idea of a treasure hunt, and enough have tried at Neahkahnie. None have found the treasure. Some found a sudden death among the tunnels and pits they dug. Others tried for a lifetime and only had disappointment and old age for their reward. The chest is still concealed somewhere about Neahkahnie Mountain—if there ever was a chest—and the treasure rock is still there, in the tall grass behind a garage. Anyone so inclined may consider its obscure instructions and follow the direction of the arrow that points toward golden wealth, or bitterness, or even death.

Part of the treasure ship's cargo had been cakes of beeswax and candles. Occasionally the sea brought some of them to the surface, preserved by the cold waters at the ocean's bottom. In 1813 Alexander Henry of the Northwest Company, visiting the site of Astoria, wrote in his *Journal*: "The old Clatsop chief arrived with salmon; with him a man with extraordinarily dark red hair, supposed to be an offspring of the ship wrecked within a few miles of the entrance of this river many years ago. Great quantities of beeswax continue to be dug out of the sand near this spot, and the Indians bring it to trade with us." Science has proved that the source of the beeswax was the region from which the *Acapulco* galleons sailed.

Is there a fortune in gold waiting for the person who can decipher the old carvings on the rocks? Will the gold bring the same bad luck to those who find it that haunted those who brought it? Are the spirits of those reckless and lawless sailors haunting the treasure and keeping it for themselves for all eternity?

The Death of Babe the Blue Ox

One day Paul got out of bed in his new logging camp and found that Babe, his beloved Blue Ox, was nowhere to be found. Now it had been raining almost every day for a year and the ground was a bit soggy, so Paul pulled on his biggest pair of boots and went looking for Babe. He called out Babe's name as he looked, but there was no sweet bellow in return. Every time Paul's boots sank too deep into the soft earth, the hole would full up with water. That's why the southwest part of Oregon has so many lakes.

He found old Babe up in the ills. The old ox was sick, and Paul cradled its huge head in his lap and cried his heart out. When Paul Bunyan cries a lot of water flows, and this day he cried like never before, By the time Paul was finished his tears had run down his face and down those hills, forming the gullies and streams that eventually flow together to form the Coos River. Now the sea gulls were hovering overhead waiting for Babe to die so they could feast on his bones. Paul got so mad that he began to pick up stones and throw them at the birds. You can still see some of those rocks strewn all over the beaches of southern Oregon. Finally Babe died, and Paul dug a grave for his old friend and buried Babe where he found him. The local folks call that place Blue Ridge, maybe because Babe is buried there, or maybe the blue color of the huge ox's hide still shines through the earth. So ended a big part of Paul's life. Babe had been with him on most of his adventures and had traveled west with him from Maine to Michigan to Minnesota to Washington and Oregon. Paul mourned his friend for the rest of his days.

Oregon Glossary

Darning needle: A long, thin needle used in repairing clothes that had been torn and needed mending.

Klamath people: A Native American people who lived east of the Cascade Mountains in the Klamath Basin, where they hunted and fished. They used dugout canoes and lived in tepees made of willow branches and tule mats in the summer and in roundhouses with conical roofs made of wood and earth and mats in the winter.

Oregon: A state whose name comes from unknown sources. It might have come from the French, who called the Columbia River "Le Fleur Aux Ouragans" or Hurricane River, due to the strong winds found in several canyons and valleys. It might also come from an engraver's error giving the name Ouaricon to the wrong river heading west in that area. The capital of Oregon is Salem.

Paul Bunyan: A fictional character who is featured in many lumberjack folktales.

Peddler: A traveling salesman in the pioneer days. Peddlers sold household items, cloth, tools, and anything they or their wagons or pack animals could carry and that pioneers needed.

Serviceberry: A small tree or shrub that blooms small white blossoms in early spring. Legend has it that it got its name from settlers who, upon seeing the white flowers, knew that spring had arrived and it was time to bury their winter dead. When the ground was too hard people often kept the dead in barns or other buildings and then buried them in the spring. The serviceberry flowers often adorned the coffins or graves.

Wasco people: A Native American people who lived on the south banks of the Columbia River, where they fished and hunted. They did not follow game but lived in fixed villages.

Story Sources

American Myths & Legends, Volumes 1 & 2

Cowboy Songs and other Frontier Ballads

Ghost Stories from the Pacific Northwest

The Greenwood Library of American Folktales, Volume 4

Heroes, Outlaws, & Funny Fellows of American Popular Tales

Indian Legends of the Pacific Northwest

Myths & Legends of Our Own Land, Volumes 1 & 2

The Parade of Heroes

The Stories We Tell: An Anthology of Oregon Folk Literature

Tales from the American Frontier

A Treasury of Western Folklore

Yankee Doodle's Cousins

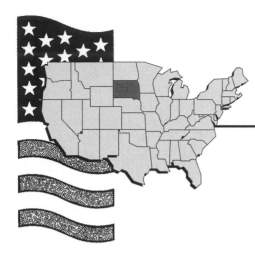

South Dakota

South Dakota was admitted to the union as the fortieth state in 1889, at the same time as North Dakota. Both states were carved out of Dakota Territory. Many Native Americans call South Dakota home and are represented here by a story from the Lakota and Dakota Sioux. Laura Ingalls Wilder's *Little House on the Prairie* and other books in that series introduced millions of readers to life on the Dakota frontier. Immigrants from all over Europe came to South Dakota to find the American dream of independence. The song "Dakota Land" gives a very different view of Dakota than Wilder's books. It talks about the suffering and privation that often accompanied coming to a new land. Mythical beasts that have never been captured roam the wilderness of America. Kevin Strauss provides us with a story about one of the most elusive creatures that haunts the wilds of South Dakota. The last story tells about a meeting between government officials and a Lakota warrior during treaty negotiations.

House on the Prairie (a True Story)

One night every week Americans would gather around their televisions and watch Michael Landon and the rest of the cast of *Little House on the Prairie* share their joys and sorrows, their tears and laughter as they struggled through the hardships of living on the American frontier in Dakota Territory. The books that inspired this series were written by Laura Ingalls Wilder, who based them on her own life growing up in DeSmet, South Dakota, and the people she met in her small town as friends and neighbors.

South Dakota was still Dakota Territory when the Ingalls family came to homestead in the late 1870s. Her father took a job with the railroad and the young family saw the small town of DeSmet rise up around them. Laura used her own childhood as the basis for her books about growing up on the frontier. Her book *The Long Winter* is based on the winter of 1880–1881, which was one of the most severe winters in recorded Dakota history. Though she used people and events from her own life, her books were not strictly autobiographical. She often combined real people to make one character and used some events in different years or seasons than when they actually occurred. She changed names and places but always kept the reality of life on the prairie in all her books.

Laura attended school in DeSmet and had a normal life for a girl of her times on the frontier. When she was fifteen, while she was still in school herself, she began to teach at one of the one-room schoolhouses in the area to help bring in some money for her family.

When she was eighteen she married Almanzo Wilder and joined him on his homestead. The early years of their marriage were both wonderful and sorrowful. She gave birth to her daughter Rose, who would follow in her mother's footsteps as an accomplished writer, but also lost a child at birth. Their farm prospered at first, but then her husband caught diphtheria and lost the use of his legs for a while. He eventually recovered but used a cane for most of his life after that illness. A manuscript called "The First Four Years," found after her daughter's death, recounts the joys and trials of Laura's early years with Almanzo. Eventually she and her husband and daughter moved from South Dakota and finally settled in Missouri.

Laura was already in her sixties when she asked her daughter Rose if she thought anyone would be interested in stories about Laura's early life in South Dakota. Rose encouraged her mother and was probably her editor as well since her own writing and editing skills were well honed by then. Harper published the first book, *Little House in the Big Woods*, sending her a royalty check for $500, which in today's economy would be about $7,500. The royalties kept coming in and, for the first time in their fifty years of marriage, Laura and Almanzo were enjoying a steady and substantial income. The *Little House* series has been in print constantly since the first book came out in 1931 and has been translated into forty languages.

The fictional books she wrote based on her youth and experiences on the prairie of South Dakota have given countless generations around the world a glimpse into the hardships, sacrifice, and happiness of those early settlers on the frontier. They have won such honors as several Newbery Awards and been turned into successful movies and television shows, including the blockbuster *Little House on the Prairie*.

Laura Ingalls Wilder once said that she wanted children to know what her life was like on the prairie of South Dakota so future generations would understand about the tremendous changes that occurred during her lifetime in America. She painted us a picture of the land, the times, and the people of that era like no other.

The Beaver Woman and the Eagle
(Lakota/Dakota People)

Long ago, there was an old Beaver Woman working by a stream bed, busily taking down saplings, stripping away their branches and leaves. But she was not so busy that she did not notice a great Eagle circling high above her in the sky. She was not so busy that she did not notice the whirring of the wind through his wings as he whistled, diving toward the earth, intending to make her his breakfast.

Quickly, she dove into the water and disappeared. The disappointed Eagle circled closer and landed on the branch of a dead cottonwood, his eyes fixed on the spot where she had disappeared under the water. Suddenly a brown head, touched with the silver of many seasons, popped up from a different spot in the stream, not where Eagle was glaring intently.

"What gives you the right to attack the grandmother of a gentle and hard-working people?"

The Eagle turned his fierce gaze on her, "I am hungry. I am Eagle."

The old Beaver Woman looked back at him, fearlessly. "Yes, but why don't you try to live as our People do? To find value in working hard and leaving others alone to live their lives?"

The Eagle scoffed, "That is easy for you to say. Not everyone can fell trees with their teeth—and who would want to be like you? Who would want to live by eating branches, leaves and bark? I am not an old woman; I am a great warrior!"

"Ah," she said, gently. "It seems it is true. Some seem to live just to cause trouble for others. But couldn't you possibly also learn to play fair? To work for a living and do something that would also help others? My work does not benefit just me and my family. I widen the streambeds. I make ponds, and there I make it possible for many others to live. But you—you use *your* power just to terrify those who are weaker and smaller than you. Perhaps there is much you could learn from *my* people."

At this, the Eagle gave her another sharp and hungry look. Before he could move even one feather, the old Beaver Woman turned and, slapping her tail on the water, dove deep to the bottom of the pond.

There, she crawled into her dry lodge of stick and mud and fed her grandchildren and ate a good meal herself. Then they slept, curled safe and comfortable in their lodge within the waters. Above them, on that cottonwood branch, Eagle waited and waited and watched the fading ripples in the water. The winds whistled and rattled the dead branches where he clung. The waters became frosted with a crust of ice.

And, though he was scornful of the old Beaver Woman's simple ways and still full of pride about who he thought he was, that day it was the Eagle who went hungry, while the old Beaver Woman was warm and well fed.

A Lakota/Dakota Story retold by Dovie Thomason. ©2006 Dovie Thomason, used with permission.

Dakota Land

This old folk song tells the story of immigrants who come to a new land only to find that its not filled with milk and honey but with hard ground and intense heat. The unknown author of this song talks about despair rather than hope: one of the two sides of the immigrant coin.

We've reached the land of waving wheat,
Where nothing grows for man to eat.
The wind it blows with feverish heat
Across the plains so hard to beat.

Chorus
Dakota land, sweet Dakota land,
As on your fiery soil I stand,
I look away across the plains
And I wonder why it never rains
Till Gabriel bows his trumpet sound
And says the rain's just gone around.

We reached the land of hills and stones
Where all is strewn with buffalo bones.
Forgotten herds, old bleached bones,
I listen to hear your sighs and moans.

Chorus
We have no wheat, we have no oats.
We have no corn to feed our shoats.
Our horses are of bronco race.
Starvation stares them in the face.

Chorus
Our neighbors are the rattlesnakes
That crawl up from the Badland's breaks.
We do not live, we only stay.
We are too poor to get away.

Jackalope Country (by Kevin Strauss)

Whenever folks travel out onto the Northern Great Plains, west of the Red River and north of Nebraska, they're likely to hear about the one species of wildlife that has never been captured in the United States. Sure, lots of folks say they've bagged one. Some will even show you an antlered head mounted on the wall. But if you look closer, you'll see that some taxidermist glued antlers onto the head of an ordinary jackrabbit.

Of course the creature I'm talking about is no other than the famous jackalope, a creature with the body of a jackrabbit, the tail of a pheasant, and the antlers of a small deer.

Now the fact that no one has ever caught a jackalope in a trap and no one has ever shot a jackalope has lead some to believe that this creature doesn't exist. They are put it in the same category as unicorns and world peace. But I beg to differ.

How else can you explain the sound of deer antlers banging together before every South Dakota thunderstorm? (Jackalopes rut and mate in the rain.) How else can you explain why cowboys and even modern hunters hear ghostlike singing under the full moon out on the prairie? Jackalopes are well known to be masters of vocal mimicry. They are even known to evade pursuers by throwing their voices and saying, "Look, it's over here!" to send hunters in the wrong direction. In my mind, if it isn't jackalopes that are doing that singing, then it must be ghosts, and I tend to believe more in talking jackalopes than talking ghosts.

What's more, the Douglas County Chamber of Commerce sells jackalope live-capture hunting licenses. Since no one knows the actual population of jackalopes in the Dakotas and Wyoming, the chamber thought it prudent to institute a "catch and release" policy in regard to the creatures. Although the season only lasts two hours, from midnight to 2:00 a.m., on June 31, folks still flock to the office to buy them, hoping to have a chance to capture such an amazing creature. Now if jackalopes don't exist, then the Douglas County Chamber of Commerce would be committing fraud, and I don't think any chamber of commerce would risk a lawsuit just to sell bogus hunting licenses.

All other evidence aside, it is a proven fact that any place that people see a jackalope prospers thereafter. Douglas, Wyoming, became a tourist boomtown after the first jackalope sighting there. Wall Drug, South Dakota, grew up out of the Badlands, some say, because a prospector saw a jackalope hopping past his camp. Right then and there, he started digging for gold and wouldn't you know, they say he found some!

After that, he started up a whole town there and to honor that jackalope, you can still see a bigger than life jackalope statue at the Wall Drug Store. Now if you ask folks in Wall about the prospector, they may not answer you straight. You see, they're still looking to see if there's any more gold in those badlands.

The fact that jackalopes bring good luck has filtered all through our society, although it did get mixed up a bit. You see, jackalopes are the source of that "lucky rabbit's foot" myth. People figured that if *seeing* a jackalope was good luck, then having a piece of a jackalope in your pocket would be even better. But after years of unsuccessful jackalope hunting, folks resorted to using jackrabbit feet for luck. But it doesn't seem to work so well, especially for the rabbit.

So the next time you're driving down I-90 through the prairie, at night and just before a thunderstorm, keep your eyes peeled. You might just see a jackalope hopping through the grass on its way to an important meeting. And if you see it and it sees you, you've got good luck coming your way.

© Kevin Strauss. Used with permission of the author.

Borrowing the Mules (Based on True Events)

The U.S. government had sent a commission to the Black Hills to negotiate a treaty with the Lakota over the leasing of the Black Hills for mining interests for a 100-year period. The government was only offering a small fee, though it knew that the profits from the gold and mineral mines would amount to a fortune. The talks for the day had come to a close, and the government wagon that was hauling senators and congressmen and other negotiators was leaving. One of the chiefs, Spotted Tail, rode up to the wagon and stopped it. One of the senators stuck his head out of the covered wagon and asked what the problem was and why the wagon had stopped.

Spotted Tail looked at the senator and said, "I want your team of mules."

The senator replied, "They're not ours. We can't sell them to you."

"I don't want to buy them, I only want to borrow them," answered Spotted Tail.

"For how long?"

"A hundred years."

"A hundred years," cried the senator. "There won't be anything left to those mules but some dried up old bones. Besides, they belong to the government; the Great Father in Washington owns those mules. He won't let you borrow them."

Spotted Tail stared at the wagon full of government officials and said, "That's what I thought you would say. But the Black Hills country doesn't belong to our chiefs, either. It belongs to all the Lakota, to all the people. We can't loan them to you or give them away so that in a hundred years you will give them back to us empty."

South Dakota Glossary

Dakota people: A Native American people who are part of the Sioux culture. They lived in tepees made of buffalo hides that were portable so they could follow the herds that they depended on for their food. The tepees belonged to the women. They lived throughout what is now Wisconsin, Minnesota, and North and South Dakota.

Lakota people: A Native American people who are also part of the Sioux culture and share the traditions of that culture with the Dakotas. The Lakota were known as fierce warriors and skilled horsemen. They also followed the buffalo herds.

South Dakota: A state that got its name after being carved out of the southern half of Dakota Territory. Both states took their name from the Dakota people.

Spotted Tail: A chief of the Brule Lakota (1823–1881). As a young man he was a great warrior, but as an elder he became an advocate for peace among his people, recognizing the futility of war.

Story Sources

American Myths & Legends, Volumes 1 & 2

Cowboy Songs and Other Frontier Ballads

Dovie Thomason

The Greenwood Library of American Folktales, Volume 3

The Hell-Bound Train: A Cowboy Songbook

Kevin Strauss

Lakota Myth

Myths & Legends of Our Own Land, Volumes 1 & 2

Outlaw Tales: Legends, Myths & Folklore from America's Middle Border

Tales from the American Frontier

A Treasury of Western Folklore

Texas

Texas entered the union in 1845 as the twenty-eighth state. Before becoming a state Texas was a republic, having fought for its independence from Mexico. Texas is home to many Native American tribes, including the Apache, the Kiowa, the Comanche, and the Caddo, whose story "The Gift of Rabbit" appears here.

"The Devil in Texas" is one of the many folktales that are part of the Hispanic heritage in Texas. "The Snake Who Loved Music" is another in that great style of the tall tale. "The Kindness of Strangers" is a story of the harsh justice and quick kindness found on the plains and comes from cowboy folklore. "The Great Turtle Drive" is a traditional story as told by the great folksinger and storyteller Art Thieme, which takes a look at what may have started the cattle industry.

The Snake Who Loved Music

One summer a drought hit Texas like it had never done before or since. Lakes and rivers, springs and creeks all dried up and blew away into the dust clouds that came across the prairie. The grass first turned yellow then brown and then followed the water up into the sky. Nothing grew, and everyone was thirsty all the time.

There was a wealthy rancher named Mr. Bradford who used other people's hardship to his own advantage. He offered to buy their land for a few dollars or sometimes even for a sack of wheat or beans. Many a farmer took his offer to keep his family from starving during the hard times.

One day Mr. Bradford rode up to old Jerry's farm. Now Jerry didn't have much, just a few cows, some chickens, and a few acres that stretched down to the riverbank. He also had a harmonica, an old mouth harp that he played every day when the sun was setting and he had finished his chores. He always told folks that the music calmed him and made him happy.

Mr. Bradford got to Jerry's house just as he was starting to play his music. Bradford got off his horse and listened for a few minutes, growing more and more impatient as Jerry just sat there playing his harmonica, ignoring him completely.

"You better sell out to me, old fellow. The drought is getting worse, and pretty soon you'll dry up and blow away like everything else."

Jerry just kept playing.

"I'll buy that land you have down near the river."

Jerry just kept on playing and never stopped to say a word.

Bradford got angrier and angrier until he finally got on his horse and yelled at Jerry over his shoulder. "Next time I come here you'll beg me to buy your land."

The next day some of Jerry's neighbors were leaving their farms and heading to the city.

They stopped and asked what he was going to do.

Jerry smiled and said, "It can't last forever. When it rains it stops, when it snows it stops. The drought will stop, too."

They shook their heads in disbelief and moved on.

It wasn't long until Jerry was alone in the small valley. All his neighbors had given up and moved away, and his only companions besides his own animals were the creatures that lived on the land. One day he was sitting on his front porch playing his harmonica.

He played one tune after another, all his favorites. He forgot about the drought and the heat, and all his troubles melted away as he played his music. He closed his eyes and he just kept playing.

When he finally opened his eyes and looked down at his feet he almost died of fright. There, in between his feet, was a giant rattlesnake, all curled up and listening to the music. Jerry was certain the big snake would bite him if he moved, so he just kept on playing every single song he knew over and over again. Now the snake really seemed to like the music, but he especially liked the old hymn "When the Saints Go Marching In" the best.

Whenever Jerry played that one the snake straightened out and swayed back and forth in time to the music, his head almost touching the harmonica.

Finally Jerry just couldn't go on any more. He was tired and shaking from playing so long and he could hardly breathe, so he stopped. He looked down at the snake and said, "You can bite me if you want to, but I can't play any more."

The snake almost looked surprised at what Jerry said. He slithered away and shook his rattle a couple times almost as if to thank him for the music.

From that day on Jerry played his harmonica every afternoon, and the snake came up on the porch to enjoy the music. Jerry grew found of the big rattler and called him Saint after his favorite song, "When the Saints Go Marching In." That rattlesnake would sway to the music, sometimes shaking his rattles to the rhythm with Jerry's harmonica. Jerry even thought he heard that old rattler humming out the tune. Jerry looked forward to these concerts and thought to himself that old Saint was just like him, too stubborn to give up and leave the land.

But one afternoon Saint didn't show up. It happened the next day and again the next. Jerry waited, but Saint didn't come back, and Jerry stopped playing his harmonica. It didn't feel the same with out his friend to listen and sway to the music.

Soon after the heat gave way and the rains came, and it rained and rained until the land began to heal and the rivers and lakes and creeks and ponds began to fill up again and the grass turned green.

Mr. Bradford came to Jerry's house one day, but this time he wasn't looking to buy the land. He needed some good pastureland to fatten up his cattle before taking them to market and wanted to rent some of Jerry's pasture down by the river for a week or two.

Jerry thought that was a good idea. He and Mr. Bradford got into Jerry's old wagon and they started down to the river land to see which acres would be best. As they traveled they heard a strange sound coming from the top of a small hill just where the river took a bend.

They climbed off the wagon and walked to the top, where they saw dozens of rattlesnakes swaying and shaking their rattles. And swaying, taller than the rest, was Saint, swaying and humming his favorite song and leading his rattlesnake band in the most unusual version of "When the Saints Go Marching In" you ever heard.

The Great Turtle Drive
(Adapted and Told by Art Thieme)

Well, yes, it had to be way over 100 years back that it happened. There was a fellow having dinner in a place in Kansas City. On the menu was this turtle soup—a very rare commodity out on the American frontier. He ordered himself a bowl of that turtle soup, spooned it down, and enjoyed it quite a bit. THEN he got the bill!

After calming down and paying the huge $50.00 price tag on the one bowl of soup, he got to thinking about all the land terrapins out there on the prairie crawling around south of there. If he could gather a bunch of those turtles together, he could make a tidy sum.

So this guy went out and hired a crew of fellows that he called *Turtle Boys*, and he sent them down to southern Texas—where all the land terrapins roamed wild down there in the desert. He gave the boys gunny sacks, and they gathered together a big herd of about 30,000 head o' turtle. It was an impressive sight: turtles just about as far as you could see. One fine summer day they got out there on the trail and headed them north—the idea being to get them all the way to the railroad up near Abilene in Kansas. Truth be told, this was a pretty strange scheme. At the rate the land terrapins moved, about four or five feet per day, it would take them more than *thirty years* to get to market. But our entrepreneur was one of those showoffs who always tried to impress people, and he was blinded to the realities of his venture by all the dollar signs in his eyes.

Now, you have to get a picture of the details of this venture. They were riding along, hooting and a-hollering, just trying anything to get the turtles to move along. Even shooting off their revolvers wasn't very effective. Turtles don't hear well. One night they fed them beans, hoping it might sort of jet propel them along. Turned out to be a bad idea.

At night the turtle boys would be riding around the herd and singing to them. Roping strays, too. It's not easy to rope a turtle. They just pull in their heads and legs and little tails so the rope slips off.

One amazing discovery they found out was that the entire herd, all 30,000 of them land terrapins, had to be flipped over—every night. The turtle boys had to get off their horses, walk over to the herd, and carefully, one by one, they had to turn over every single turtle onto its back. That was to keep the turtles from stampeding! After a week or two of doing this the turtle boys realized that the turtles' little legs waving around in the air all night tired them out so bad that the next day the animals could only make one or two feet. So they had to cut that out. It was all trial and error, since a trail drive like this had never been tried before.

The one good thing that came out of all this was that, while they were all bedded down for the night, the females would all lay eggs. Three weeks later they would hatch out into a secondary herd following the first herd. Our headman just got more and more dollar signs in his eyes. He had a picture in his mind of a whole long string of hurtle turds, I mean *turtle herds,* stretched out (as it were) all the way to the railhead up north in Abilene.

Well, eventually they got to the banks of the Red River—that fabled stream that was infamous in the tales and songs of Texas. Sunning himself on the banks of the river was an impressive scholarly-looking mud turtle named Studs, Studs Turtle. Now, he saw this thundering mass of turtle flesh barreling down the bluff at him with their nostrils all flared and the steam pouring out, and he got a little spooked! He jumped right into the river and swam away. But the land terrapins, being a few straws short of a bale, followed him into the river. And them being land terrapins, of course they all sank like a rock and drowned. They couldn't swim a lick!!

Folks, as you might imagine (and I hope you are doing just that), this would've put a quick end to what has, through the years, come to be known in the annals of western history as *The Great Turtle Drive*. But the turtle boys, being quite resourceful, wouldn't let it end there. They started digging these huge pits, which they filled with red-hot coals. They pushed boulders into the pits and heated those rocks up until they were just glowing red hot with heat. Then, using small trees as levers, they pushed the hot rocks right into the waters of the Red River. V-e-r-y s-l-o-w-l-y the water started to heat up and then it started to seethe, boil, steam, and froth. For the next year, at least, the Red River ran with pure turtle soup. It kept the Indians fed through a very bad winter. Everyone turned out pretty happy when it was all over.

A year later, in that very same restaurant in Kansas City where this adventure began, that same guy, this time having a nice bowl of beef stew, had another big idea. He told his partner, "I just thought of something. If we could do it with turtles, maybe we ought to try it with COWS."

And that was the start of the whole cattle and beef industry in the American West.

Used with permission.

The Kindness of Strangers

During the summer of 1860 a man was moving a herd of cattle in the country near Helena, Texas. As he was passing a nearby stream some strays that were lured by the water on a hot day mixed with his herd. The next day, about a dozen armed men who demanded their cattle overtook the man. They accused him of stealing the strays.

Now in those days it was a greater offense to steal a horse or cattle than it was to kill a man. The herdsman tried to explain, but the men wouldn't listen. He offered to cut the strays from his herd and turn them over on the spot, but they said that the time for talking was over. They thought that perhaps they should take the whole herd and leave him there hanging from a tree as a warning to others.

The cowboys turned to him and said that they would give him ten minutes to defend himself.

The herdsman turned to the men and asked, "How many of you have wives?" A few nodded.

"How many of you have children?" Heads nodded again.

"You'll understand me then, so I'll tell you my story. I have never stolen any cattle. I came here from New Hampshire out east where my business failed in the Panic of 1857. I've been here in Texas for about three years now, where I have worked hard saving my money. My family is still out east, and I send them every spare cent that I earn. I have no home but sleep on the ground, working where I can and hiring myself out as I travel from place to place. I look hard because I live hard and this is a hard country. If it wasn't for the letters from home I would have gone mad long before this." The herdsman pulled out a packet of worn and often read letters from the inside of his canvas coat. "I finally made enough money to buy this small herd, which I had intended to sell in the markets in Helena. Here are the receipts from my purchase of these cattle." He handed over the proper bills of sale to the cowboys. "Now here is the last letter from my wife. In it she tells me how happy she will be to see me soon when I sell this herd. Here is a letter from my aged mother, who also looks forward to my homecoming. Here is a picture of my daughter. If you intend to kill me for a crime I am innocent of then go ahead, but I beg you to send these back to my family and tell them of what happened so they know I have not deserted them of my own free will. If you could find it in your hearts, could you please send them some of the money from the sale of this herd?"

The cowboys sat uneasily in their saddles. Most were looking down at the ground.

Finally one of them spoke.

"Hold on, stranger," he said. "Your letters and picture have done the trick for me and my friends. Give us your hand and be on your way. You can go free, but remember how lucky you are this day."

"I have a better idea," one of the cowboys said. "Let's buy his cattle here and now and let him go home to his family out east."

Money was exchanged and soon the herdsman was riding toward Helena to catch a stagecoach that would take him to the nearest railroad line. He had money in his pocket to start a new life back home. Watching him ride away was a band of smiling cowboys who had made a family whole again.

The Devil in Texas (Hispanic)

Much of Texas was at one time part of Mexican territory, and today it is home to many people of Spanish and Mexican heritage. This is one of their stories.

It was a hot day in Hell. The big devils and the little devils were all busy feeding the fires, making final preparations to give a warm reception to a politician, a student, and a banker who were arriving soon. A knock sounded on the door, and Satan, who was sitting on a throne of flames, sent one of his henchmen to see who it might be. In walked four men. One, who held a book filled with the names of folks who owed him favors, gave away his profession; the second held on to a wallet filed with money that wasn't his; the third exhibited an empty notebook. The three were men were terrified. The fourth did not appear a bit impressed by the fiery reception, but with the coolness of one accustomed to such things glanced around with a look of curiosity. He was an athletic sort of a man, wore a five gallon hat, chaps, and spurs, and played with a lariat he held in his hands. He seemed to be as much at home as the others were terrified. Before he was assigned any particular work, he walked to where a devil was shoveling coals, and taking the shovel from his hands, began to work. Satan was so much impressed that he paid no attention to the others but went to where the stranger was. He did not like this man's attitude at all. He liked to watch the agony on the face of the condemned, but here was this man as cool as a September morn. He went through the flames, over the flames, into the flames, and did not mind the heat at all. This was more than his Satanic Majesty could take. He commanded him to stop and listen to what he had to say. But the man would not listen and kept on working.

"I really would like to know something about you and where you come from," said the Devil.

"If that's the case," the stranger replied, "then I feel I must satisfy your curiosity. I am Pedro de Urdemanas by name. I have lived through the ages deceiving people. I trick them into believing my stories and they reward me with money. I have traveled the world living by my wits and the foolishness of others. As a gypsy and a horse trader in Spain, then as a soldier of fortune in the New World, I have managed to live without working. I have lived through the equatorial heat of the Amazon, the cold of the Andes, and the desert heat of the Southwest. I am immune to the heat and the cold, and really bask in the warmth of this place. I like it here."

The Devil was more impressed than ever and wanted to know more of this strange person. "Where was your home before you came here?" he asked.

"Oh, in the most wonderful land of all. I am sure you would love it. Have you ever been in Texas?"

The devil shook his head.

"Well, that's where I come from. It is a wonderful country."

"Really?" said the Evil One, "and what is it like?"

Pedro described the land in such glowing terms that the Devil was getting interested in seeing Texas with his own eyes. "And what's more," continued Pedro, "there is plenty of work for you down there. Lots of souls to harvest."

At this Satan cocked his ears, for if there was one thing he liked better than anything else it was to get more workers for his shops.

"But listen," the Devil confided, "you say there are many cows in Texas. Well, I have never seen one and wouldn't know what to do if I saw one."

"Don't worry about that. Both of you have horns and a tail. I am sure you and the cows will become very good friends."

After this comparison, Satan was eager to go to this strange land called Texas where cows lived. So early the next day before the Hell fires were even started, he set out for Texas. Since he usually found what he needed in the cities, he knew nothing of ranch life. Satan left for Texas dressed in the latest New York City style.

Finally, he set foot on a little prairie surrounded by thorny brush, near the lower Rio Grande. It was a hot day indeed. The sand that flew in whirlwinds was hotter than the flames of Hell. It burned the Devil's face and scorched his throat. His tongue was swollen. His temples throbbed with the force of a sledgehammer. As he staggered panting under the noonday sun, he saw a ray of hope. A muddy stream glided its way across a sandy bed. The Devil caught sight of a small plant bearing red berries. Here was what he most wished for—water and fresh berries to eat. He picked a handful of the ripest and freshest, and with the greediness of the starved put them all into his mouth. With a cry like the bellow of a bull he ducked his head in the stream. He was burning up. The heat that he was used to was nothing compared to the fire from chili peppers that erupted like a volcano in his mouth.

This made him even more curious about Texas. That afternoon he saw something that, had he not been a devil, would have reminded him of heaven. The ripest of purple figs were growing on a plant that was not a fig tree. "Here," thought Satan "is something I know I can eat. I remember seeing figs like these in the Garden of Eden." Hungrily he reached for one, but at the first bite he threw it away with a cry of pain, his mouth and tongue full of thorns from the prickly pear.

Later that same day, just before sunset, he heard the barking of dogs. He continued in that direction and soon he came to a ranch house. A group of men dressed like Pedro de Urdemanas were on horses and chasing some animals. The animals they were chasing must be the cows that Pedro had told him about. The big animals had horns and a tail. One of the mounted men threw a cow down by merely touching its tail. At least that's what it looked like to Satan; he didn't see the long rope in the cowboy's hands.

"I'd like to learn that trick so I can have fun with the other devils when I go back home."

He approached one of the *vaqueros* and said, "My friend, will you tell me what you did to make the lady cow fall?"

The cowboy looked at the city man in surprise, and with a wink at those around him replied, "Sure, just squeeze its tail as hard as you can."

Satan approached the nearest cow—an old gentle milk cow—gingerly, and squeezed its tail with all his might. Now, as all of you know, no decent cow will allow anyone, even the Devil himself, to squeeze her tail. She ceased chewing her cud, and, gathering all her strength in her hind legs, that cow shot out a kick that sent Satan whirling through the air and smashing into the side of the barn.

Slowly the Devil got up and dusted himself off as the cowboys hooted and hollered and laughed until they cried. Embarrassed and sore, the Devil ran hell-bound for home and did not stop until he got through the fiery gates. The first thing he did upon his arrival was to throw Pedro out of Hell. He would have nothing to do with the man who had been the cause of his humiliation in front of those Texas cowboys.

Since then Satan has never been back to Texas, and Pedro de Urdemanas still wanders through Texas visiting towns and ranches, always a smile on his face, the fun-loving *vaquero* he's always been.

The Gift of Rabbit (Caddo People)

At one time, Fox and Rabbit lived together. It was when the Earth Mother was very young.

One day the Great Mysterious was walking around in the form of a two-legged (a human being), enjoying the sweetness of creation, when Fox and Rabbit happened along. The three visited through the day, sharing stories, wisdom, nonsenses, and humor, and they became fast friends. They walked with no particular destination or direction—whichever way they turned seemed to be the right way. They munched on the ripe strawberries and huckleberries that grew in abundance along the path, accepting the hospitality of Mother Earth.

The warm midsummer morning sun was on its way to hot as the trio sat in the shade, resting. A cool breeze passed, refreshing them with a story that moved the needles and leaves in the surrounding trees and made the grasses and flowers nod their heads. The air filled with mountain music. The humming of insects' wings led the chorus of chirping birds and chattering squirrels, singing mice and whistling marmots.

The music was sweet, and soon all the people were dancing.

Young and old shared the dance ground:

> twirling, twisting, moving feet,
>
> round and round in steady beat,
>
> everyone was dancing!

They danced and danced and danced some more, until it was late afternoon.

People were still dancing when Fox, Rabbit, and their new friend walked up the path. No one knew who the Great Mysterious was, for that was the Great One's wish.

The three walked on, but stopped frequently to absorb the freshness of the world around them. The smells of pine and fir mixed with wildflowers and sweet berries lingered leisurely around them. Whenever they stopped someone always came along and another story would be shared—the hospitality of listening, extended to all.

This is the way it was until sunset, and directly opposite sunset was moonrise, full and round, big and bright.

"Stories, music, dancing, stories—what a grand way to spend the day," said Fox. "You honor us with your stories. We will honor you by passing them on."

"Please, join us for supper," said Rabbit invitingly, "our home is close by."

"It would be my pleasure," said the Great Mysterious. "Lead the way."

Rabbit and Fox lived in a cave high on the eastern slope of a mountain, with a view overlooking the valley to the mountains on the other side.

Fox built a small fire while Rabbit went straight to the kitchen—only to discover that there was no food.

"Oh, no!" thought Rabbit. "It's my day to gather."

Rabbit called Fox into the kitchen.

"I forgot to gather food today," said Rabbit. "We have nothing to feed our guest! Do you have one of your food bags stored somewhere?"

"I munched it out two days ago," replied Fox, "and I haven't replaced anything yet."

Rabbit and Fox sat drumming their fingers and thinking.

"We cannot let our company go away hungry," said Rabbit:

> "because my meat is good and sweet,
>
> I'll give myself to our guest to eat!"

Rabbit ran to the fire and jumped in.

The Great Mysterious reached quickly into the flames, and taking Rabbit in both hands, tossed Rabbit out of the cave.

"Why did you do that?" cried Fox, running to the mouth of the cave. "Rabbit was to be your food."

"Rabbit was hospitable and generous," replied the Great Mysterious, "and that will never be forgotten. Because Rabbit was willing to be my food, from now on Rabbit shall be a special part of the diet of the two-leggeds."

Fox and the Great Mysterious stood silent for a moment, basking in the moonglow. The night songs of Frog and Cricket could be heard rising from the valley, and somewhere in the distance, Fox's twin brother Coyote added a voice to the serenade.

"Rabbit will have to be cunning," observed Fox, "and plentiful, for the two-leggeds are always hungry."

"For this reason, Rabbit's population will increase rapidly, and will need the opportunity to do so. Therefore, Fox, tell the story to all and say this: that Rabbit is only to be consumed on this night and the three surrounding it, and this shall be the sign; when the full body of Rabbit jumps high in the night's sky, there will also be a moon, full and round, big and bright. That is where I have placed Rabbit for all time." The Great Mysterious raised a hand, gently pointing—inviting Fox to look. There, cradled in the full of the moon, was Rabbit. "This is my will."

Turning, the Great Mysterious said, "Remember, Fox, they are never to hunt Rabbit in the dark of the moon; that is Rabbit's time."

Rabbit's gift of sacrificial hospitality will not be forgotten, as long as the story is told and with each full moon it happens: we see Rabbit, and we remember.

Used with permission of Dayton Edmonds, Caddo storyteller.

Texas Glossary

Apache people: A Native American people found throughout the Southwestern desert country. The name is actually Zuni. The original name for the Apache tribe was "Ndee," which means "the people." Though they could not be warriors, girls learned how to ride and shoot and it was not uncommon for them to help protect their villages. In the old days the Apaches lived in wickiups, small houses about the size of a camp tent made of light wooden frames covered with brush mats or buffalo hide.

Caddo people: A Native American tribe who lived in the Arkansas/Texas area.

Comanche people: A Native American people who call themselves "Numinu," which means "the people." They lived in tepees made of buffalo hides. An entire Comanche village could break down their tepees and pack and be underway in less than an hour. The Comanche Nation stretched from Oklahoma across Texas and into New Mexico. The Comanche warriors were known as excellent horsemen.

Drought: An extended period of little or no rain when the underground water table gets seriously low.

Kiowa people: The English pronunciation of the tribal name "Gaigwu." The Kiowa's ancestral home covers parts of Texas, Oklahoma, New Mexico, and Colorado. As in many plains tribes, the women owned and the tepees and kept the family secure with cooking and child rearing while the men provided the food and protected the tribe.

Pedro: Often a trickster among the Hispanic people.

Texas: A state whose name comes from the Caddo people's word "taysha," which means "friends" or "allies." The capital is Austin.

Vaqueros: The Spanish term for cowboy or ranch hand.

Story Sources

American Fairy Tales

American Myths & Legends, Volumes 1 & 2

Art Thieme

Buying the Wind

The Corn Woman, Stories and Legends of the Hispanic Southwest

Coronado's Children: Tales of Lost Mines & Buried Treasures of the South West

Cowboy Songs and other Frontier Ballads

The Eagle and the Cactus: Traditional Stories from Mexico

The Folklore of Spain in the American Southwest

The Greenwood Library of American Folktales, Volume 3

Mexican Folktales from the Borderland

Mexican-American Folklore

Montezuma's Serpent & Other True Supernatural Tales of the Southwest

Myths & Legends of Our Own Land, Volumes 1 & 2

Myths & Tales of the Jicarilla Apache Indians

Outlaw Tales: Legends, Myths & Folklore from America's Middle Border

Stockings of Buttermilk

Tales from the American Frontier

Tales of Old-Time Texas

Texas Ghost Stories

Yankee Doodle's Cousins

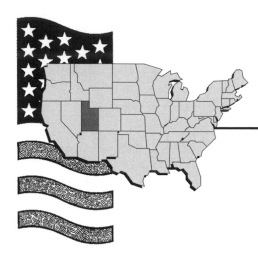

Utah

Utah became a state in 1896. Before European settlers came to this area it was and still is home to many Native American tribes. The story "The White Trail in the Sky" by the Shoshone is part of this heritage. Mountain men roamed the West before the great wave of immigrants and settlers moved from the east. "Jim Bridger and the Winter of 1830" is a traditional story, told here by folksinger and storyteller Art Thieme, about Utah winters. Members of the Church of Jesus Christ of Latter Day Saints moved to Utah to avoid the persecution they were experiencing in Illinois and other eastern states. "The Mormon Legend of the Gulls" depicts not only their hardship in the new land but also their faith. Utah was the meeting place for the Union Pacific and Central Pacific railroads and the beginning of a nation connected by steel. Every state seems to have a monster or creature or two lurking about, and Utah's lives in the bottom of Bear Lake.

The Mormon Legend of the Gulls
(Based on True Events)

The grain had sprouted early and had a rich color, which promised a needed good harvest. But before May had passed an unexpected pest put in its appearance in the guise of millions of large black crickets, which marched into the new fields of grain. (These were Mormon crickets, which are not true crickets, but related to the katydid. They have ornamental wings, but do not fly.) They devoured every blade of grain as they went, cutting day and night with huge appetites that left the fields bare and brown behind them. The men, women, and children came and dug holes, burying bushel after bushel of the pests, but this didn't seem to affect their numbers. Then ditches were ploughed around the fields and an effort was made to drown the crickets, but even greater numbers descended from the hills. Fire was tried, but even the flames and smoke didn't seem to keep the hungry insects off the crops. The people were exhausted and had run out of ideas to stop the invasion. They might as well try to stop the sun from rising or to try to stem the tide with their bare hands. They remembered the days of ancient Egypt's curse of locusts and felt that they were reliving that horror. If they could not defeat this indestructible pest, it meant starvation, not only to those already living in the Great Salt Lake valley, but to the thousands of men, women, and children who were traveling across the plains to join them. Their resourcefulness and their courage were worn down to the point of admitting defeat.

Then the miracle happened. Early one morning the people heard the shrill half scream of thousands of seagulls circling over the wheat fields. Soon the winged avengers landed and began devouring the crickets. Day after day the birds came and ate their fill, until every last cricket was eaten, and the crops of the Mormon pioneers were saved.

Those early Utah settlers held the lake sea gulls as sacred, and later they were protected by the state legislature.

Jim Bridger and the Winter of 1830
(as Told by Art Thieme)

One of my favorite stories has to do with a fellow named Jim Bridger. There are a lot of great tall tales about Bridger. He was one of the early members of the Ashley Expedition that left St. Louis in 1822 and headed up the Missouri River after furs. Later on in life he discovered—well, he was the first white man into the Great Salt Lake area, the first one to see the Great Salt Lake and tell people about it. And later on he was a guide for the U.S. Army, and the new recruits kind of made fun of Jim. They saw him as a rustic old has-been and they teased him a lot. So when Jim would tell them about things he'd seen, like a glass mountain, they would make fun of it and think he was lying and so Jim would expand on these stories. He became known as one of the great tall tale tellers. If you've ever been to Yellowstone, you know that out there's an entire cliff of obsidian—volcanic glass. So there is a glass mountain, but these guys, they said, "A glass mountain? How'd you find it—if it's made of glass, you couldn't see it, could you?" And Jim would say, "Well, I'd look along the base where the birds would run headlong into it and killed themselves. And then I'd feel for it. And there it would be, sure enough . . . . Of course you couldn't see it, but the dead birds would give it away." And Bridger told a story about taking a wagon train across the plains, and they were camped opposite a box canyon. His alarm clock story was a favorite one, told all around the West. They camped opposite this box canyon and at around eight o'clock at night when the sun was going down, he'd walk outside of the wagon train and yell, "Time to get up!" Eight hours later the echo would come back and wake everybody.

Tall tales were a way of dealing with hard times, and if you could laugh at nature it helped a lot. My favorite story about Jim Bridger had to do with the winter of 1830 in the valley of the Great Salt Lake. A thousand feet of snow fell that winter.

Trouble was, it all fell in one day.

Jim was sound asleep in his cabin, and when he woke up there was no sign of light in the cabin. The snow was way over the roof, of course—a thousand feet of snow. So he went back to sleep. He slept for about a week and a half and finally he woke up and said, "I think I've got enough rest. Think I better go check things out."

He got up and tried to push the door open (the door wouldn't open). He ate up all the food he had in the next few days, then he burned up all the wood he had, and burned up all the furniture. He was putting the last table leg on the fire and, realizing he was in quite a predicament, he happened to glance up the chimney as he was putting that last piece of wood on the fire and there was a spot of light—way, way up there, shining like a single star in a coal bin.

He was seeing daylight. He had melted a tunnel right up through that snow, and he was seeing daylight up way above the snowfall.

"Well," he said, "I better get my ax and cut some handholds." And he cut these handholds, and climbed and climbed and climbed until he finally got up top. His idea was to cut down a tree, and chop it into smaller pieces, and drop it down into the cabin to have firewood so he could keep himself warm. He hadn't thought about the fact that most of the trees would be under the snow, too.

He got up there, and there was no sign of any trees—except one lonesome pine way up on the left ridge. He trudged up to it and cut off some of the big lower branches and threw them down the tunnel to his cabin. Then he cut down the huge tree and let it slide into his valley, where he was going chop it into smaller pieces . . . . Trouble was, it didn't stop, it went right on up the other side, then teetered up there until it shot right back to where he'd cut it down. He sat up there for three hours, watching that tree go back and forth, back and forth. Finally he got fed up and went right back down into his cabin, got under a bearskin rug, and fell asleep listening to that tree tear overhead, counting the passes, *shoo-shoo—shooo-shooo—shooo-shooo.* It sounded like a freight train tearing through the valley over his head.

Well, he must've slept a long time or else it was a quick thaw, because when he woke up there was daylight streaming in through the windows. There were puddles of water on the floor where some of the snow had melted. He could hear the birds chirping and singing outside the cabin. He said, "Well, I better go out and check to see what this great snowfall and thaw has done to the countryside."

He pushed the door open, walked out into his yard, and almost fell down a chasm as deep as the Royal Gorge. It hadn't been there before.

"Well," said Jim. "I better climb on down there and explore."

So he climbed down that chasm and found some drowned rabbits from the meltwater, and since he hadn't eaten in quite a while he picked them up, figuring he'd make a stew later. He was walking around and happened to glance around a boulder—a bit of motion had caught his eye. He walked back there, and there was a twig going about two inches this way, two inches that way, two inches this way, two inches that way. That was all that was left of the tree he had cut down. It had dug that entire canyon, and worn itself down to a little twig.

"Well," said Jim, "I always needed a good pine toothpick."

He picked it up and he took it with him.

A few years later my great-great-grandfather was riding with Bridger—they were doing some scouting for the U.S. Army—and they happened to be camping. At supper they were eating some buffalo meat cooked over a fire, when my relative got a piece of that meat stuck in his tooth and had to borrow that toothpick from Jim. Somehow he never did give it back, and we've passed it down in our family. *This* is *that* toothpick . . . . Tall tale tellers always have to have proof, you know.

Used with permission.

The Golden Spike (a True Story)

The railroad crisscrossed America in the nineteenth century and the intercontinental railroad would be the last great link in that chain. Working westward the Union Pacific moved from Omaha, Nebraska, while moving eastward the Central Pacific Railroad started from Sacramento, California. The muscle of Irish immigrants moved the Union Pacific railroad track, while mostly Chinese immigrants built the Central Pacific. Each faced hardship and danger, and each persevered, moving toward their meeting place at Promontory Point, Utah. The Central Pacific faced the challenge of building their stretch of the track through the mountains of the Sierra Nevada and Rocky Mountain ranges. The Chinese workers employed the same techniques that they had used in China, suspending workers from baskets over the sides of cliffs to chip away at the mountain and place explosive charges into the rock face to build the countless tunnels. The Irish workers faced the danger of increased Native American opposition to the "iron horse," and their attacks slowed the railroad's progress the deeper the tracks drove into Indian Territory.

Finally ,after the Union Pacific had laid 1,085 miles across the prairies and the Central Pacific had laid 690 miles through the rugged mountains, they met in Utah. A golden spike was driven into the last tie that secured the two rail lines, and two engines, the Jupiter from the Central Pacific line and Engine Number 119 from the Union Pacific, slowly edged forward until they touched each other, and the United States was finally connected from the Atlantic Ocean to the Pacific Ocean, connected by immigrants from Asia and Europe, connected by hardship and dreams.

The White Trail in the Sky (Shoshone)

No one can remember any more exactly how it came about that the black bear Wakini overpowered the strong grey grizzly Wakinu. The black bears say that Wakini was just feeding on the contents of an anthill when Wakinu came up to him and quite rudely stuck his paw in as well. It was a rude thing to do, and one that Wakini could not ignore.

A great fight ensued, with grey and black hairs flying on every side. Wakini was, of course, in the right, for no animal may ever touch another's food without permission.

Wakinu thus received a just punishment; but that was by no means all. Like a defeated warrior, he had to leave his tribe forever.

Wakinu wailed and lamented, but the Indian laws are inexorable. And so he had to go, wading through familiar streams, taking a last look at the familiar pines, and saying farewell to the valley he had lived in all of his life.

He could not see for tears, and so he failed to notice that he was making straight for the Snow Country. Suddenly he fell into a deep snowdrift. Clambering out with difficulty, he wiped his eyes and took a look round. In every direction there was nothing but white, unblemished snow everywhere.

"I'm sure to find a trail soon," the bear said to himself, and set out on his way once more. His grey coat had turned completely white with the snow, ice, and fierce wind.

But Wakinu took no notice of anything and walked on and on, until he reached a strange land in which a deep, frosty night reigned supreme. Somewhere in the far distance the gale could still be heard, yet here there was no sound but that made by his own footfalls on the frozen snow.

Above him glowed the night sky, while not far away, on the very fringe of the Snow Country and the heavens, a broad white trail could be seen ascending the sky.

Wakinu ran, hardly touching the ground, mesmerized by that beautiful trail. Another leap and he found himself in the air, shaking the snow from his coat; light as a feather, he soared up and up.

The animals who were awake that night saw, for the first time, a wide white trail in the sky, and on it a grey bear running joyously through the night sky.

"Wakinu has found the Bridge of the Dead Souls and is on his way to the Eternal Hunting Grounds," said the wise black bear Wakini.

And the grizzly really did go to the Eternal Hunting Grounds. The only thing he left behind was the snow he had shaken from his coat. And that white snow is there in the sky to this day.

The Europeans speak about the Milky Way, but every Indian knows that that is the way to the Eternal Hunting Grounds, the path taken by the grey grizzly Wakinu, and the stars are the snowflakes he shook from his coat.

Used with permission of the Shoshone-Bannock Tribes.

The Creature That Waits

The newly arrived settlers were going to town in their wagons when they saw something streaking across the water. They stopped and stared as the beast swam faster than any horse could run, leaving a plume of water in its wake. When they got to town they excitedly told their story to anyone who would listen, but not many people really seemed that surprised. Most of the folks who had been in the area for a while had already heard or in some cases seen the Bear Lake Monster, so one more sighting was not news.

The Native Americans who lived or visited the area had told early Mormon settlers about the creature that lived in Bear Lake. They told the settlers that they never bathed or went near the water unless absolutely necessary. They were warned that the beast could easily kill and swallow a man. It wasn't long before the new settlers also started to see the monster. First reports say that the creature was as long as ninety feet with small legs or flippers at its side that propelled it through the water. Its mouth could swallow a person whole and it appeared snakelike. Reports started to come in that more than one creature had been seen, a smaller one following the bigger one, and another following that one. Was there an entire family of these animals living in the depths of Bear Lake?

Some people described it as walruslike, while others said it was more like a dinosaur. Reports began to vary as to its size, ranging from 40 feet up to 200 feet long. One fact that seemed consistent was that the creature was fast in the water.

The creature has found its way into folklore as one of Pecos Bill's adversaries in one of the popular stories about the Western cowboy hero. Stories are also told about how one farmer caught a small beast, perhaps one of the monster's young, but no proof exists to back up this tale. Sightings still occur, with the latest as recent as 2002.

Is there a monster living in Bear Lake, perhaps a relative of Scotland's famous Loch Ness monster, Nessie, haunting the waters? Is it some creature left over from ancient days when Lake Bonneville covered the entire basin, or is it a legend that has grown with time and imagination? Could it be a hoax by the tribes that lived in the area to scare away the new settlers from their lands? Whatever it is it makes a visit to Bear Lake an exciting adventure. Who knows, you might be the next person to see the Monster of Bear Lake.

Utah Glossary

Black crickets: Insects belonging to the family Gryllidae that are related to both grasshoppers and katydids.

Gulls: Water birds most commonly associated with the sea, though there are some found on large lakes. The gulls mentioned in this story migrate to the Great Salt Lake in the spring and leave for the south when the weather turns cold.

Jim Bridger: A mountain man, guide, and explorer who roamed the mountains of the West trapping and hunting in the early days of the European expansion. He spoke French, Spanish, and several Indian languages as well as his native English. He was born in 1804 and died on his farm near St. Louis in 1881. Fort Bridger, Wyoming, and Bridger, Montana, are named after the great storyteller.

Mormon: The popular name for a member of the Church of Jesus Christ of Latter Day Saints.

Shoshone people: A Native American people who were found in Idaho, Montana, Nevada, and Utah. The more eastern and northern Shoshone had a horse culture dependent on following herds of buffalo and elk, whereas the western and southern band relied more on smaller animals and roots and berries and often didn't have horses.

Utah: A state that took its name form the Native American tribe the Utes. The capital is Salt Lake City.

Story Sources

American Indian Tales & Legends

American Myths & Legends, Volumes 1 & 2

Art Thieme

Ballads & Songs from Utah

Buying the Wind

Cowboy Songs and other Frontier Ballads

The Greenwood Library of American Folktales, Volume 3

Montezuma's Serpent & Other True Supernatural Tales of the Southwest

Myths & Legends of Our Own Land, Volumes 1 & 2

The Parade of Heroes

Shoshone-Bannock Tribes

Tales from the American Frontier

A Treasury of Western Folklore

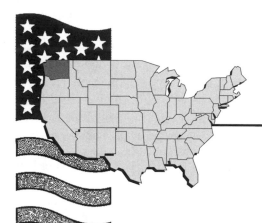

Washington

Washington, which became the forty-second state in 1889, is home to several Native American tribes, including the Spokane and Quinalt peoples.

Included in this chapter is a fanciful version of how Paul Bunyan became involved in creating Puget Sound, "Paul Bunyan and Puget Sound." In "The Gooey Duck" we see the age-old story of "never telling the truth to strangers" turned on its head. Washington, because of its position on the Pacific Coast of the United States, has a large Asian population, represented here by a traditional Korean story, "The Fountain of Youth." When the volcano Mount St. Helen's erupted in 1980, stories circulated about a lady in white who tried to warn people of the coming disaster. Her story is included here.

Paul Bunyan and Puget Sound

Now Paul Bunyan had logged his way across the country and was working the forests up the Columbia River. He and his men had been working hard and had harvested a good load of timber by the end of the season. One day when he got back from the river after sending another raft on down the Columbia to the sawmills he had a visitor waiting for him at the camp. Mr. Rainier had come to see Paul. Now they talked about the price of timber and they talked about the weather and they drank some coffee and talked about the weather some more, until Rainier finally got down to what he had come to Paul's camp for in the first place.

"Paul, I am part of a group pf businessmen who have a contract to build the bay and sound off the coast to make a safe and big harbor for the state of Washington. We had two years to finish this project and now we only have about two months left, and we've hardly made a dent. We were wondering if you could help us?"

"Well," said Paul, "logging is winding down this time of year, so I guess I could come on down and take a look at the situation and see what I can do for you."

Now Rainier and Puget and Hood and Elliot and a few other powerful men had a contract to build this bay, but they were so far behind schedule they knew they could never finish on time and that the government would never give them the money if it wasn't done on time. People back east were asking for progress reports, but there wasn't any progress, so they did the only thing they could think of and sent Rainier to ask for Paul's help.

When Paul arrived he took one look at the work they'd done and just shook his head. "Do you have a plow? Do you have a scraper?" he asked. The engineers and construction men said no. Paul decided to send for a plow and scraper that would be just right for his beautiful Blue Ox Babe. He sent all the way to the steel mills in Pittsburgh. It took all the steel that all the mills in Pittsburgh could make in two months, and it took sixteen freight engines to haul it across country on a special flatbed railroad car. People at every town along the railroad line came out to see the giant plow and scraper that Paul had designed for the job.

When the plow and scraper finally got to Seattle, Paul hitched the plow up to Babe's harness. The plow was enormous, but still it could only plow about forty feet deep and wasn't big enough for the job. Paul thought and thought about what he could use to dig out this bay and sound, when he finally got an idea.

"Why haven't I thought of this before, Babe?" he said to his Blue Ox. "How did all those lakes and rivers and bays get made back east and in the Midwest? They were made by ice by a glacier, that's how. What we need is to go up to Alaska and get a glacier and bring it down here where we can use it to dig out the bay in no time at all."

Paul and Babe traveled up to Alaska and looked around until they found the biggest glacier. They brought it back down to Washington and hitched it up to Babe's harness and began to plow. They didn't need a scraper because the glacier just smoothed out everything as it moved along behind Babe. There were a couple rough spots where Paul had to do a little pulling and tugging himself to help Babe out, but soon the sound was almost finished.

One afternoon while they were moving that glacier a lady passing by with a pink parasol spooked Babe. It was the first umbrella that Babe had ever seen, and Babe hated the color pink. Babe took off, and before Paul could put on the brakes Babe had dug out Hood's Canal.

Now all that dirt had to be put somewhere. The businessmen had another contract to build a something for Tacoma. They told Paul where to put the dirt and soon a mountain started to rise on the horizon. By the time the sound and bay were finished Mount Rainier was towering over the landscape.

Now the people of Bellingham asked Paul if he could come up to their city and while he still had the glacier with him dig a bay for them, too. Well, Paul dug out their bay and made a mountain for them too that's still there, Mount Baker.

Now when the sound was all finished there was a bit of controversy as to the name. Some folks wanted it named Whidby Sound, while others, including Paul, thought it should be named after Mr. Puget. Well, the settlers at Whidby were so mad when they finally called it Puget Sound that they wanted the entire thing filled back up. Paul got so angry that he took a shovel and dug a trench across the land and the water from the sound rushed in and cut off Whidby Peninsula from the mainland.

When it was finally time to pay Paul for digging Puget Sound the businessmen had a really hard time parting with the money they had promised him. They came to Paul and started hemming and hawing and saying that costs went over budget and that they really didn't have the money they had promised him and could he take less.

Paul never said a word. He just picked up his shovel and started throwing dirt back into the sound. As they watched the men knew that Paul could fill the whole place up in no time at all. They ran back and got the rest of the money and paid Paul exactly what they had promised. All that dirt that Paul had thrown back into the sound became the San Juan Islands. Even though it's hard for some of the ships to get around them, they do look nice now, all covered with trees and berry bushes.

Paul went back to being a lumberjack after that adventure, and I think that he was happiest in the woods with Babe and his men. It's where he belonged.

The Gooey Duck

No matter where you live, there is always that one local legend or tall tale or yarn that the folks who live there have to tell a stranger when they come to visit. Most of the time, the unsuspecting stranger catches on and everyone has a good laugh. Most of the time.

The folks in Washington never seem to take themselves too seriously, at least that's what's been said about them. Its no surprise that a group of older men whose most active morning sport was sitting on a bench near the wharf just happened to catch an unsuspecting visitor from "back east" as he strolled along the water's edge.

"Young man," one of them asked, "have you ever hunted a gooey duck?"

"A what kind of duck?" said the young man.

"Well, I guess the proper name might be a geoduck, but around here we call them gooey ducks. You've never heard of them?" another of the old-timers asked.

"How are they caught?" asked the stranger.

"Well, you hunt them with a shovel and a length of stove pipe. You see a gooey duck isn't a duck at all but a very large type of clam that's found on the beaches around here. Its got a neck about four or five feet long and a shell body about six or eight inches in diameter. They can weigh in at about eight or nine pounds sometimes."

The young man had figured out by this time that the old men were pulling his leg, and he decided to get into the spirit of the fun. "Maybe I'll get a shovel and a piece of stove pipe and join you gentlemen tomorrow morning and we can hunt some gooey ducks together."

"Now be sure to be here early," said one of the gentlemen of the bench. "You see the clam burrows into the sand at low water. It'll dig four or five feet down if its neck is long enough. That's why you need the stove pipe."

"After we catch some of these gooey ducks, what do we do with them?" he asked.

"Well, you chop the neck up and put it into chowder. It's awfully good in chowder. The rest of the clam you can steam or even cut up into steaks if you like. Now the tide is out about 5:00 a.m., so be here early tomorrow. We'll meet you down on the beach right over there." The man pointed a few yards away.

"Sure thing," said the stranger. "I'll be there for sure."

But you know the next morning the young man didn't show up to hunt the gooey ducks. I guess he thought that the whole thing was just so unbelievable and that the old men were just playing a trick on him. Too bad, because they were waiting for him at 5:00 a.m. down at the beach just like they said they would be. You see everything that they had said was true. Too bad, he missed a great meal later on.

The Fountain of Youth (Korean)

Washington is home to many people of Asian ancestry. This story, of Korean origins, was brought to this country by Korean immigrants.

Once in a village deep in the mountains there lived an unusually kind, elderly couple. Since they had no children to help them in their old age, they cut wood and sold it to others in the village. Their neighbors admired the way the old couple patiently accepted their lot in life and the kindness they showed toward everyone they met.

Near the humble couple lived another elder of the village who was childless, but unlike them, this man was a greedy and spiteful person. No one in the village except the old couple had a kind word to say about him.

One day when the kind old man was cutting firewood in the forest he heard the sound of a bird singing. He had never heard a song more beautiful and, pausing in his work, he sat down and listened as the bird serenaded him.

Much to his disappointment, his musical friend soon flew away. But the old man, hearing its song not far away, followed the bird. When he reached the tree where it had perched, it flew away again. Over and over, the old man followed the bird only to have it fly away singing and enticing him to follow. Finally, after hours of following the bird, the old man saw that it had perched on a tree that stood near a clear spring. The bird was singing more beautifully than ever.

The old man sat down under the tree to listen, and this time the bird did not fly away but sat, happily singing to its new friend. The old man, feeling thirsty, knelt by the pool of water and drank. The water was cool and sweet, and the old man drank his fill.

Soon he was very relaxed, the way he felt when he was with friends and they had just had some good rice wine. At once he began to feel drowsy, so he lay down his head and fell into a deep sleep.

When he awoke the sun was setting and darkness was creeping its way into the forest. He remembered following the bird and its song and drinking from the spring. He hurried toward home and soon came to the place where he had been cutting wood. It seemed as if his body was lighter and he noticed that his arms and legs felt stronger. He picked up the frame of firewood that he had cut and was surprised by how light it was. With a spring in his step, he followed the path toward his home.

Meanwhile, the old man's wife had become worried when he didn't return before dusk. She imagined accidents or wild beasts or thieves and soon she was beside herself with fear. She went next door.

"Neighbor," she said, "my husband has not returned from the forest and I am so worried. Could he have had an accident or fallen prey to wild animals or brigands?"

Instead of helping his neighbor, the old man simply dismissed her. "It's late and he probably was devoured by wolves or a tiger."

The old woman asked if he would go with her into the forest and help her look for her husband, but the thoughtless man refused and told her it was a waste of time. She went back to her cottage and was preparing to go alone in search of her husband when she heard him whistling as he often did as he neared his home. She rushed out to meet him and saw him walking through the darkness, his wood on his back.

Once they were inside and she saw him in the light, she couldn't believe her eyes. She stammered and tried to speak, but nothing came out of her mouth.

"What is it, dear one?" cried her husband. "What is the matter with you?"

"Is it really you?" she asked.

"Of course it's me. Why do you ask?"

"You are so young. There's not a single wrinkle on your face," she cried in amazement.

The old man put his hands up to his face and felt his skin. It was true. "So that's why I felt so strong."

"How did this happen to you?"

Her husband told her about the bird and its song, and how he followed it through the forest. He told her about drinking at the spring and falling into a deep sleep.

"That must be it," he said. "The water from the spring tasted so cool and sweet, and I felt so good after drinking it."

His wife looked up at him and said, "Everyone will laugh at us, an old woman and a young man living together. Do you think the water might do the same for me, husband?"

The next morning the two of them went into the forest to find the magic water. When they found the pool the old woman knelt beside it and drank her fill. Almost at once she began to grow younger. Soon she was a young woman, full of life and strength just like her husband. Filled with relief and joy, the couple walked back to the village.

When their greedy old neighbor saw them and heard about the magic that had made them young again, he was filled with jealousy. When they told him about the spring and where to look for it, he immediately set off to find it.

All afternoon the couple watched for their neighbor's return. When it grew late, they decided to go and look for him. As they neared the pool they heard the sound of a baby crying. As the spring came into view they saw the infant lying in the grass next to the magic waters.

"It must be our ill-tempered neighbor," the man cried. "He was so anxious to be young again. He must have had too much of the water."

Together, the couple laughed at what had happened.

Then, suddenly, the wife turned to her husband. "What about this baby?" she said. "We can't just leave it in the woods, and besides, we are in some way responsible for what has happened."

Smiling, her husband replied, "Let's take the infant home and raise him as our own."

"A wonderful idea," replied the wife.

The couple, now young and strong, worked harder than ever and through the years their child grew to be kind and caring, just like his parents.

A Warning (an Urban Legend)

The young couple was driving up Interstate 5 in Washington when they saw a woman dressed in white standing at the side of the road waving hopefully at them. The couple didn't normally pick up hitchhikers, but they pulled off the road and stopped, wondering if she needed assistance. She told them that she was stranded. The couple offered her a ride to the next town and thanking them for stopping she got into the back seat. They had barely gotten back on the road when she started to talk to them.

"You need to be careful soon," she said in a low voice as if she was telling them a secret. "The mountain is going to erupt soon, and when it does you have to be far away. In mid-May the whole top of the volcano is going to blow apart. It will be horrible, horrible. I know it will. Please tell me you'll stay away from there in May." The woman began to cry.

The young folks tried to calm her down, but it seemed the more they tried to reassure her the more frantic she got until the young woman turned around in her seat to take her hand and to talk to her gently. She never uttered a word, for the back seat was empty. They had not stopped or even slowed down during the whole time since she had entered the car, but the woman was gone. Windows closed, doors shut, and the back seat totally empty.

Who was this woman dressed in white? Was she a ghost who had come to warn those who took pity on strangers? Was she Pele, the goddess of Hawaii, come to test her mettle against the volcanoes of the mainland? Or was she a messenger who had warned others down through the centuries? Perhaps she had warned the people she met on the road to Pompeii or Krakatoa, too.

Washington Glossary

Geoduck: Panopea abrupta. It is a very large saltwater clam with a very long siphon or neck. It is edible and is found on the beaches at low tide.

Krakatoa: A volcano that erupted in August 1883, one of the most violent volcanic eruptions in modern history, estimated to be four times more powerful than the biggest atom bomb ever built. Official estimates of 36,000 killed are probably low, and some place the death toll at more than 100,000.

Paul Bunyan: A fictional character that was featured in many lumberjack folktales.

Pompeii: One of two cities that were totally destroyed by the eruption of Mt. Vesuvius in AD 79. The other town was Herculaneum. A total of more than 30,000 people were killed during the nineteen-hour eruption.

Quinalt people: A coastal tribe that fished and hunted. They lived in longhouses. They called the red cedar "the tree of life" because it provided logs for their canoes, planks for their longhouses, bark for their clothing, and much more.

Spokane people: A Salish-speaking people who lived along the Spokane River. They were hunters and fishermen.

Washington: A state that was named after the first president, George Washington. The capital is Olympia.

Story Sources

American Myths & Legends, Volumes 1 & 2

Cowboy Songs and other Frontier Ballads

Ghost Stories from the Pacific Northwest

The Greenwood Library of American Folktales, Volume 4

Haboo: Lushootseed Literature in English

Heroes, Outlaws, & Funny Fellows of American Popular Tales

Indian Legends of the Pacific Northwest

Myths & Legends of Our Own Land, Volumes 1 & 2

The Parade of Heroes

A Treasury of Western Folklore

Yankee Doodle's Cousins

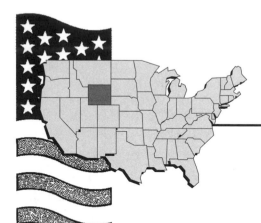

Wyoming

Wyoming became the forty-fourth state in 1890. One of its earliest European explorers to come to Wyoming was Jim Bridger. He brought the stories of the western mountains to those "back east," but no one believed him so he started to tell them tall tales, some of which are told here. Many Native American people call Wyoming home, including the Crow, the Shoshone, and the Northern Cheyenne; they are represented here by a story from the Shoshone people. Nellie Ross became the first woman elected as a governor of a state in the United States and went on to a long career in public service. Children often became separated from their families due to illness, attacks by Native American bands, and just the "wandering off" that most children do. "The White Mustang and the Lost Child" is a beautiful legend from the days of the early settlers as they crossed the mountains and prairies. The chapter ends with a Jim Bridger story about a memorable fight in the mountains and an unexpected outcome.

The White Mustang and the Lost Child

The family moved across the flat plains slowly, their wagon loaded with all the possessions they could carry from their old home in the east. Their three daughters sat on top of the bedding, which was laid over the furniture that was piled up in the back of the wagon. Mary, the youngest, was so tired of being bumped and jostled and cooped up in the wagon. She begged her parents to let her ride on their old mare, which followed the wagon, loaded down with sacks of corn meal, grain, and seed. They finally gave in and tied her to the mare in between the sacks. Now Mary could watch the scenery and have the wind in her hair and the sun on her face and feel just a little more free.

As they traveled along they came to a stream and the wagon got stuck in the mud. As her father tried to coax the mules into pulling the wagon out, Mary's mare wandered off a bit to eat some fresh grass that grew along the side of the stream. Mary fell asleep. When she woke up she was moving so fast she felt as if she was on a comet soaring through the sky. The old mare was galloping along, following a beautiful white mustang. The white horse galloped along as if leading the mare, enticing her to follow him. They traveled until they came to a small, hidden valley covered in grass, a small stream crisscrossing it.

The valley was home to a herd of wild horses that all rode up to greet the white mustang and inspect the visitors. They sniffed at Mary and at the bags filled with grain and corn meal. They began to bite at the ropes that held the sacks and their teeth came so close to the little girl's legs, which were still tied to the mare, that she became frightened and began to cry. The huge white stallion moved close to her and drove the other horses away. He carefully bit the ropes that held her to the mare and then gently lifted her off the back of the mare, holding on to her dress with his teeth. He set her under a tree near the stream and then set the corn meal bags next to her. Mary was so hungry that she opened the sacks and ate the corn meal uncooked. When she did that the other horses came up and looked at her so mournfully that she began to give each one a handful of meal. They took it gently from her hand, and Mary and her new friends had a picnic there under the tree in the valley of the wild mustangs. The horses stayed with her all day, and when the sun set they wandered off to find a safe place to spend the night. All but the white mustang, which stood near Mary all night as she curled up under the tree and slept.

When the sun came up in the morning the girl woke to the muzzle of the old mare as she quietly pushed against Mary's face. Mary realized how much she wanted to see her family, and she tried to get on the back of the old mare. She was too short, and she stood there and cried. The white mustang walked over and again grabbed the back of her dress and lifted her onto the back of the mare. The white stallion snorted at the mare and then turned and raced out of the valley and across the endless prairie. Mary held on for dear life. There were no ropes tying her to the horse, and she was so afraid that she might fall off. She was so tired she thought she couldn't go on any more, when she saw the white top of her family's covered wagon.

Her father had searched all the day before and was just about to go out again and start his search once more when the mare slowly walked into their camp. The white mustang stood at the top of the hill and watched as Mary's family embraced her. Mary turned from them for a moment and waved at the white stallion. He tossed his head and galloped off, a white streak across the vast prairie.

The Rainbow Snake (Shoshone)

A long time ago it was so hot that the air shimmered with the heat. The lakes and rivers dried up, and the plants withered, and the trees lowered their branches in defeat. The people knew that if the drought continued they would all perish.

"The game is gone and the water has disappeared," they cried. "The plants are all dying, and soon we will follow them."

A small snake heard their distress and crawled out from his hiding place and spoke to the people. "I can help you," the snake said. "I have great powers. I don't want you to die. Please, all you have to do is to throw me up into the sky."

One of the shamans said, "But you will fall down and be killed."

The snake laughed and replied, "No, I won't fall back down. I will hold on with my scales, and I will use them to scratch the rain and snow off the sky meadows and you will have water again."

Another shaman said, "But you are so small."

"I can stretch myself across the sky from one horizon to the other. Please just throw me up into the sky and watch what I can do for you."

The snake coiled itself up and the first shaman picked up the small snake and hurled it with all his strength high into the sky. As the snake flew into the air he uncoiled himself and grew longer and longer and longer, until at last his tail and his head curled back toward the earth and his body arched high into the sky. He began to scrape off the blue ice that clung to the sky meadows.

As he scraped the little snake changed color from red to yellow to green and blue and to purple. The ice in the sky meadows melted and raindrops began to fall to the earth.

Life came back to the earth. Water rushed through the riverbeds and filled up the lakes. The animals returned and plants sprouted anew. Roses bloomed, and the trees lifted their branches up to the sky as if they were thanking the small snake.

The rainbow is the sign that the small snake sends the people after it has scraped the ice from the sky meadows to send us the water of life.

Used with permission of the Shoshone-Bannock Tribes.

Nellie Ross, Political Pioneer (a True Story)

Nellie Davis Tayloe was born in Missouri. Her family moved to Kansas. While visiting family in Tennessee she met a young shopkeeper, William Ross, and fell in love. William's dream was to move west and open up a law practice so the young couple moved to Cheyenne, Wyoming, where he became a successful lawyer. He became very active in the Democratic Party and ran for several offices, always losing in the heavily Republican state. In 1922 his luck changed and he won the race for governor by appealing to the progressive wings in both parties. After about a year and a half in office William Ross died from complications after surgery. A special election was held, and Nellie Ross was nominated by the Democrats to run for her husband's office. Even though Nellie refused to campaign, she still won the race easily and became the first woman governor in the history of the United States. She continued her husband's progressive reforms and called for tax cuts; laws protecting children, women, and miners; and assistance for farmers in financial trouble. She called for Wyoming to ratify a federal law prohibiting child labor. She also called for the continuation of Prohibition laws that banned the making, sale, and distribution of alcohol. When she ran for reelection she was narrowly defeated. Nellie stayed active in politics and in 1933 President Franklin Roosevelt appointed her as the first woman to direct the U.S. Mint. She served as director of the Mint for twenty years. After she retired she traveled and spoke and wrote articles on social issues. She died in 1977 at the age of 101.

If They Won't Believe the Truth, Then...

Jim Bridger was a mountain man and a traveler in the early days of European exploration of the west. When he would encounter folks from "back east" they would often scoff at his stories and say he was the biggest liar that ever lived. Well, if they wouldn't believe the truth, Jim Bridger would make sure his tall tales were even more romantic and outrageous. When he first saw Yellowstone he saw geysers that would shoot out of the ground and rise to heights of seventy feet or more. He saw geysers that erupted so regularly that you could set your watch to them if you happened to carry one. He saw hot springs that could cook your meat in a matter of minutes. He saw waterfalls that cascaded down mountains and crystal pools of water. He was one of the first if not the first European to encounter the beauty and wonders of Yellowstone, but most folks wouldn't believe him. That's when the real tall tales started to be told.

One day Jim was out hunting and came across the trail of an elk. After what seemed a short time he saw the creature. Bridger took careful aim and fired at the giant elk, but nothing happened. His gun fired, but the elk just stood there unharmed as if it hadn't heard the noise of the rifle. He fired again, but once more the elk just stood there grazing as if nothing had happened. It was if Jim and his rifle were not even near the animal. After two or three more attempts Jim was so angry and frustrated that he took his rifle in his hands like a club and rushed toward the beast. Suddenly he crashed into a wall, a wall that he couldn't see. It was a mountain of solid glass that stood between Jim and that elk. The elk was about twenty-five miles away, but that glass mountain acted like a telescope and made the elk look only a couple hundred yards from where Jim was standing.

Jim would tell "newcomers" about the wonderful glass mountain but then would shake his head sadly and say, "The shame of the thing is that it would be a waste of time to take you there because you'd never be able to see it." He said that the only time you could find it was when the birds flew into it at sunset and their dazed bodies were flapping around at the foot of the invisible mountain.

Jim knew the country better than anyone except the Native Americans who had lived there for generations. He found places that suited his odd sense of humor. One day he had to be up early, so before he went to sleep he walked over to the edge of a canyon and shouted out "Get up!" Early the next morning a loud, "Get up!" resounded through the camp and woke every one. It was Jim's echo that bounced off the canyon wall a hundred miles away and finally made its way back to him. The perfect alarm clock, you might say.

Jim told a story about when he was camping once near the edge of a deep gorge. In horror his friends watched as he rode his horse right off the edge of the cliff. But Jim didn't fall to his death; instead he rode calmly across the gorge to the other side. He told them later that he had discovered the "petrified" air that existed between the two edges of the gorge and allowed him to travel safely from one side to another. Jim also had a favorite place to go fishing. A hot pool discharged into a deep lake, and the upper three or four feet of the water was boiling hot while the bottom of the lake was cold, as are most mountain lakes. Jim would toss his bait into the deep part of the lake, hook his fish, and bring it out slowly through the boiling hot water. By the time he finally had landed his trout, it was already cooked just the way he liked it.

Jim told stories about an entire mountain and valley that had been cursed by a Crow medicine man. The mountain and everything on it and in the valley were turned to stone. The flowers were beautiful crystals, frozen in their flower shape and color but solid stone. The animals and trees and every living thing in that valley and on that mountain were petrified. Birds are caught in flight and suspended as beautiful soaring crystals, hanging in the air and catching sunlight and moonlight both. Even the light of the sun, moon, and stars is petrified in a solid world of lighted stone.

Jim Bridger was a storyteller. He was a man who saw the West as few have ever seen it and kept most of its beautiful stories to himself. Let the folks "back east" have the tall tales; Jim had the real West.

The Duel in the Mountains
(Retold by Dan Keding)

It was a rendezvous in the mountains, a gathering of mountain men. They came together to swap their stories and exchange information about the best places to hunt and trap and which areas were getting too popular with settlers. The men showed each other prize pelts that they were on their way with to trading outposts. They swapped each other for knives and guns and most of all, stories. Now everyone knew that Jim Bridger was the best of the mountain storytellers, and as the evening gathered around the men they drew close to the campfire and listened. A few of the men told a story or two, but they were just priming the pump so Jim could get started. After a long pause that followed one story they heard a familiar voice speaking from the dark side of the circle.

"Well boys, I'm here to tell you it has been one scary year," began Bridger. "I was up in the mountains and I was set upon by a band of Indians. They were determined to have me, and they chased me without stopping for over a week. I had to start a campfire on the saddle of my horse just to make myself a bit of breakfast and have a cup of coffee. We raced on until we came to a canyon that spanned a river. I tell you the drop from the edge of that canyon to the bottom must have been at least three or four miles deep. Knowing that if I turned around I'd be a dead man, I just closed my eyes and spurred my horse forward. Wouldn't you know it, boys, but completely by accident I had found the famous canyon with reverse gravity. Things fall up instead of down, and since my horse and I were so heavy we just floated on over to the other side of the canyon's rim. All but one of the Indians chasing me gave up at this point. One brave, though, just kept on following me, and we raced on for another three or four days until our horses grew a bit tired. We finally took aim and we shot each other's horse out from under the other man and both of us tumbled to the ground. Then the fight commenced. It was bowie knife against tomahawk, and it was a bloody affair. We fought for two straight days. Whenever I thought I was winning he just roared back, and whenever he thought he was getting the best of me I charged to meet him. I tell you he was the strongest, most skilled, and bravest man I have ever fought. Finally, my foot caught in the roots of an old tree and I fell to the ground, losing my knife. I stared up at that fierce warrior, who stood over me with his tomahawk raised and then . . . ." Bridger paused and looked around the campfire. Finally one man, new to the mountains, said, "What happened then, Jim?"

Jim looked across the flames and in a sad and quiet voice said, "Well boys, he killed me."

There was a long pause and then the laughter rolled from the men and into the woods and across the mountains and valleys. Jim Bridger had proved again that he was the greatest of storytellers.

Wyoming Glossary

Cheyenne people: A Plains tribe originally found throughout Colorado and Wyoming. The mothers used cradleboards, like modern backpacks, to carry their infants on their backs. Before they became horse people they were farmers, but after they acquired horses they followed the buffalo herds in a more nomadic lifestyle, living in tepees.

Crow people: A Native American people who called themselves the "Apsaalooke" (pronounced opp-sah-loh-kay), which meant the bird people. An anomaly among Native American tribes, on rare occasions a Crow woman, especially a widow, could ride into battle with the warriors.

Jim Bridger: A mountain man, guide, and explorer who roamed the mountains of the west trapping and hunting in the early days of the European expansion. He spoke French, Spanish, and several Indian languages as well as his native English. He was born in 1804 and died on his farm near St. Louis in 1881. Fort Bridger, Wyoming, and Bridger, Montana, are named after the great storyteller.

Mustang: A wild horse.

Shoshone people: A Native American people found in Idaho, Montana, Nevada, and Utah. They were at first farmers and hunter-gatherers, but after the introduction of the horse they began to follow buffalo and elk herds.

United States Mint: The department that is in charge of printing and minting all paper and money and coins and distributing them. The Mint also guards and stores the U.S. gold and silver assets.

Wyoming: A state that got its name from the Munsee people. It means "at the big river flat." The capital is Cheyenne.

Story Sources

American Indian Tales & Legends

American Myths & Legends, Volumes 1 & 2

By Cheyenne Campfires

Cowboy Songs and other Frontier Ballads

The Greenwood Library of American Folktales, Volume 3

Myths & Legends of Our Own Land, Volumes 1 & 2

Outlaw Tales: Legends, Myths & Folklore from America's Middle Border

Shoshone-Bannock Tribes

Tales from the American Frontier

A Treasury of Western Folklore

The Way of the Warrior: Stories of the Crow People

Yankee Doodle's Cousins

Crossing the Borders: Stories That Touch Many States

Included here are several stories that can't really be told as belonging to one state. These stories cross the borders of several states.

The Pony Express (Based on True Events)

It only lasted sixteen months, but the Pony Express is part of the legendary opening of the West and one of the most enduring stories of America. It started on April 3, 1860, when the first rider rode at breakneck speed for the first stop. Along the way riders would get fresh horses and new riders would take over to get the mail from the east to the west and then back again. Most of the riders were young, including a fifteen-year-old Bill Cody, later known to the world through his Wild West Shows as "Buffalo" Bill Cody. The young riders braved heat and exhaustion, blizzards and floods, outlaws and Native American warriors as they rode across the West, bringing the news from the Atlantic to the Pacific in ten days. They left St. Joseph, Missouri, and traveled through parts of Kansas, Nebraska, Colorado, Wyoming, Utah, and Nevada and on to Sacramento, California. There were 190 relay stations along the 1,966-mile route, approximately one station every ten miles, the distance they thought that a fast pony could maintain a steady gallop. The horses were small, sturdy, fast animals that earned the name pony.

Bill Cody told the story of how he was stopped by robbers on his leg of the route. Now Cody had heard that some outlaws had wounded a rider, but the man had stayed on top of his horse and they hadn't gotten the sack that contained the mail and any valuables he had been entrusted with. The young Express rider died at the next station stop. Now Bill Cody decided to carry two sets of pouches, one with the mail in it and the other as a decoy that was filled with rocks. He was in a lonesome valley when two men came out from behind some rocks and stopped him. They both had rifles, and they were both aimed at Bill's chest.

"Now, son," said one man, "just hand over the pouches and we'll leave you alone."

"These pouches are the property of the Pony Express, and it's a hanging offence to steal them," replied Bill. "There's nothing valuable in them anyway."

"We'll be the judges of that, boy. Now hand them over."

The two men were right in front of Cody, and to resist them would mean a bullet. He unfastened the false pouches and threw them into the face of the first robber. The man dodged, and as he did Bill shot the other man in the arm. Cody spurred his horse on and rode down the first man and made his escape. Bill Cody whooped in triumph as he rode away from the wounded men, the real Express pouches safely tied to the back of his saddle.

The Trail of Tears (a True Story)

The long line of people stretched out for almost a mile. They wore no chains and yet they were prisoners. They were born here in the United States, and yet they were not citizens. The soldiers who escorted them were grim faced, as if this was an unpleasant duty. The people did not look defeated, for defeated people still have a spark of defiance. These people had lost too much. They had been taken from the land of their birth, the land of their ancestors, the land of their stories, and forced to leave it all behind. This was one of the worst atrocities committed against the Native American people. This was the Trail of Tears.

The people traveled for over 1,200 miles from homes in Georgia, Alabama, North Carolina, and Tennessee to Oklahoma. They had left their homes, their livestock, and all their belongings that they couldn't carry behind. Some 17,000 Cherokees were forced from their homes at gunpoint and sent west to Indian Territory, later the state of Oklahoma. Some rode in wagons; most walked. Along the way many died of disease and exposure. Some never left their homes but died at their front doors, shot dead for refusing to leave. It is estimated that 4,000 Cherokees died on their way to Oklahoma.

How did it all happen? What caused friendly neighbors to turn on the Cherokees? How did a nation turn a blind eye to such a miscarriage of justice? The answer is gold and land. In 1829 the first American gold rush started when gold was discovered in Georgia. Prospectors began encroaching on Cherokee land, and the Cherokee people asked the state of Georgia to honor its commitment to secure the borders of their tribal lands. Instead, the state of Georgia moved to extend its laws to the Cherokee, to satisfy gold and land speculators. The Supreme Court said that Georgia had no jurisdiction over the Cherokee and that only the federal government had authority in tribal affairs. The weakness of the court decision was that John Marshall and the Supreme Court had no army. The president did.

In 1830 Congress passed the Indian Removal Act of 1830 and gave President Andrew Jackson the right to negotiate treaties to remove eastern Indians to lands across the Mississippi River. President Jackson and later President Martin Van Buren used this act to remove native people from their lands. The fate of the Cherokee was sealed. Removal began in 1838, and General Winfield Scott was put in charge of the force that would oversee it. The lands of the Cherokee in Georgia became state lands, and those lands were used to help create the Western and Atlantic Railroad of the State of Georgia. The railroad went from Atlanta, Georgia, to Chattanooga, Tennessee. The line is still owned by the state of Georgia. That railroad and the wealth of the Cherokee lands transformed Atlanta, Georgia, into the commercial powerhouse it still is today.

The treaty that the government used as its basis for the legal removal was the Treaty of New Echota. Chief John Ross, the principal chief of the Cherokee, refused to recognize the treaty, and not one member of the Cherokee Council signed it.

The soldiers who carried out these removals often wrote the most telling accounts of what really happened. Following are excerpts from a letter written by John Burnett to his family on his eightieth birthday:

> I was sent as interpreter into the Smoky Mountain Country in May, 1838, and witnessed the execution of the most brutal order in the History of American Warfare. I saw the helpless Cherokees arrested and dragged from their homes, and driven at the bayonet point into the stockades. In the chill of a drizzling rain on an October morning I saw them loaded like cattle or sheep into six hundred and forty-five wagons and started toward the west. . . . Many of these helpless people did not have blankets and many of them had been driven from home barefooted.
>
> Murder is murder whether committed by the villain skulking in the dark or by uniformed men stepping to the strains of martial music. Somebody must explain the streams of blood that flowed in the Indian country in the summer of 1838. Somebody must explain the 4,000 silent graves that mark the trail of the Cherokees to their exile. I wish I could forget it all, but the picture of 645 wagons lumbering over the frozen ground with their cargo of suffering humanity still lingers in my memory.

The Cherokee were not the only Native American tribe to be removed. All of the Five Civilized Nations, so called because they had embraced the European way, were removed to Indian Territory west of the Mississippi River. This included the Choctaw, who lost between 2,000 and 4,000 people during their removal; the Creeks, who lost about 3,500; the Chickasaw; the Seminole; and the Cherokee. Further north more tribes were removed from ancestral homes and moved across the Mississippi River, including the Shawnees, Ottawas, Potawatomis, Sauks, Foxes, and Miami. Though most of these tribes were smaller, the death tolls were still horrible.

During the nineteenth century more than 100,000 Native Americans were removed from their lands, their homes, the place of their ancestors in the east and sent west to Indian territory.

The Underground Railroad (a True Story)

The three people huddled in the bottom of a wagon underneath some sacks of grain, a father and mother and their little girl. The wagon was fitted with a false floor to keep prying eyes away from its human passengers. They rode down country lanes and through small towns, stopping at the homes of people they didn't know but whose kindness they would never forget. They stayed at one home for a week in a small room that was hidden in the attic of a wealthy family, while the bounty hunters looked everywhere in the area. They just didn't look there. They traveled by foot and wagon, by mule and by boat. Finally they crossed the border into Canada, and they were safe. Here the bounty hunters had no power. Here there were no slaves. They had been passengers on the Underground Railroad.

The Underground Railroad was the desperate attempt of a few to try in some small way to help end the horrors of slavery. It was a series of safe houses and secret routes to help escaped slaves get to freedom that was run by abolitionists, former slaves, and people of conscience. Every day folks gave runaway slaves shelter in their homes, barns, secret rooms in their basements, or attics. From 1810 until 1850 it was estimated that 30,000 to 40,000 slaves escaped to free states and Canada through the efforts of the Underground Railroad. It gave us heroes like Sojourner Truth and Harriet Tubman, who made nineteen trips back to the South and helped free over 300 people. People like William Still, often called the Father of the Railroad, who went south and came back with as many as sixty slaves a month, often hiding them in his Philadelphia home before they continued north.

The Underground Railroad had its own special language: guides were called "conductors" and hiding places were "stations." The Railroad itself was often referred to as the "Freedom Train" or the "Gospel Train," headed toward "heaven," which was Canada.

To this day you can find in old homes the hidden rooms and the tunnels that led from homes to barns that helped bring a desperate people to freedom. They are in houses in Illinois and Wisconsin, Pennsylvania and Ohio, Indiana and Massachusetts, all over the north, the south, and the Border States. They still exist as a silent testament to courage.

The Great Adventure (a True Story)

It was a journey to fire the imagination. Thirty men going into the wilderness to explore the new lands purchased by the young American government. In May 1804 they left St. Louis and started down the Missouri River. This was the beginning of the first great American journey of exploration since the new country had won its independence from England. This was the Lewis and Clark Expedition.

Captain Meriwether Lewis and Lieutenant William Clark led the expedition, officially known as the Corps of Discovery, as it explored the Louisiana Purchase. Almost bankrupted by his many wars, Napoleon had sold the vast wilderness that was part of France's empire in North America to the United States. President Thomas Jefferson had always wanted to send someone to explore the vast continent of North America and had even discussed it with his friend John Ledyard. Now with this expedition it was a reality. The expedition traveled along the great rivers of the west from what is now Missouri through what would become the states of Kansas, Nebraska, South Dakota, North Dakota, Montana, Idaho, Washington, and Oregon. They met over three dozen indigenous tribes. The expedition had friendly relations with most of these tribes, and because of this they were helped along the way with food and shelter. The expedition would never have been a success if they hadn't been received in friendship.

A great deal of the credit for the success of Lewis and Clark must be given to their guide and interpreter, Sacajawea, the teenage bride of a French trapper whom they had hired as a guide. She had been kidnapped from her own people and brought up in another tribe. Later she was married to the French trapper Chaboneau. It was because of her that the expedition was met with peace rather than with weapons. She carried her infant in a cradleboard on her back, and the sight of a woman and her baby was a sign that this was not a war party. She guided the expedition all the way to the Pacific Ocean, and in the course of the journey was reunited with members of her family, the Shoshone people. Probably one of the most wonderful moments for her was when she was asked to interpret for the Shoshone chief Cameahwait. She heard his voice and turned and threw herself into the surprised chief's arms. She had found her brother.

When Captain Lewis saw his first buffalo herd, he decided to shoot one for his hungry band's meal. As the wounded animal started to stagger, Lewis saw another animal he had never seen before, a grizzly bear. Lewis decided to walk out toward the beast and scare him off. Grizzly bears don't scare off, and the huge beast reared up on its hind legs and roared its disapproval. The bear had been master here for centuries, not man. Lewis aimed to fire but then realized that he had not reloaded his musket. Captain Lewis was not about to show fear, so he turned and walked away from the grizzly. Then he heard the sound of huge paws pounding the prairie behind him and turning, he saw the giant bear coming at him, all fangs and claws. Lewis started to run, but the bear was gaining. Suddenly he turned sharply and dove into the nearby river. The bear, having chased off his competition, went back to feast on the buffalo.

The expedition lost only one member, Sergeant Charles Floyd, who died of appendicitis and is buried at Floyd's Bluff near present-day Sioux City, Iowa. That only one man died over the miles and years is a testament to the leadership qualities of the two men, especially Captain Lewis.

When the Lewis and Clark Expedition returned they brought back 140 maps they had charted of the new territory. They also documented over 100 new species of animals, 68 mineral specimens, and 176 new species of plants. Over their two-year journey they had made more scientific discoveries than any expedition up to that time.

Ships of the Desert (a True Story)

Before he ever became famous as the first and only president of the Confederacy, Jefferson Davis was Secretary of War in the mid-1850s. He had an idea that he thought just might prove to be an easy and efficient way to transport troops and supplies across the Great American Desert, as the Southwest has often been called. He decided to bring camels to America. The shipment of animals and a few native handlers arrived in Texas, and Davis decided to have a trial run of the beasts by sending them across Texas, New Mexico, Arizona, and into California. Critics of the plan called it "Jeff Davis's Folly."

The American soldiers were not at all impressed by the social skills of the camels. They were more stubborn than mules, they spat and bit, and they smelled awful. But they were great at their jobs. The average camel could carry twice what a mule could and not get tired. They were steady and fast and could walk day after day without more than a few hours' rest. You didn't have to carry food for them because they ate anything. Their stomachs were the garbage cans of the desert, eating any plant that they came across; even cactus didn't seem to bother their mouths or their stomachs. Water was never a problem because they could go for days without any at all.

Well, they made the trip to California with no problems at all and faster than anyone had ever expected. All twenty-four camels arrived and had proven Jeff Davis right. More camels arrived in 1860, but the army soon lost interest in them. President Lincoln had announced plans for a transcontinental railroad to connect the two coasts of America. No one seemed interested in the poor beasts, and they were sold off to zoos or circuses or to a few people who thought they might still use them for freight. Some folks who bought them later just turned them loose in the desert to live out their lives as best they could in a strange land.

For years stories were told of folks coming across camels walking calmly through the desert heat or the ghosts of the camels and their native drivers running across the desert, the men talking to their animals in their native tongue. Prospectors told of coming across the camels calmly lying in the shade of a tree or near a watering hole.

Maybe their ghosts are still out there in the Great American Desert trying to get back to their desert homes across the sea, to a place where they are loved and honored.

Taking the Herds to Market (a True Story)

The cattle industry in Texas depended on getting the herds to market. Before the coming of the railroads the only way to do that was to drive the herds north. The great cattle trails passed through many states. The Chisholm Trail started in San Antonio, Texas, and ended in Abilene, Kansas. The Sedalia and Baxter Springs Trail started in southern Texas and went through Oklahoma and Arkansas before arriving at the markets in Sedalia, Missouri. The Goodnight-Loving Trail started in Texas and went through New Mexico before ending in Denver, Colorado. These were all long, hard journeys for both the cattle and the men and horses that drove them to market. The dangers that waited were usually from nature, but not always. Violent storms could cause a herd to stampede, while swollen rivers could take their toll in lives trying to ford them or in time trying to go around them. Rustlers were always a threat, stealing a few cattle or, if there were enough of them, taking the entire herd and leaving the bones of the cowboys to rot in the sun. We can glamorize the life in story and song and movies, but it was a hard life being a cowboy. You slept rough and ate rough, and the work was endless and often life threatening. The following song sums up the life on the trail better than most.

John Garner's Trail Herd

Come all you old timers and listen to my song.

I'll make it short as possible and I'll not keep you long.

I'll relate to you about the time we all remember well,

When we with old John Garner drove a beef herd up the trail.

When we left the ranch it was early in the spring.

We had as good a corporal as ever rope did swing.

Good hands and good horses, good outfit through and through,

We went well equipped we were a jolly crew.

We had no little herd: two thousand head or more

And some as wild as brush beeves as you ever saw before.

We swung them all the way and sometimes by the tail.

Oh you know we had a circus as we all went up the trail.

All things went on well until we reached open ground

And then the cattle turned in and gave us merry hell.

They stampeded every night that came and did it without fail.

Oh you know we had a circus as we all went up that trail.

We would round them up next morning and the boss would make a count
And say "Look here old punchers, we're down by a large amount.
You must make all losses good and do it without fail,
Or you'll never get another job driving up the trail."

When we reached the reservation how squirmish we did feel,
Although we had tried old Garner and knew him true as steel.
And if we would follow him and do as he said do,
That old bald-headed cow thief would surely take us through.

When we reached Dodge City we drew our four months' pay.
Times were better then boys, that was a better day.
We slept and ate and gambled and danced the girls around.
Yes a crowd of Texas cowboys had come to take their town.

The cowboy sees many hardships although he takes them well.
The fun we had upon that trip no human tongue can tell.
The cowboy's life is a dreary life though his mind it has no load,
And he always spends his money like he found it in the road.

If you ever meet old Garner you must meet him on the square,
For he is the biggest cow-thief that ever tramped out there.
But if you want to hear him roar and spin a lively tale,
Just ask him about the time we all went up on the trail.

Crossing the Borders Glossary

Abolitionists: People who favored ending slavery in pre–Civil War America.

Camels: Desert animals with long legs that can store water in the fat of the humps on their backs. Their feet are suited for walking in the sand, and they can go for days with no water and little food. They are referred to as "ships of the desert."

Cherokee people: The largest Native American tribe in America today. They used to be referred to as one of the Five Civilized Tribes and at one time had occupied parts of Tennessee, Kentucky, Georgia, the Carolinas, Virginia, and Alabama. They were the first Native American people to have a written alphabet and a newspaper in their own language.

Cradleboard: A board that had a cloth or soft leather pouch attached to it to hold an infant. The cradleboard was worn on the mother's back.

Head: The number of animals in a herd. The number was determined by counting their "heads." If there were 2,000 cattle in a herd, they were referred to as 2,000 head.

Puncher: Another name for a cowboy working with cattle, especially on the trail.

Stampede: A headlong rush of startled or frightened cattle. It was very difficult to stop.

Story Sources

Amazing American Women

Native American Testimony

The Trail of Tears

A Treasury of Western Folklore

Undaunted Courage

Commonwealths and Territories

The United States has territories in the Caribbean Sea and the Pacific Ocean. The Caribbean territories are Puerto Rico and the Virgin Islands. Puerto Rico gives us two stories, "Aunt Misery" and "Juan Bobo and the Princess Who Answered Riddles," from the Spanish tradition. "The Race Between Crab and Fox" comes from the Virgin Islands, where you can find several types of crabs, including hermit crabs and land crabs, as featured in the Samoan story. In the Pacific Ocean the United States has several territories, including Midway Island, American Samoa, the Federated States of Micronesia, the Marshall Islands, Palua, and Guam. The story "The Sandpiper and the Crab" from Samoa represents those Oceanic people.

Aunt Misery (Puerto Rico)

There was an old woman, a very old woman whose only companion in this world was a beautiful pear tree that grew near the front door of her cabin. When the pears were ripe the neighborhood boys would scamper up the tree and steal them and taunt her if she tried to stop them. The only pears she ever tasted were the ones that grew within reach of her frail arms or the ones the boys dropped as they stole her fruit.

Once a traveler stopped by and asked if he could spend the night at her cabin. Aunt Misery, that's what the boys called her, said to the man, "You are welcome. Please come in and stay." The man slept by the fire. In the morning when he was ready to leave he turned to the old woman and said, "Ask for anything you want and your wish will come true."

Aunt Misery thought for only a second, then replied, "I wish that anyone who climbs my pear tree would have to stay there until I give them permission to come down."

"Your wish will come true," said the stranger with a slight smile on his lips.

The next time the pears were ripe the boys in the town came to steal them. They climbed high into the tree and taunted Aunt Misery. She just stood there calmly and said nothing. When they tried to climb down they couldn't. They were stuck in her tree. They begged and they pleaded, but she wouldn't let them come down. Finally she made them all promise to leave her alone and never climb her tree again. When they swore an oath to her she let them free, and they ran for home as fast as they could move. Aunt Misery was now able to enjoy her pears by herself, and if she wanted to share them, that was her business.

The days went by and one evening anther stranger stopped at her door. The man seemed in a hurry. Aunt Misery invited him in and asked his business with her.

"I am Death, and I've come for you," he replied.

She was silent for a moment and then she said, "I am ready to come with you, but before we go, could you do me one favor?"

Death agreed.

"Would you pick me a few pears to take along on my journey? I am so old and I can't reach the really tasty ones that grow near the top."

Death climbed up the pear tree and dropped a few down to Aunt Misery. Then he tried to climb back down, but he was stuck. Just like the neighborhood boys, Death begged and pleaded, but Aunt Misery was content to let him stay in that tree for many years.

As the years passed there were no deaths. Everyone who was alive when Death climbed the tree was still alive. The gravediggers and undertakers, the doctors and druggists all complained that Death was not doing his job. There were so many old people who were ready to die but couldn't. Little did they know where Death was all that time.

Finally Aunt Misery made a deal with Death. She would let him down if he left her alone and did not claim her life. Death agreed and hurried off to tend to the dying and the old. That is why to this very day people die, but Aunt Misery is still in this world.

Juan Bobo and the Princess Who Answered Riddles (Puerto Rico)

Once there was a king who was very fond of riddles, who had a daughter who could solve any riddle she heard. Now the king wanted her to marry someone who was just as smart as she was, so he devised a plan to eliminate any suitors who weren't up to his intellectual standard. If they presented a riddle to the princess and she solved it, they lost their heads. But if she couldn't solve it she would marry that suitor. It seemed like a good plan to the king.

Suitors came from all around, since the princess was also as beautiful as she was smart. Sadly the walls of the castle were soon lined with the heads of all those suitors, for she had solved every riddle they presented. It wasn't long until young men stopped coming to the king's court to win her hand.

Now in a small village there lived a widow with her only son, Juan. Everyone called him Juan Bobo, which meant Simple John, because he was a very foolish young man and didn't have much sense at all. One day he was walking past the castle walls and saw all those heads of all the men who had tried to win the princess's hand and had failed. That night over their evening meal Juan told his mother that he was going to try his luck and see if he could win the hand of the king's daughter. His mother cried and begged him not to be so foolish, but the idea was now stuck in Juan's head, and once that happened it was hard to get it out.

The next morning he was still just as determined to try his hand with a riddle. His mother knew it was useless to try to stop him, so she made him some food for the road. She was crying so hard as she mixed up some cakes that she seasoned them with poison instead of spices. When it was time for him to leave she gave him the bundle of food and still crying, said good-bye, knowing she would never see her simple son again.

Juan traveled toward the city on his old donkey Panda and after several hours he dismounted and stretched out on the grass to take a rest. While Juan dreamt of the princess his donkey got into the food parcel his mother had sent Juan off with and ate the poison cakes. In a few minutes the old donkey rolled over and died. Three vultures landed and started to pick on the dead animal, and they also died from the poison.

When Juan Bobo woke he saw the dead donkey and the dead vultures and he also saw that the cakes were missing and put it altogether, realizing he was one lucky young man. Juan was hungry but couldn't trust anything that was in his mother's food bundle, so he took his gun and tried to shoot a rabbit for his meal. The one he aimed at jumped out of the way, but another rabbit jumped right into the path of the bullet. After he had eaten Juan was thirsty but couldn't find and well or stream, so he climbed a coconut tree and drank the milk from one of the coconuts. Now his head was full of Panda and vultures and rabbits and coconuts. Since he had no riddle for the princess yet he decided to make one up from the adventures he had had so far in his journey.

When Juan Bobo reached the castle, he told the guards that he was there to put a riddle to the princess. The guards knew all about Juan, and they laughed until it hurt at the idea that he could pose a riddle that she couldn't solve. At first they would not let him in, thinking it was cruel to allow someone so simple to lose his head over the princess, but Juan insisted and they finally let him in to see the king. When the king saw that the young man who came to test his daughter was not a prince or a king but a country fool he was angry. But then he remembered his own words, that she would marry the man, rich or poor, noble or common, who could give her a riddle she could not solve. Juan walked right over to the princess and said:

> "I left home with Panda.
> But two killed her and
> Then she killed three.
> I shot at what I saw
> But hit what I didn't see.
> I was thirsty and drank
> Water, which had never sunk
> Into the earth nor fell from the sky.
> If you guess my riddle,
> I'm done with my head."

The princess thought and thought but had no idea what this riddle was all about. The king and the court were amazed. They had never seen her stumped by a riddle before. Now the rules were that she had three days to figure out the answer to the riddle. Juan Bobo was made welcome in the castle while she tried to figure out its meaning.

The first night she sent one of her servants to Juan's room to see if she could find out the answer, but even though the servant was beautiful Juan paid her no attention at all.

The second night she sent an even more beautiful servant to his room, but he would not say a word.

The third night the princess went herself to Juan Bobo's room. She begged and pleaded, and finally Juan told her that he would tell her the meaning of the riddle if she gave him the ring from her finger and one of her shoes. She consented and gave him the small ring off her finger and her left shoe. Juan told her all about the poisoned cakes, the donkey and the vultures, the two rabbits, and the coconut. She was so happy that she clapped her hands and ran out of the room.

The next day the princess told the whole court the solution to Juan's riddle.

The king was especially happy, since the last thing he wanted was a village fool for his son-in-law. He called the executioner to come into the courtyard and take off Juan Bobo's head. Juan asked the king if he could say a few words, and the king granted his request. He told the king that the princess had come to him and he had given the answer to her. He told the king that he had asked for a ring and her left shoe, knowing it would be hard for him to get both items without her permission. He showed the ring and the shoe to the king.

Now the king was a just man, so instead of an execution there was a wedding, and Juan Bobo married the princess and became a prince. Many years later he became the king, and if not a wise one or a clever one, I think he was a just one.

The Race Between Crab and Fox
(Virgin Islands)

"Why are you always in a rush, Mr. Fox?" asked Brother Crab.

Brother Fox just looked at the Crab and said nothing.

"Why don't you slow down and walk like me? I take my time in life and enjoy the view," said the Crab.

"I walk fast because I am fast," replied Brother Fox.

"You're not as fast as I am," said the Crab. "If we had a race I could beat you every time."

The Fox laughed and said, "We can race if you want, but I know who's going to win."

They started their race near a tall tree. Crab looked up at Brother Fox and said, "Mr. Fox, I'm going to let you start first since I know I can beat you."

When Fox started to run Crab just reached up with one of his claws and took hold of Fox's tail. It was so full and bushy that Brother Fox never felt a thing. Fox ran so fast that the sand shot up like a wave around him. Mr. Fox never looked behind him, he just ran as fast as he could so he could prove how speedy he was to the Crab.

When he got to the finish line he whipped around to see where Brother Crab was, and as his tail passed over the line Crab let go. Brother Fox looked down the beach and stretched his neck to see if he could spot Crab. Just then he heard a voice.

"What took you so long, Mr. Fox? I've been waiting here for a long time."

Fox turned and there was Brother Crab smiling up at him. "Now we know who the fastest is, don't we?" said Crab.

Crab won the race, but Fox was sure he had cheated; he just never knew how.

The Sandpiper and the Crab (Samoa)

It was early evening when Land Crab came out of the forest and went searching for food along the reef. He looked for fallen coconuts, and when he found them he broke them with his huge claws and took out the tender meat inside. It was that time when Land Crab shed his shell and grew a new one. His old shell would be left behind, the sun and the wind would harden his new skin into a hard shell, and he would go to the reef and tell everyone that he was lord of the reef.

As he crawled down the beech he met Sandpiper ,who had flown down from his nest and was also walking along the beech looking for food.

"Where are you going?" asked Land Crab.

Now Sandpiper also wanted to be lord of the reef but didn't want his rival to know. "Nowhere in particular," said Sandpiper. "I'm just walking around looking for a friend."

"Well, I can be a good friend," said Land Crab.

They wandered together, picking at shells until it became dark. "Let's find a place to sleep," said Land Crab.

Now Sandpiper wanted to get rid of Land Crab so he could fly over to the reef and make his claim as lord. He devised a cunning plan. "Let's spend the night in a tree so we can be safe from our enemies."

Land Crab was puzzled, "But I can't climb trees. You have wings, but I don't."

"I'll fly to the top branches of a tree and let down a vine. You can take hold with your powerful claws ands I'll pull you up." The two friends came to a tall tree and Sandpiper flew up and lowered a vine down to Land Crab, who took hold of it with one of his giant claws. Sandpiper hauled him up into the top branches.

Land Crab looked around and got dizzy. "I can't stay up here," he said. "I'll fall off as soon as I fall asleep. Let me down."

"I went to a lot of trouble getting you up here. You have to stay with me now. Besides, you can't get down by yourself."

"Yes I can," said Land Crab. "Getting up here is much harder than getting down." With his huge claws he grabbed a branch and swung himself down to the next branch and slithered down to the next, keeping hold with his claws. "You'll have to sleep alone old friend," called Land Crab.

Sandpiper was worried that Land Crab would get away and called down, "I have an idea. I'll come down and join you and we can sleep on one of the big bottom branches. You can lean your back against the trunk and I'll put my wing over you to keep you safe."

Land Crab reluctantly agreed. They settled down on a big bottom branch and Sandpiper placed his wing over Land Crab. Soon Sandpiper was sound asleep, but something was happening to the crab: his shell was getting loose. Land Crab waited until Sandpiper was fast asleep, then he crawled out of the shell and very quietly dropped down into a pile of leaves. He crept out of the forest and onto the beech where the sun and wind could dry his new skin until it was thick and hard.

Sandpiper woke up but felt Land Crab's shell under his wing and felt safe that he was still there and went back to sleep. The next time he woke up the sun was high in the sky, and when Sandpiper stood up the empty shell fell off the branch. He flew as fast as he could to the reef, but Land Crab was there already.

He waved his big claws at Sandpiper and called, "Sandpiper, I think you need another friend. You sleep much too late to ever be lord of the reef."

Commonwealth and Territories Glossary

American Samoa: Part of an island chain in the Pacific Ocean. Both Germany and the United States had claims to the islands, and in 1899 a treaty was signed that divided the islands between the two powers. The western islands became independent in 1962 and form the Independent State of Samoa. The other islands make up American Samoa and are considered an unincorporated territory.

Juan Bobo: A trickster character in many Spanish cultures.

Land crabs: Crabs that have adapted to living on land and breathing oxygen. They do go to the sea to breed, and the young larvae are kept in the water until they mature. Usually one claw is larger than the other.

Puerto Rico: An island that was visited by Christopher Columbus on his second voyage to the Americas. It was captured from Spain by the United States during the Spanish–American War. As a commonwealth, its people elect their own local government, but the United States handles all foreign affairs for the island.

Sandpipers: Wading birds that find their food in the mud and sand along the shore. They have long legs and long beaks to dig for their food.

Virgin Islands: A group of islands located in the Caribbean Sea. The eastern islands are under the protection and administration of the British government, while the western islands are an unincorporated territory of the United States.

Story Sources

Greedy Mariani & Other Folktales of the Antilles

The Greenwood Library of American Folktales, Volume 2

Latin American Folktales

The Magic Calabash: Folktales from America's Islands and Alaska

Myths & Legends of the Pacific

Myths and Legends of the Polynesians

Tala o le Vavayu: The Myths, Legends & Customs of Old Samoa

The Three Wishes: A Collection of Puerto Rican Folktales

Bibliography

Story Sources

People and Organizations

Jimm GoodTracks, Baxoje Jiwere Language Project

Shoshone-Bannock Tribes

Kevin Strauss

Art Thieme

Dovie Thomason

Tim Tingle, Choctaw Storyteller

Publications

Amazing American Women, by Kendall Haven. Libraries Unlimited, 1995. ISBN 1-56308-291-8.

American Fairy Tales, by Vladimir Stuchl. Octopus Books, 1979. ISBN 0-7064-0860-8.

American Indian Tales & Legends, by Vladimir Hulpach. Paul Hamlyn Publishing, 1965.

American Myths & Legends, Volumes 1 & 2, by Charles M. Skinner. J. B. Lippincott Company, 1903.

And It Is Still That Way: Legends Told by Arizona Indian Children, collected by Byrd Baylor. Cinco Puntos Press, 1976. ISBN 0-938317-36-9.

Arkansas Voices, by Sarah M. Fountain. University of Central Arkansas Press, 1989. ISBN 0-944436-09-9.

Back in the Beforetime: Tales of the California Indians, by Jane Louise Curry. Margaret K. McElderry Books, 1987. ISBN 0-689-50410-1.

Ballads & Folk Songs of the Southwest, by Ethel & Chauncey O. Moore. University of Oklahoma Press, 1964. LC 64-11329.

Ballads & Songs, by H. M. Belden. University of Missouri Press, 1940. ISBN 0-8262-0142-3.

Ballads & Songs from Utah, by Lester A. Hubbard. University of Utah Press, 1961. ISBN 0-87480-134-6.

Blackfoot Lodge Tales: The Story of a Prairie People, by George Bird Grinnell. University of Nebraska Press, 1962. ISBN 0-8032-5079-7.

The Bodega War & Other Tales from Western Lore, by Hector Lee. Capra Press, 1988, ISBN 0-88496-279-2.

Buying the Wind, by Richard M. Dorson. University of Chicago Press, 1964. LC 63-20903.

By Cheyenne Campfires, by George Bird Grinnell. University of Nebraska Press, 1926. ISBN 0-8032-5746-5.

The Cactus Sandwich & Other Tall Tales of the Southwest, by Don Dedera, Northland Press, 1986. ISBN 0-87358-406-6.

The Charm Is Broken: Readings in Arkansas & Missouri Folklore, by W..K. McNeil. August House, 1984. ISBN 0-935304-67-3.

Chinese Fairy Tales & Fantasies, by Moss Roberts. Pantheon Books, 1979. ISBN 0-394-42039-x.

The Corn Woman, Stories and Legends of the Hispanic Southwest, by Angel Vigil. Libraries Unlimited, 1994. ISBN 1-56308-194-6.

Coronado's Children: Tales of Lost Mines & Buried Treasures of the South West, by J. Frank Dobie. University of Texas Press, 1958. ISBN 0-292-71052-6.

Cowboy Songs and Other Frontier Ballads, by John A. Lomax and Alan Lomax., Collier Books, 1966 (originally printed in 1910). ISBN 0-02-061260-5.

The Devil's Pretty Daughter & Other Ozark Folktales, by Vance Randolph. Columbia University Press, 1955. LC 55-6179

The Eagle and the Cactus: Traditional Stories from Mexico, by Angel Vigil. Libraries Unlimited, 2000. ISBN 1-56308-703-0.

The Eskimo Storyteller, by Edwin S. Hall Jr. University of Tennessee Press, 1975. ISBN 0-87049-603-4.

Febold Feboldson: Tall Tales from the Great Plains, by Paul R. Beath. University of Nebraska Press, 1962. ISBN 0-8032-5012-6.

Filipino Children's Favorite Stories, by Liana Romulo. Periplus Editions, 2000. ISBN 962-593-765-X.

Folk Tales from Portugal, by Alan S. Feinstein. A.S. Barnes & Co., 1972. ISBN 0-498-01031-7.

Folklore from the Working Folk of America, by Tristram Potter Coffin and Hennig Cohen. Anchor Press, 1973. ISBN 0-385-038747-4-7.

The Folklore of Spain in the American Southwest, by Aurelio M. Espinosa and J. Manuel Espinosa. University of Oklahoma Press, 1986. ISBN 0-8061-2249-8.

Folktales from the Japanese Countryside, by Hiroko Fujita. Libraries Unlimited, 2008. ISBN 978-1-59158-488-9.

Folktales of Japan, by Keigo Seki. University of Chicago Press, 1963. LC 63-13071.

The Ghost of Mingo Creek & Other Spooky Oklahoma Legends, by Greg Rodgers. Forty-Sixth Star Press, 2008. ISBN 0-9817105-0-1.

Ghost Stories from the Pacific Northwest, by Margaret Read MacDonald. August House, 1995. ISBN 0-87483-437-6.

Ghosts of the Mississippi: Dubuque to Keokuk, by Bruce Carlson. Quixote Press, 1988.

Ghosts of the Mississippi: Keokuk to St. Louis, by Bruce Carlson. Quixote Press, 1988.

Greedy Mariani & Other Folktales of the Antilles, by Dorthy Sharp Carter. Atheneum Books, 1974. ISBN 0689-30425-0.

The Greenwood Library of American Folktales, Volume 1, edited by Thomas Green. Greenwood Press, 2006. ISBN 0-313-33773-X.

The Greenwood Library of American Folktales, Volume 2, edited by Thomas Green. Greenwood Press, 2006. ISBN 0-313-33774-8.

The Greenwood Library of American Folktales, Volume 3, edited by Thomas Green. Greenwood Press, 2006. ISBN 0-313-33775-6.

The Greenwood Library of American Folktales, Volume 4, edited by Thomas Green. Greenwood Press, 2006. ISBN 0-313-33776-4.

Haboo: Lushootseed Literature in English, by Vi Hilbert. Lushootseed Press, 1996.

Hawaiian Mythology, by Martha Beckwith. University of Hawaii Press, 1940. ISBN 0-8248-0514-3.

Hawaiian Myths of Earth, Sea & Sky, by Vivian L. Thompson. University of Hawaii Press, 1988. ISBN 0-8248-1171-2.

Hearts of Fire: Great Women of American Lore & Legend, by Kemp Battle, Harmony Books, 1977. ISBN 0-517-70397-1.

The Hell-Bound Train: A Cowboy Songbook, by Glenn Ohrlin. University of Illinois Press, 1973. ISBN 0-252-00190-7.

Heroes & Heroines in Tlingit-Haida Legend, by Mary L. Beck. Alaska Northwest Books, 1989. ISBN 0-88240-334-6.

Heroes, Outlaws & Funny Fellows of American Popular Tales, by Olive Beaupre Miller. Doubleday, 1939.

Heroes, Villains & Ghosts: Folklore of Old California, by Hector Lee. Capra Press, 1984. ISBN 0-88496-223-7.

How the Morning & Evening Stars Came to Be & Other Assiniboine Indian Stories, by The Assiniboine & Sioux Tribes of Fort Peck Reservation. Montana Historical Society Press, 2003. ISBN 0-917298-96-9.

The Hurricane's Children, by Carl Carmer. David McKay Company, 1965. LC 67-17525.

Image of a People: Tlingit Myths & Legends, by Mary Helen Pelton and Jacqueline DiGennaro. Libraries Unlimited, 1992. ISBN 0-87287-918-6.

Indian Legends of the Pacific Northwest, by Ella Clark. University of California Press, 1953.

Indian Sleep-Man Tales: Legends of the Otoe Tribe, by Bernice G. Anderson. Greenwich House, 1967. ISBN0-517-062534.

The Inland Whale: Nine Stories Retold from California Indian Legends, by Theodora Kroeber. University of California Press, 1959.

It's Good to Tell You: French Folktales from Missouri, by Rosemary Hyde Thomas. University of Missouri Press, 1981. ISBN 0-8262-0327-2.

Kauai Tales, by Frederick B. Wichman. Bamboo Ridge Press, 1985. ISBN 0-910043-11-6.

Lakota Myth, by James R. Walker. University of Nebraska Press, 1983. ISBN 0-8032-9706-8.

Latin American Folktales, by John Bierhorst. Pantheon Books, 2002. ISBN 0-780375-42066-5.

The Legends & Myths of Hawaii, by His Hawaiian Majesty King David Kalakaua. Charles E. Tuttle Co., 1888. ISBN 0-8048-1032-X.

Legends of the Yosemite Miwok, by Frank La Pena, Craig D. Bates, and Steven P. Medley. Yosemite Association, 1981. ISBN 0-939666-57-X.

The Magic Calabash: Folktales from America's Islands and Alaska, by Jean Cothran. David McKay & Co., 1956. LC 56-90093.

Mexican Folktales from the Borderland, by Riley Aiken. Southern Methodist University Press, 1980. ISBN 0-87074-175-6.

Mexican-American Folklore, by John O. West. August House, 1988. ISBN 0-87483-060-5.

Montezuma's Serpent & Other True Supernatural Tales of the Southwest, by Brad Steiger and Sherry Hansen-Steiger. Paragon House, 1992. ISBN 1-55778-474-4.

Myths & Legends of Our Own Land, Volumes 1 & 2, by Charles M. Skinner. J. B. Lippincott Company, 1896.

Myths & Legends of the Pacific, by A. W. Reed. Reed Books, 1969. ISBN 0-7900-0739-8.

Myths and Legends of the Polynesians, by Johannes C. Andersen. Dover Books, 1995 (first published in 1928). ISBN 0-486-28582-0.

Myths & Tales of the Jicarilla Apache Indians, by Morris Edward Opler. Dover Press, 1994 (first published in 1938). ISBN 0-486-28324-0.

Native American Testimony, by Peter Nabokov. Penguin Books, 1978. ISBN 0-14-028159-2.

Navaho Folk Tales, by Franc Johnson Newcomb. University of New Mexico Press, 1990. ISBN 0-8263-1231-4.

Navajo Coyote Tales, by Bernard Haile, O.F.M. University of Nebraska Press, 1984. ISBN 0-8032-7222-7.

Northern Tales: Traditional Stories of Eskimo and Indian Peoples, by Howard Norman. Pantheon Books, 1990. ISBN0-394-54060-3.

Outlaw Tales: Legends, Myths & Folklore from America's Middle Border, by Richard Young and Judy Dockery Young. August House, 1992. ISBN 0-87483-195-4.

Ozark Folksongs, by Vance Randolph. University of Illinois Press, 1982. ISBN 0-252-00952-2.

The Parade of Heroes, by Tristram Coffin and Hennig Cohen. Anchor Press, 1971. ISBN 0-385-09711-5.

Pawnee Hero Stories & Folktales, by George Bird Grinnell. University of Nebraska Press, 1961. ISBN0-8032-5080-0.

Polihale & Other Kaua'i Legends, by Frederick B. Wichman. Bamboo Ridge Press, 1991. ISBN 0-910043-24-8.

Portuguese Fairy Tales, by Maurice Michael and Pamela Michael. Follett Publishing, 1965. LC 67-10700.

Pueblo Stories & Storytellers, by Mark Bahti. Treasure Chest Books, 1996. ISBN 1-887896-01-5.

Stars Is God's Lanterns: An Offering of Ozark Tellin' Tales, by Charles Morrow Wilson. University of Oklahoma Press, 1969. LC 75-88142.

Sticks in the Knapsack & Other Ozark Folk Tales, by Vance Randolph. Columbia University Press, 1958. LC 58-13670.

Stockings of Buttermilk, edited by Neil Philip, Clarion Books, 1999. ISBN 0-395-84980-2.

The Stories We Tell: An Anthology of Oregon Folk Literature, by Suzi Jones and Jarold Ramsey. Oregon State University Press, 1994. ISBN 0-87071-380-9.

Tala o le Vavayu: The Myths, Legends & Customs of Old Samoa, adapted from the collections of C. Steubel & Bros. Herman. Polynesian Press, 1976. ISBN 0-908597-03-7.

Tales from the American Frontier, edited by Richard Erdoes. Pantheon Books, 1991. ISBN 0-394-51682-6.

Tales of a Basque Grandmother, by Frances Carpenter. Amereon House, 1930.

Tales of Molokai, by Harriet Ne with Gloria L. Cronin. Institute for Polynesian Studies, 1992. ISBN 0-939154-50-1 .

Tales of Old-Time Texas, by J. Frank Dobie. Castle Books, 1955. ISBN 0-7858-7732-X.

The Talking Turtle & Other Ozark Folk Tales, by Vance Randolph. Columbia University Press, 1957. LC 57-6382.

Tewa Tales, by Elsie Clews Parsons. University of Arizona Press, 1994. ISBN 0-8165-1452-6.

Texas Ghost Stories, by Tim Tingle and Doc Moore. Texas Tech University Press, 2004. ISBN 0-89672-519-7.

The Three Wishes: A Collection of Puerto Rican Folktales, by Ricardo E. Alegria. Harcourt Brace & World, 1969. LC 69-13770.

Traditional Narratives of the Arikara Indians, Volumes One, Two, Three, and Four, by Douglas R. Parks. University of Nebraska Press, 1991. ISBN 0-8032-3698-0 (set).

The Trail of Tears, by Michael Burgan. Compass Books, 2001. ISBN 0-75650937-8.

A *Treasury of Iowa Tales: Unusual, Interesting & Little-Known Stories of Iowa,* by Webb Garrison with Janice Beck Stock. Thomas Nelson Books, 2000. ISBN 1-55853-751-1.

A *Treasury of Mississippi River Folklore,* by B.A. Botkin. Crown Publishers, 1955.

A *Treasury of Nebraska Pioneer Folklore,* compiled by Roger L. Welsch. University of Nebraska Press, 1984. ISBN 0-8032-9707-6.

A *Treasury of Railroad Folklore,* by B..A. Botkin and Alvin F. Harlow. Bonanza Books, 1968. ISBN 0-517-168685.

A *Treasury of Southern Folklore,* by B. A. Botkin. Crown Publishers, 1949.

A *Treasury of Western Folklore,* by B. A. Botkin. Crown Publishers, 1951.

Undaunted Courage, by Stephen E. Ambrose. Touchstone Books, 1996. ISBN 0-684-82697-6.

The Way of the Warrior: Stories of the Crow People, edited by Phenocia Bauerle; compiled and translated by Henry Old Coyote and Barney Old Coyote. University of Nebraska Press, 2003. ISBN 0-8032-6230-2.

Way Out in Idaho, by Rosalie Sorrels. Confluence Press, 1991. ISBN 0-917652-83-5.

We Always Lie to Strangers: Tall Tales from the Ozarks, by Vance Randolph. Columbia University Press, 1951.

Yankee Doodle's Cousins, by Anne Malcolmson. Houghton Mifflin, 1941. LC 41-24262.

General Reading about American Folktales, Folklore, and Folk Music

Afro-American Folktales, by Roger D. Abrahams. Pantheon Books, 1985. ISBN 0-394-72885-8.

American Folk Classics Retold, by Charles Sullivan. Harry N. Abrams, 1998. ISBN 0-8109-0655-4.

American Folklore & Legend, by Jane Polley. Reader's Digest Association, 1978. ISBN 0-89577-045-8.

The American People, by B. A. Botkin. Transaction Publishers, 1998 (first published in 1946). ISBN 1-56000-984-5.

The Ballad of America: The History of the United States in Song and Story, by John Anthony Scott. Southern Illinois University Press, 1966. ISBN 0-8093-1061-9.

Flying with the Eagle, Racing the Great Bear, by Joseph Bruchac. Troll Medallion, 1993. ISBN 0-8167-3027-X.

The Folk Songs of North America, by Alan Lomax. Doubleday & Company, 1960. LC 60-15185.

Folklore in America, selected and edited by Tristram Coffin and Hennig Cohen. Doubleday & Company, 1966. LC 66-17450.

Folklore of the Great West, by John Greenway. American West Publishing, 1969. LC 74-88202.

From My People: 400 Years of African American Folklore, by Daryl Cumber Dance. W.W. Norton & Company, 2002. ISBN 0-393-04798-9.

Further Tales of Uncle Remus, by Julius Lester. Dial Books, 1990. ISBN0-8037-0610-3.

The Girl Who Married the Moon: Tales From Native North America, by Gayle Ross and Joseph Bruchac. BridgeWater Books, 1994. ISBN 0-8167-3480-1.

Great American Folklore, by Kemp Battle. Barnes & Noble Books, 1986. ISBN 0-88029-902-9.

The Great American Liar, by James E. Myers. Lincoln-Herndon Press, 1988. ISBN 0-942936-13-2.

The Greenwood Encyclopedia of African American Folklore, Volumes 1–3, edited by Anand Prahlad. Greenwood Press, 2006. ISBN 0-313-33035-2 (set).

Hearts of Fire: Great Women of American Lore & Legend, by Kemp Battle. Harmony Books, 1997. ISBN 0-517-70397-1.

Heroes & Heroines, Monsters & Magic: Native American Legends & Folktales, by Joseph Bruchac. The Crossing Press, 1998. ISBN 0-89594-995-4.

Heroes, Outlaws & Funny Fellows of American Popular Tales, by Olive Beaupre Miller. Doubleday & Company, 1940.

The Hurricane's Children, by Carl Carmer. David McKay Company, 1965. LC 67-17525.

The Last Tales of Uncle Remus, by Julius Lester. Dial Books, 1994. ISBN 0-8037-1303-7.

Latin American Folktales, by John Bierhorst. Pantheon Books, 2002. ISBN 0-375-42066-5.

Legends and Lore of the American Indians, edited by Terri Hardin. Barnes & Noble Books, 1993. ISBN 1-56619-039-8.

More Tales of Uncle Remus, by Julius Lester. Dial Books, 1988. ISBN0-8037-0420-8.

Myths, Legends, & Folktales of America, by David Leeming and Jake Page. Oxford University Press, 1999. ISBN 0-19-511783-2.

Myths of Native Americans, edited by Tim McNeese. Four Walls Eight Windows Publishing, 2003. ISBN1-56858-271-4.

Native American Legends, edited by George E. Lankford. August House, 1987. ISBN 0-87483-041-9.

Sidewalks of America, by B. A. Botkin. Bobbs-Merrill, 1954. LC 54-9485.

Spirits Dark & Light: Supernatural Tales from the Five Civilized Tribes, by Tim Tingle. August House, 2006. ISBN 0-87483-778-0.

A Treasury of Afro-American Folklore, by Harold Courlander. Smithmark Publishers, 1996. ISBN 0-7651-9733-2.

A Treasury of American Folklore, by B. A. Botkin. Bonanza Books, 1983. ISBN 0-517-420570.

A Treasury of North American Folktales, edited by Catherine Peck. W. W. Norton, 1999. ISBN 0-393-04741-5.

A Treasury of Railroad Folklore, by B. A. Botkin and Alvin F. Harlow. Bonanza Books, 1968. ISBN 0-517-168685

Voices of the Wind, by Margot Edmonds and Ella E. Clark. Facts on File, 1995. ISBN 0-8160-2067-1

Featured Storytellers

Phillip Allen, writer
(580) 916-6392
pallen@choctawnation.com

Ceil Anne Clement
PO Box 1
Hettinger, ND 58639-0001
(701) 567-4218
    Ceil Anne is a performer and educator and is available for programs in schools, libraries, and festivals. She is also on the roster of the North Dakota Artists in Residence Program.

Donald Davis
PO Box 397
Ocracoke Island, NC 27960
(252) 928-2587
donald@ddavisstoryteller.com
www.ddavisstoryteller.com
    Donald has published several books and CDs and is available for concerts, workshops, and festivals.

Dr. Tina L. Hanlon
    AppLit: Resources for Readers and Teachers of Appalachian Literature for Children and Young Adults: www/ferrum.edu/AppLit

Alan Irvine
2704 Tilbury Avenue
Pittsburgh, PA 15217
(412) 521-6406
alanirvine@aol.com
http://members.aol.com/alanirvine
    Alan has published recordings and is available for concerts, workshops, festivals, and residencies.

Greg Rodgers
6104 NW 54th Street
Warr Acres, OK 73122
(405) 361-2619
grodgers3@cox.net
www.gregdrodgers.com
    Greg has published recordings and books and is available for concerts, festivals, school appearances, and workshops.

Bob Sander
(317) 255-7628
mail@bobsander.com
www.bobsander.com
    Bob is available for concerts, workshops, festivals, school appearances, and residencies.

R. Rex Stephenson
Artistic Director of the Blue Ridge Dinner Theatre
Ferrum College
Ferrum, VA 24088

Jenifer Strauss
1061 West Sager Road
Hastings, MI 49058
(269) 945-4943 or (269) 838-8361 (Cell)
E-mail: jenifer@storybetold.com
www.storybetold.com
    Jenifer has published CDs and is available for work in schools, libraries, concerts, and festivals.

Kevin Strauss
PO Box 6511
Rochester, MN 55903
(507) 993-3411
kevin@naturestory.com
www.naturestory.com
    Kevin has published CDs, DVDs, and books and is available for concerts, school appearances, library appearances, and festivals.

Art Thieme
705 Calhoun, Apt. 7-B
Peru, IL 61354
folkart@ivnet.com
Art has published several CDs.

Dovie Thomason
PO Box 6351
Harrisburg, PA 17112
dovestory@earthlink.net
www.doviethomason.com

Dovie has published several CDs and is available for concerts, festivals, residencies, and workshops.

Tim Tingle
4417 Morningside Way
Canyon Lake, TX 78133
(830) 899-5678
timtingle@hotmail.com
www.choctawstoryteller.com

Tim has published books and CDs and is available for concerts, festivals, workshops, and school appearances.

Index

About the Author

DAN KEDING has been a professional folksinger and storyteller for almost forty years. He has written several books, made over a dozen recordings, and has been a regular columnist for *Sing Out: The Folk Music Magazine* for over twenty years. His recordings and books have won numerous awards, including The American Library Association Notable Recording for Children, The Anne Izard Storytellers' Choice Award, and nine Storytelling World awards. In 2000 he was inducted into The Circle of Excellence of the National Storytelling Network. He is also an Adjunct Lecturer at the Graduate School of Library and Information Science at the University of Illinois. One of his hobbies is collecting books on folktales, fairy tales, folklore, and ballads. He has over 2,200 volumes in his library. He lives in Urbana, Illinois, with his wife Tandy and his two Australian shepherds, Jack and Maeve. You can visit him at www.dankeding.com.